BATH PUBS

by

Kirsten Elliott & Andrew Swift

AKEMAN PRESS

Published by AKEMAN PRESS
www.akemanpress.com

ISBN 0 9546138 0 5

Designed by Niall Allsop in Bath
Printed by SRP in Exeter

Set in Frutiger, Perpetua and Trajan

ACKNOWLEDGEMENTS

Special thanks to Stuart Burroughs of the Museum of Bath at Work and Colin Johnstone, Lucy Powell and Mary Blagdon of the Bath Record Office. Thanks also to the staff of the Buckinghamshire, Somerset and Wiltshire Record Offices, Bath Central Library, Bristol Reference Library and the British Newspaper Library.

Picture credits: Thanks to Stuart Burroughs of the Museum of Bath at Work for archive photographs of the *Beaufort Arms*, the *Bear* (after bombing in 1942), the *Crown & Anchor*, the *Seven Dials*, and the *Ring of Bells*; to Colin Johnson of Bath Record Office for the archive photograph of the *Alehouse* and help with old maps and licensing records; and to Paul De'Ath for photographs of jars and flagons from the *Bear*, the *Bell*, the *New Inn*, the *Cleveland Wine Vaults*, the *White Horse*, the *Crown*, the *Devonshire Arms*, the *County Wine Vaults*, the *Talbot*, the *King's Arms*, the *Porter Butt*, the *Star*, and the *White Hart*. All other photographs are from the Akeman Press Archive. Thanks to Nick Luke and Tim Bethune for the plans of the *Old Green Tree*, and to Mark Palmer for the painting of the *Cross Keys*.

Thanks also to Jim Alcock for the recipe for hartshorn jelly.

Finally, a big thank you to all the landlords and locals with whom we have chatted and picked up stories. We hope you enjoy the book

CONTENTS

INTRODUCTION

For centuries, people have come to Bath to take the waters. This book, however, deals with liquid refreshment of a different kind. It is the first in a series on the history of Bath's inns and pubs, and covers all those still open in 2003.*

Lost pubs will feature in future volumes in the series, but, to whet your appetite, we survey the pubs that have disappeared over the last 100 years. It makes grim reading, and, if the trend of shutting pubs down continues, many of those featured in this book may soon follow them into history. The message is simple – get out there and visit them before it's too late.

This is not so much a drinking guide as a history of Bath's pubs. We have tried to give an impression of what each pub is like, but have not included detailed descriptions of opening hours, facilities, prices, etc., simply because things change so rapidly. The last comprehensive guide to Bath's pubs was produced in 1976. It was not an historical survey, but a guide to which pubs served the best beer, which had the best atmosphere, and so on. It was written by Fred Pearce, who visited all of Bath's pubs during a six-week period and reported his findings. Over a quarter of a century later, it is an historical artefact in its own right. As a guide to where to go, however, it is worse than useless. We refer to it many times in this book to give an idea of how much things have changed. It is sobering to ponder what Bath's pubs will be like a quarter of century hence, and how many will be left.

For the record, 14 of the pubs visited by Fred have gone – the *Beaufort* in Princes Street, *Broadley's* in the Sawclose, the *Empire Bars* on the Grand Parade, *Fortt's* in Milsom Street, *Fuller's* in Broad Street, the *Heath Robinson* on St James's Parade, the *Golden Fleece* on Pulteney Road, the *Royal Oak* on the Lower Bristol Road, the *Seven Stars* in Twerton, the *Windsor Castle* on the Upper Bristol Road, the *Bladud's Arms* on the Gloucester Road, the *Mason's Arms* at Combe Down, the *Railway* on the Wells Road and the *Beehive* at Southdown. On the credit side, however, six new pubs have opened – the *Ha! Ha! Bar*, *Lambretta's*, the *Litten Tree*, *O'Neill's*, the *Pig & Fiddle*, and the *Slug & Lettuce* – as well as a slew of wine bars. Admittedly, four out of those six fall into the superpub category, but the two that do not – *Lambretta's* and the *Pig & Fiddle* have both managed to get into the *Good Beer Guide*. So it is not all doom and gloom. But think on this as you down your next pint – if the price of beer continues

---

* This means that we have had to leave out some of our favourites, such as the *Paragon Wine Bar*, winner of the *Venue* award for bar of the year in 2002. However, we had to draw the line somewhere, otherwise we would have ended up having to decide whether we should include restaurants that served wine. Hotels with bars open to non-residents have also been excluded, with the exception of the *Royal Hotel*, which we regarded as a special case.

to rise at the same rate as it has in the last 27 years, then by 2030 the cheapest pint in Bath will set you back around £20.

As this is primarily an historical guide, we have avoided star ratings. We have, however, added a final chapter indicating which pubs appear in the 2003 edition of the Good Beer Guide and the Good Pub Guide, and suggesting, for those whose stay in Bath is limited, a few watering holes that no visitor to the city should miss. We would stress, however, that this selection is very subjective. The only real answer to the question which are Bath's best pubs is to go and try them out for yourself. One person's dream pub, as they say, is another person's nightmare.

THE GREAT BATH PUB CRAWL

The Great Bath Pub Crawl is a unique project. As well as publishing a series of books, we also have a website (www.greatbathpubcrawl.com) with a message board for anyone interested in the history of Bath's pubs. Here information can be sought, provided and exchanged, so that, in time, it will build up to a compendium of information about Bath's boozy past. Finally, there is the GREAT BATH PUB CRAWL, a guided walk through Bacchanalian Bath, with ample stops for liquid refreshment. It runs throughout the summer (although we take pre-booked parties throughout the year), and details of it can be found on our website. So, as you can see, the Great Bath Pub Crawl project is very interactive. We hope you like the first book in the series and will get in touch with us on our message board, especially if you have – or are seeking – information on Bath's pubs, past or present. We also hope to see you on the Great Bath Pub Crawl.

Details of the Great Bath Pub Crawl are correct at time of going to press. Please check our website (www.greatbathpubcrawl.com) or call 01225 310364 for latest update.

BACCHANALIAN BATH

There have been pubs in Bath for much longer than anyone can remember. They ranged from lofty coaching inns to squalid single-roomed alehouses. The only thing they had in common was that they all served beer. Beer was the national tipple – and in the days when water was likely to come laced with a lethal cocktail of diseases, drinking beer was a far healthier option.

As far back as you care to go, however, the authorities were trying to stop people drinking. In 1623, for example, the Mayor of Bath launched a campaign to suppress all unnecessary alehouses and reduce the strength of the ale sold in them. It worked for a time, but alehouses – licit and illicit – always seem to have had a habit of bouncing back.

By 1749, there were 150 inns and alehouses in the city – one for every 67 people. To put that another way, one in every ten houses served alcohol. Faced with such lavish over-provision, the authorities decided to act. By 1762 the number of alehouses had fallen to 120. Bath's population was growing rapidly, so this reduction was even more drastic than it first appears.

Having purged the city of its most notorious drinking dives, the authorities relaxed and the numbers started to climb again. By 1780, there were 163 licensed houses in the city.

Then came the Gordon Riots.

The Gordon Riots were probably the closest this country ever came to a full-blooded revolution. More damage was done in London during one week of mob rule than in Paris throughout the whole of the French Revolution. Bath was the only provincial city to experience anything like the devastation suffered by London. Its one night of rioting was one of the worst ever seen in England.

The riots were sparked off by the government's attempts to extend greater tolerance to Catholics, but the authorities in Bath had no illusion as to the underlying cause. "It is remarked," wrote a correspondent in the *Bath Chronicle* shortly afterwards, "that the great number of public houses, particularly those in many of the obscure parts, are most of them harbours for the rendezvous of the idle and profligate, who when assembled together generally excite one another to many daring, riotous and illegal acts, to the great dismay and terror of the public in general, as it is too well known by daily experience."

In the wake of the Gordon Riots, the number of licensed premises in Bath fell from 163 to 100. In the following decades, Bath's population continued to rise, but few new licenses were granted. By the end of the century, the number of inns and alehouses stood at 116 – one for every 284 people. This was quite a reduction from the figures for 1743, but it still meant that around one in every 30 houses sold alcohol.

Nothing much happened for the next 30 years, until the Prime Minister, the Duke of Wellington, concerned about the number of people drinking gin, decided to encourage them to drink more beer. His government proposed to allow any householder to open a beerhouse upon payment of two guineas (£2.10). Temperance campaigners and local authorities were horrified, warning of the dire consequences that would follow if the act were passed. Despite these protests, it was passed anyway, and the number of licensed premises doubled almost overnight. Most of the new beerhouses were in poorer areas and many soon became the centres for the sort of vice and depravity the authorities had spent so long trying to eradicate.

The government soon realised that it had made a tremendous blunder and amendments to the act began to appear. Not until 1869 was the legislation repealed, however, and control for all licensed premises handed over to local authorities. So began a campaign of suppression that has continued, almost unabated, to the present day. Bath expanded rapidly in the second half of the nineteenth century, but there was a virtual ban on new licences. Breweries could only get licences for new pubs in the suburbs if they agreed to close city centre pubs and transfer their licences to them.

Meanwhile, the arrival of the railway in 1841 signalled the end of the coaching trade which Bath's inns relied upon. Many closed immediately. Others struggled on, trying to adapt to a new role as family or commercial hotels. A century and a half later, none of Bath's inns survives in anything like its original form. Most were demolished years ago. The two that are still open – *All Bar One* (formerly the *Christopher*) and the *Rat & Parrot* (formerly the *Angel*) – have changed so much as to be unrecognisable.

By 1903, there were 240 pubs in the City of Bath (which at that time still excluded Twerton and Weston). As Bath had a population of just under 50,000, this meant there was a pub for every 208 residents, much higher than the ratio a century earlier, and well over three times higher than the ratio today.

For the first five years of the twentieth century, nothing much happened on Bath's pub scene. In 1901, the Bath Brewery Company, having surrendered the licences of three beerhouses – the *Fountain* in Avon Street, the *Malakoff* in Claverton Street, and the *Engineer's Arms* on the Lower Bristol Road – opened the *Moorfield's Park Tavern* in Oldfield Park. Between 1901 and 1905 only two other pubs closed – the *St George's Brewery* on the Upper Bristol Road and the *Rising Sun* in Union Passage, which was in the building now occupied by Thornton's.

In 1903, however, the licensing authorities commissioned a detailed report on the state of Bath's pubs. It provides a fascinating insight into what they were like, and we refer to it frequently in this book. The licensing authorities were not acting in a spirit of disinterested enquiry, however. They wanted a hit list, and in 1906 they started using it.

Forty-four pubs closed in between 1906 and 1914, an average of almost five a year. They included the following:

The *King's Arms* in Lilliput Alley after closure in 1906. Today, bay windows have been added to the building, part of which is occupied by *Tilley's Bistro*.

1906	*Military Arms*, Union Passage
	Peep O'Day, Sawclose
	King's Head, Lilliput Alley
	Newmarket Tavern, Walcot Street
	Corn Street Brewery, Corn Street
	Lord Nelson (Pig & Whistle), Avon Street
	Woolpack, Prospect Buildings, Twerton
	Wheatsheaf, High Street, Twerton
1907	*Owl's Nest*, Upper Borough Walls
	Don Cossack, Walcot Street
	Bunch of Grapes, Morford Street
	Boatman's Arms, Waterloo Buildings, Widcombe
1908	*Wheatsheaf*, Broad Street
	Chatham House Tavern, Walcot Street
	Black Horse, Kingsmead Square
	Greyhound, Claverton Street
	Prior Park Tavern, Coburg Place, Claverton Street
	Canal Tavern, Ebenezer Terrace, Claverton Street
	Old Fox, Holloway
1909	*Catherine Wheel*, Walcot Street
	Somerset Arms, Somerset Street
	Prince Frederick, Beauford Square
	Caledonian, Albion Buildings, Upper Bristol Road
1910	*Midland Arms*, Monmouth Street
	Exeter Inn, Southgate Street
1911	*Freemason's Arms*, Abbeygate Street
	Southgate Hotel, Southgate Street
	Manvers Arms, Philip Street
	Malt & Hops, Corn Street
1912	*Queen*, St Michael's Place
	Fuller's Wine Vaults, Upper Borough Walls
	Queen Square Wine & Spirit Vaults, Chapel Row
1913	*Lion Brewery*, Dolemeads
	New Inn, Widcombe Hill
	Queen's Head, Waterloo Buildings, Twerton
	Chequers, Peter Street
	Queen Square Tavern, Barton Street
	Rising Sun, Circus Mews
1914	*Mason's Arms*, Dolemeads
	Mason's Arms, High Street, Weston

1914	Queen's Head, Trafalgar Road, Weston
	Chandos Arms, Chandos Buildings
	Walcot Wine Vaults, Walcot Street
	Somerset Arms, Winifred's Lane

Bath was not alone in the savagery of its crackdown. The loss of almost one in five of the city's pubs in this brief period was spurred on by government legislation. An Act passed by the Conservative government in 1904, in an attempt to appease the temperance campaigners while keeping the brewers happy, established that local authorities could close down any pub they liked as long as they compensated the brewery and the landlord. Two years later, the Liberals, with strong links to the temperance movement, swept to power in a landslide victory. The following year, they proposed cutting the number of pubs by a third and started hiking the duty paid on alcohol to help pay for a programme of social reform. On average, 600 pubs a year closed in Britain between 1904 and 1934.

Opening hours also came under the spotlight. At the beginning of the twentieth century, pubs could open at five or six o'clock on weekday mornings and stay open till eleven o'clock at night. The only day on which there was any sort of restriction was Sunday. All this changed with the coming of war and Lloyd George's contention that munitions workers were spending all day in the pub. Whatever truth there was in the claim, to a veteran of a party committed to temperance, the war provided the perfect pretext to stop people drinking.

Early in 1915, Lloyd George declared that, "we are fighting Germany, Austria and Drink and, as far as I can see, the greatest of these deadly foes is Drink." The government passed emergency measures to restrict the production and strength of beer, and put prices up. Opening hours were drastically reduced. Pubs could not open before noon, had to close at 2.30 or 3pm, and were only allowed to open for a couple of hours in the evening. These measures were supposed to be temporary, but in 1921 an act was passed making them permanent. This stayed in force, with minor modifications, for most of the twentieth century, only being repealed in 1988.

The campaign to cut the number of Bath's pubs slowed dramatically with the outbreak of war. The Fox & Hounds in Walcot Street was the only pub to close in 1915, and 1916 was the first year since 1903 with no closures. 1917, however, saw five pubs disappear – the Three Crowns in London Street, the Shakespeare in Old Orchard Street, the Black Dog in Walcot Buildings, the Gardener's Arms on Primrose Hill, Weston, and an unnamed beerhouse in Claremont Buildings. The Edinburgh Arms on James Street West closed the following year.

The magistrates' drive to reduce the number of pubs continued after the First World War. It was helped by an ongoing programme of slum clearance. Areas that were full of pubs were bulldozed and replaced by new developments with no pubs at all. New estates in the suburbs were also provided with very few pubs. As a result, the number of pubs in Bath (including Combe Down, Twerton and Weston) fell from 186 in 1918 to 156 in 1938. Only two pubs opened in the interwar period – the

Englishcombe Inn on Englishcombe Lane and the *Trowbridge House* on Coronation Avenue. The thirty-two that closed included the following:

Albert Tavern, Union Passage
Albion Brewery, Corn Street
Barley Mow, Margaret's Hill
Bath Arms, Kingsmead Street
Beefsteak Tavern, Newmarket Row
Bladud's Head, Walcot Street
Cabinet Maker's Arms, Trim Street
Cleveland Arms, Sydney Wharf
Coach & Horses, Barton Street
Duke of Cambridge, Grove Street
Edinburgh Arms, James Street
Full Moon, Southgate Street
Garibaldi, Avon Street
Golden Lion, Southgate Street
Highbury Arms, Snow Hill
Lower Bristol Road Tavern, Lower Bristol Road
Lyncombe Brewery, Claverton Street
Mason's Arms, Peter Street
North Parade Brewery, North Parade Buildings
Old Bridge Tavern, Holloway
Queen, St Saviour's Road
Robin Hood, St George's Place, Upper Bristol Road
Seven Dials, Westgate Place
Smith's Arms, Winifred's Terrace, Dolemeads
Somerset Arms, Pulteney Place, Dolemeads
Somerset Wine Vaults, Southgate Street
Sumsion Brewery, Corn Street
Trafalgar Tavern, Calton Road
Turk's Head, Broad Street
Victoria Arms, Eldon Place, Larkhall
Waterman's Arms, Broad Quay
White Hart Vaults, Upper Borough Walls

The *Red Lion* in Kingsmead Street, destroyed by enemy action in 1942.

The pubs that went in the Second World War owed their demise to the Bath Blitz rather than the Bath magistrates. The *Half Moon* on Holloway, the *Bear* on Wellsway, the *Folly* beyond Hampton Row, the *Red Lion* in Kingsmead Street, the *Circus Brewery* in Circus Mews, the *Oxford Brewery* in Julian Road, and the *Railway Inn* in Twerton were among the pubs either destroyed by enemy action or so badly damaged that it was decided to demolish them. The *Livingstone* in Moorland Road was also destroyed but the pub stayed in business by moving up the road.

Since the Second World War, Bath's pubs have closed at the rate of one a year. In the 1960s and 1970s redevelopment accounted for many of the casualties, but since then it has been more a case of breweries realising their assets. In 1913, when the magistrates refused to renew the licence of the *New Inn* on Widcombe Hill, which had been closed for over a year, the owner protested, saying that he wanted to sell the pub as a going concern, as it was worth far more as a pub than as a private house. How times have changed! Today, many pubs would be worth far more as private houses or shops. They only manage to stay open because local authorities – the same local authorities who were doing their best to close them a century ago – refuse to grant change of use.

The *Coeur de Lion* and the *Beehive* on Belvedere, both of which were earmarked for conversion into shops, were only saved after vigorous lobbying and heated debate. Others were not so lucky. The list of pubs which have closed in the last five years makes depressing reading – the *Bladud Arms* in Swainswick, *Broadley's Wine Vaults* in the Sawclose, the *Golden Fleece* on Pulteney Road, the *Railway Tavern* on Wells Road, the *Royal Oak* on the Lower Bristol Road, the *Seven Stars* at Twerton, and the *Windsor Castle* on the Upper Bristol Road. *Broadley's* may yet reopen, and the *Seven Stars* has found a new use as a social club, but, for the rest, last orders have been called for the last time. It is even more depressing if we look further back. In the last 50 years, the number of pubs in Bath has fallen by over a third. The roll call of lost pubs is as follows:

Angel Tavern, Holloway
Atlas Brewery, Fielding Terrace, Twerton
Beaufort Arms, Princes Street
Beehive, Belvedere
Beehive, Mount Road, Southdown
Beehive, Walcot Street
Bell, Gloucester Street
Berkeley Arms, Berkeley Street
Bladud Arms, Gloucester Road, Lower Swainswick
Broadley's Wine Vaults, Gascoyne Place
Claremont Arms, George's Road, Fairfield
Claverton Brewery, Claverton Street
Coachmaker's Arms, Snow Hill
Crown Brewery, New Orchard Street
East Twerton Hotel, St Peter's Terrace, Lower Bristol Road
Edinburgh Castle, Newark Street
Gay's Hill Tavern, Gay's Hill
Globe, High Street, Weston
Golden Fleece, Queen's Place, Pulteney Road
Great Western Hotel, Dorchester Street

The *Beaufort Arms* in Princes Street, one of around 60 pubs that have closed in Bath since the Second World War.

Grove Tavern, Padley Bottom
Horse & Jockey, Beau Street
Jupiter Inn, Prospect Place, Combe Down
King's Arms, Bailbrook
Kingsmead Wine Vaults, Kingsmead Street
Lamb Hotel, Stall Street
Lansdown Brewery, Belle Vue Buildings, Lansdown Road
Masons' Arms, Claremont Row, Tyning Lane
Masons' Arms, Bradford Road, Combe Down
New Inn, Southgate Street
New Moon, Upper Borough Walls
Newbridge Tavern, Lower Bristol Road
Old Ship, St James's Street South
Olivers, Southgate Street
Portland Arms, Portland Place
Queen Victoria, Hampton Row
Railway Inn, Charles Street
Railway Hotel, Wells Road
Retreat, Primrose Hill
Ring o'Bells, High Street, Twerton
Rising Sun, Gloucester Road, Upper Swainswick
River's Arms, Camden Road
Rose, Morford Street
Royal Oak, Lower Bristol Road
Royal Oak, Monmouth Place, Upper Bristol Road
Royal Sailor, Wells Road
Seven Stars, Avon Buildings, Twerton
Seven Stars, Upper Borough Walls
South Pole, Dorchester Street
Three Blackbirds, Little Stanhope Street
Three Crowns, North Road, Combe Down
Three Cups, Walcot Street
White Lion, Lambridge Buildings, St Saviour's Road, Larkhall
Windsor Castle, Upper Bristol Road
Young Fox, Old Orchard, Holloway

There is no indication that the rate of closure – over one a year – is about to slacken. The pub is a unique British institution, but, with the fate of so many of them now in the hands of accountants and image consultants in distant lands, it is one that faces a growing threat. One sector of the pub business is booming, however – the superpub. But while the multi-portfolioed companies that have taken over from the big breweries press for more and bigger superpubs, the traditional local is under threat as never before.

WHO BREWS BATH'S BEER?

The first big brewery in Bath was built by Ralph Allen at Widcombe in 1736. After his death in 1764, most of his estate was inherited by his niece, Gertrude Tucker, who was married to William Warburton, Bishop of Gloucester. Not considering it seemly to be associated with trade she closed down the stone quarries, sold the tramway for scrap, and disposed of the brewery. So ended Bath's first encounter with large-scale brewing. Others, however, quickly stepped into the breach.

At the beginning of the eighteenth century, most of the beer drunk in Bath's inns and alehouses came from small brewhouses in their back yards. By the end of the century, a cluster of large and medium-sized breweries had sprung up in and around the city, and the licensed trade had been transformed from a cottage industry into one controlled by wealthy businessmen. By 1822, only one in five of Bath's pubs was still a free house. The others were tied to local brewers. Not surprisingly, a lot of high profile wheeler-dealing went on. In 1825, for example, the Large Brothers (William and Joseph), whose portfolio already included the *Argyle Tap* in Argyle Street, the *Sydney Tap* in Sydney Gardens and the *Plough* in Southgate Street, agreed to pay £18,640 (around £1M in today's terms) to James Grant Smith for the Anchor Brewery in Southgate Street, together with 13 tied pubs. These included the *Angel Inn* and *Angel Tap* on Holloway, the *Hare & Hounds* on Lansdown, the *Red Lion* in Kingsmead Street, the *Lord Nelson* in Avon Street, the *Bird in Hand* in Corn Street, the *Horse & Groom* in Princes Street, the *Three Blackbirds* on the Upper Bristol Road, the *Packhorse* in Widcombe, the *Full Moon* by the Old Bridge, the *Bath Arms* on Southgate Street, the *Bird Cage* in Westgate Street and the *White Horse* in Stall Street. Three years later, in 1828, William Large decided to retire, the partnership was dissolved, and the property they had acquired from James Grant Smith, but which was only partly paid for, reverted to him. In 1842, he went bankrupt and the Anchor Brewery was advertised for sale. However, there were no takers, and the brewery, along with the *Bath Arms* and the *White Horse*, closed down. The other pubs were bought out by the licensees or taken over by other brewers. The only one still open today is the *Hare & Hounds*. After standing empty for several years, in 1850 the Anchor Brewery was demolished to make way for Rainey's Cabinet Works.*

Bath's biggest brewery was where Waitrose is today. Known as the Northgate Brewery, it was founded in the 1770s by Samuel Sayce, and brewed porter, for which

---

* The Anchor Brewery features in a Panorama of Bath painted by JW Allen in 1833, on display in the Building of Bath Museum on the Vineyards.

there was an almost insatiable demand. Due to a combination of luck and astute business acumen, it soon became the biggest brewery in the West of England. When it outgrew its site, a tramway bridge was built across the river so that it could continue to expand along Grove Street. The Northgate Brewery's contribution to the pollution of the river was a constant source of irritation to the council. There were other problems as well. In 1853, for example, the owners were summoned for using "the chimney flue of their brewing furnace without taking means to consume the smoke thereof."

In 1868, however, two of the partners who owned the brewery died within a short time of each other, and the third, "a gentleman of large fortune," decided to sell up. The brewery, together with 28 tied houses, was put on the market, but, although most of the pubs were snapped up, there were no takers for the brewery. Its equipment was sold off piecemeal and the site was redeveloped.

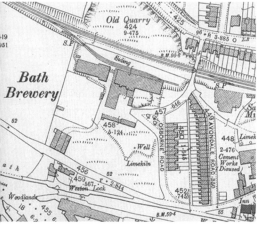

The Bath Brewery in Lower Weston, next to the Midland Railway. A garage now occupies the site.

Bath's other big breweries closed during the nineteenth century for various reasons – bankruptcy being a common one – and by the beginning of the twentieth century there was only one major brewery left – the Bath Brewery at Lower Weston, opened in 1898.

The Bath Brewery owned 56 pubs in the city, well over a quarter of the total. Other major pub owners were the Oakhill Brewery, with ten houses, Wilkins Brothers & Hudson of Bradford on Avon with eight, the Charlton Brewery of Shepton Mallet, the Stokescroft Brewery of Bristol, and the Lamb Brewery of Frome, with seven each, and the Anglo-Bavarian Brewery of Shepton Mallet with six. Frome United Breweries, the Old Market Brewery in Bristol, and Charles Stride of the Albion Brewery in Corn Street had five each, while George Biggs of the Crown Brewery in New Orchard Street had four.

Brewers with only one or two pubs in the city included the Batheaston Brewery, Bass, Ratcliff & Gretton of Burton on Trent, Eldridge Pope of Dorchester, Shepherd's of Warminster, Blake's of Trowbridge, J&T Usher's of Bristol, Pointing's of Weston, Ruddle's of Bradford on Avon, the Southstoke Brewery, Usher's of Trowbridge, and Welton Breweries. At least 28 pubs in the city still brewed their own beer. Bath's drinkers had a formidable array of different beers to choose from. What is more, apart from one pub owned by Bass and one owned by Eldridge Pope, it all came from no more than 20 miles away.

With 22 breweries represented in the city, and 28 home-brew houses, there were more different beers available in Bath 100 years ago than there are on offer at many beer festivals today. Their quality is a different matter, but a story from 1916 shows that Bath's drinkers were just as partisan and particular about their beer as they are today. The licensing magistrates had decided that there were too many pubs on Holloway and recommended the *Angel* for closure. The Welton Brewery Company, who owned it, put up a strong defence, pointing out that it was their only outlet in Bath. Several customers appeared before the magistrates, saying they had a particular liking for Welton beer and would miss it if the *Angel* closed. So strong was local feeling that the magistrates gave in, and the *Angel* survived for another 42 years. However, the victory was somewhat hollow. Two years later, Welton Brewery was taken over by George's of Bristol.

It is remarkable, given their later prominence, that George's owned no pubs in Bath in 1903. They gained a foothold in the city in 1911 when they absorbed the Stokescroft Brewery with seven tied houses. In 1923, they took over the Bath Brewery Company, and overnight George's became Bath's biggest-selling beer. George Biggs of the New Crown Brewery sold out to George's the following year. In 1931, the Ashton Gate Brewery (which had taken over the Old Market Brewery in 1911) was also taken over by George's.

Oakhill Brewery was taken over by another Bristol giant, Bristol United Breweries of Lewin's Mead, in 1925, although brewing continued at Oakhill until 1938. The two-and-a-half-mile-long narrow-gauge railway that linked the brewery with the Somerset & Dorset Railway at Binegar, however, succumbed to road competition in 1921. Charlton Brewery was the next to be absorbed by Bristol United Breweries. Brewing continued at Charlton until 1961. By then, Bristol United Breweries had been taken over by George's, who turned the Lewin's Mead Brewery into a sugar factory. George's themselves were swallowed up by Courage's in 1961, but the brewery stayed open.

Courage's now had the lion's share of Bath's pubs, but Usher's of Trowbridge, who had only one pub in the city in 1903, came a respectable second.. They had taken over Wilkins Brothers & Hudson of Bradford on Avon in 1920, and in 1957 teamed up with Stroud Brewery to take over the two Frome breweries (Frome United and Lamb) which had merged two years previously. Pubs previously owned by the Frome Breweries were divided up between the Stroud Brewery and Usher's. In 1960, Usher's merged with Watney Mann, but the Trowbridge brewery stayed open. In 1972, Watney Mann was taken over by Grand Metropolitan and the brewery and pubs were managed separately. Stroud Brewery merged with Cheltenham & Hereford Breweries in 1958 to form West Country Breweries and became part of Whitbread's five years later.

When Fred Pearce went round Bath's 112 pubs in 1976, 58 were owned by Courage's, 17 by Watney's/Usher's, eleven by Bass, seven by Whitbread, two by Ind Coope, two by Wadworth's, two by Gibbs Mew, two by Berni's, one by Devenish's, and one by Eldridge Pope. Nine were free houses.

Things remained much the same until the end of the 1980s. The old George's brewery in Bristol continued to brew the bulk of Bath's beer. Usher's continued to be brewed at Trowbridge. Drinking tastes changed, pubs closed, the threat of keg beer came and went, but, by and large, Bath's drinkers could have been forgiven for thinking that the future looked relatively bright. Courage's confirmed their commitment to keeping George's brewery going as a dedicated real ale brewery and, after plans to close Usher's Brewery were dropped in the mid-1970s, Grand Metropolitan seemed no less keen to maintain it as a going concern.

Then the Government had a Really Good Idea. Whenever the powers that be have had a Really Good Idea, it has almost always gone terribly wrong. Take William of Orange. When he overthrew James II in a coup in 1688, he hit on the bright idea of cutting the tax on spirits and increasing the number of distilleries. Result - the gin epidemic. In 1830, the Duke of Wellington, anxious to cut gin consumption, decided that it would be a jolly good thing if people drank more beer and passed the Beer Act. Result – the number of licensed premises doubled and the gin epidemic was replaced by the beer epidemic.

What happened in 1989 was not epidemic but meltdown – or something very near it. The Monopolies and Mergers Commission, enquiring into the state of the brewing industry, found much to displease them. Their recommendations were draconian. No brewer should own more than 2,000 pubs, loan ties should be abolished to prevent the effective takeover of free houses, and every pub should have at least one guest beer. The Government watered down the proposals, ignoring the bit about loan ties, but the big six breweries (Allied, Bass, Courage, Grand Metropolitan, Scottish & Newcastle, and Whitbread) who were responsible for around 80% of beer production, were told they had to turn many of their pubs into free houses and introduce guest beers into the rest. As the guest beers had to be cask-conditioned, this seemed like a dream come true for Britain's real-ale drinking fraternity.

It soon turned to nightmare. The big brewers were not going to be told what to do by the Government. They proceeded to turn the "beer orders" into an irrelevance. Courage and Grand Metropolitan (the owners of Usher's) made the first move. Their solution was breathtakingly simple. They agreed to swap pubs and breweries. Courage would concentrate on brewing, while Grand Met would form a company called Inntrepreneur to run the pubs.

In this new climate, Usher's suddenly found itself facing closure. This was averted by a management buyout in 1991. After 31 years, Usher's was once again an independent brewery with a tied estate of 433 pubs. For a time all went well. Then, in 1999, Usher's merged with the Alehouse company. A year later the company changed its name to Innspired Pubs PLC. Shortly afterwards, the Trowbridge brewery, despite running at full capacity, was closed because the Innspired accountants considered it "not cost effective." What this meant was that, because it was in the town centre, it was ripe for development. Plans submitted to West Wiltshire Council in 2003 outlined a scheme to convert the old brewery site for housing, retail and leisure use.

After the closure of Usher's Brewery, a company called Refresh UK was established to market beers under the Usher's brand name. Usher's beer was initially brewed under contract by the Thomas Hardy Burtonwood Brewery (the old Eldridge Pope Brewery) at Dorchester, until this too closed in 2003, another victim of being in a town centre. Some was also brewed at the Wychwood Brewery in Witney, which was taken over by Refresh UK in 2002. Latest news is that Usher's is now being brewed under contract by Wadworth's Brewery in Devizes.

The year before the closure of Usher's Brewery in Trowbridge, Scottish Courage closed George's Brewery in Bristol, which had a history dating back to 1702. They blamed the closure on a steady decline in real ale sales, failing to point out that the company had virtually ceased promoting the stuff, although they had spent a fortune on trying to get people to drink John Smith's Extra Smooth. Beer production was transferred from Bristol to John Smith's Brewery at Tadcaster in Yorkshire.

The rest of the "big six" soon followed Courage and Grand Metropolitan's example. In 1989, most British pubs were owned by the "big six" breweries. Today, the "big six" have been reduced to four – Scottish Courage, Coors, Interbrew, and Carlsberg-Tetley, and their pubs have been hived off to new pub-owning conglomerates, such as Pubmaster, Punch and Enterprise Inns. Links between the pub-owning companies and the brewers mean that, to all intents and purposes, there is a greater monopoly in 2003 than in 1989. The "beer orders" had precisely the opposite effect to that intended.

Having failed to foist keg beer onto us, the big breweries are trying once again to undermine real ale sales by promoting nitro-keg "smooth" beers such as John Smith's. The reason is straightforward. The Marketing Director of one of the big breweries is upfront about the rationale behind this: "From the retailer's perspective, they don't want a living organism (real ale) to look after in their cellars. They haven't got the time – they want ease of use and no worries. Basically, with cask ale, you wouldn't want to invest your money personally in it."

Fortunately, not everybody takes this view. Brewing terrific beer does not require the outlay of vast sums of money, nor is looking after a barrel of real ale when it turns up from the brewery in the rocket science league. However, both processes resist automation and require a degree of hands-on involvement which is anathema to the accountants and the flow-chart optimisation mob.

One brewery has bucked all the trends. Founded in 1875, still brewing, and owning around 250 pubs, including several in Bath, Wadworth's is a family firm which has resisted the blandishments of the buy-it-up-and-close-it-down brigade, showing rare commitment not only to its employees but also to its customers. Its red-brick tower brewery in Devizes, built in 1885, with its original copper, is a rare survival. Wadworth's also has a cooper – one of only five in the country working exclusively on beer barrels. Bucking another trend, Wadworth's is increasing the amount of beer sent out to pubs in wooden barrels. 6X is the company's flagship brew, but Henry's IPA and Summersault and seasonal beers are also popular. Wadworth's can be found in Bath at the *Curfew*, the *Long Acre Tavern*, the *New Inn*, the *New Westhall*, the *Rose & Crown*, the *Old Farmhouse*, and the *Wansdyke Inn*. Another family-owned brewery which has an outlet in Bath is Brain's of Cardiff, founded in 1882. It now owns the former *Royal Oak* – now renamed the *Brains Surgery* – in Larkhall.

The upsurge in small breweries in the last twenty years is one of the great success stories of local enterprise – and a reassurance that we are not quite ready to be submerged in a grey sludge of blandness and mediocrity.

The first small brewer to set up in this neck of the woods, in the wake of the real ale revival, celebrated its 25th anniversary in 2003. It was on 2 April 1977 that Smile's, a traditional tower brewery, was set up in Colston Yard in Bristol. To celebrate its 25th birthday on 2 April 2003, an Anniversary Ale was launched at the splendid *Brewery Tap* in Bristol.

The following year, Simon Whitmore, a former Courage director, set up Butcombe Brewery at his home near Bristol. It has expanded steadily, and now has six pubs, as well as supplying around 350 other outlets. In March 2003, Simon Whitmore retired and the brewery was sold to the former owners of the Beer Seller distribution company. Butcombe Bitter is found in several Bath pubs and is offered, along with Bass, in many pubs in North Somerset. Butcombe was a one-beer brewery until 1999, when a new premium-strength bitter, Butcombe Gold was introduced.

RCH Brewery was set up behind the Royal Clarence Hotel in Weston-super-Mare in the early 1980s. Problems with the water supply (at times the brewery was using the hotel's entire water supply, leaving guests without the wherewithal for a quiet scrub) led to a move to a former cider mill at nearby West Hewish. RCH Pitchfork, a hoppy bitter which won title of Best British Bitter in 1998, is a popular fixture in several Bath pubs. Other RCH beers include Old Slug Porter, East Street Cream and Firebox.

Oakhill Brewery was set up in 1984 in a fermentation room at the old Oakhill Brewery, which it later outgrew and moved to the old maltings. It now has five pubs and around 200 other outlets. Its range includes Oakhill Bitter, Mendip Gold and Yeoman 1767 (the date referring to the year the original Oakhill Brewery was founded).

Wickwar Brewery opened in 1990. Its founder, Ray Penny, had run pubs as a tenant for Courage's, and when the law about pubs having to serve a guest beer came in, he saw an opening in the market. After a quick but intensive apprenticeship, he opened a brewery in an old cooper's shop at Wickwar in Gloucestershire. It has gone from strength to strength, with an impressive line-up of beers, including BOB (Brand Oak Bitter), Station Porter, Olde Merryford, and Mr Perrett's Traditional Stout (dedicated to Arnold Perrett who brewed on the same site until the 1950s).

Bath Ales was founded in 1995 by two former employees of Smile's Brewery, using the same plant as the Henstridge Brewery (which closed in 2000). It moved to Webb's Heath, between Bath and Bristol in 1999. It owns six pubs, including the *Hop Pole* and the *Salamander* in Bath. Its range of beers include three regulars – Spa, Gem, Barnstormer (short-listed by CAMRA for best bitter of the year in 2003) – and three seasonal beers – Festivity, Rare Hare and Spa Extra.

There are other recent arrivals. The Milk Street Brewery in Frome opened in 1999 at the back of the *Griffin*. Glastonbury Brewery started production at Somerton in May 2002. Its Mystery Tor is a stunning addition to the Somerset beer scene. Breweries from somewhat farther afield whose products can regularly be found in Bath's top real ale pubs include Stonehenge Ales, set up in an old electricity generating station at Netheravon in 1984. Originally called Bunce's, it was taken over by Danish master brewer Stig Andersen in 1994 and renamed in 1998. Sign of Spring is a green-tinted seasonal beer brewed in March and April, while brews such as Danish Dynamite and Old Smokey are deservedly popular among the real-ale fraternity. Great Dane is one of the few cask-conditioned lagers brewed in this country and well worth seeking out. Hopback Beers from Downton near Salisbury – and their perennially popular Summer Lightning – is another brewery well worth checking out.

These small breweries – there are many others – are taking brewing back to its roots as a small-scale industry. With all the hi-tech equipment at their disposal, the hit and miss brewing methods of the eighteenth and nineteenth centuries, are a thing of the past. The success of local breweries demonstrate that there is a strong demand for beer that has a local identity, brewed according to traditional methods by people who are concerned about creating a high-quality product and not just about making a fast buck.

Finally, there is Abbey Ales, Bath's own brewery, founded by Alan Morgan at the back of the *Old Farmhouse* in 1997. Bellringer Bitter, its flagship beer, winner of numerous accolades and awards, is now the best-selling real ale in Bath, and can be found in most of the top pubs within a 20-mile radius. Winner of several regional and national awards, it is deservedly popular and, in just six years, has become among just about most famous brand in the city. Seasonal brews from Abbey Ales include Bath Star, Chorister, Twelfth Night, White Friar and Black Friar. The brewery now owns the *Star* on the Vineyards.

When Fred Pearce wandered round Bath's pubs in 1976, he found that less than half of the pubs owned by Courage's served real ale. For Usher's the figure was just over a third. The CAMRA bandwagon was already rolling, but that is how close we came to losing real ale to keg. There is not much keg around these days. Even with all the advertising hype, drinkers just realised that it was not very good. And so we got nitrokeg. . . .

The percentage of pubs that serve real ale is much higher these days than it was in 1976. Wine bars and youth-orientated superpubs tend not to stock real ales (although some youth-oriented pubs like *Lambretta's* and the *Pig & Fiddle* go so far to buck the trend as to merit entries in the *Good Beer Guide*). It is not so much keg beer that has replaced real ale, but bottled beer, vodka, alcopops, wine, cocktails and myriad concoctions that just were not around a quarter of a century ago.

Virtually all the traditional pubs in Bath serve real ales. Most of them take care to look after it, but in some the quality is decidedly questionable. Some of these pubs are the ones in which visitors from abroad are most likely to end up. For many of them, trying out a pint of traditional English beer is likely to be an experience they will be unlikely to repeat. Like the American servicemen who came over here in the Second World War, they will return home with tales of warm, unpleasant beer, courtesy of indifferent landlords. Given the unprecedented interest in microbreweries and traditionally-brewed beers in America, it is a pity that one of this country's chief cultural assets and tourist attractions should sometimes be in the hands of such careless ambassadors. The publicans who do take care to serve good real ale – and, thankfully, they are in the majority – not only give visitors a taste of something uniquely English, but provide those of us who live here with one of the best possible reasons for staying.*

---

* For more information on the history of brewing in Bath, see Mike Bone's article in *Bath History VIII* (Bath, 2000). The Museum of Bath at Work in Julian Road, Bath, also has a permanent exhibition on the history of brewing in Bath, as well as related industries. Phone 01225 318348 for details of opening times, or see their website, www.bath-at-work.org.uk.

PUB LISTINGS

ALEHOUSE 1 York Street

York Street was built in 1796 and named after the Duchess of York, the first person to ride along it in a carriage. On the corner of York Street stands the *Alehouse*, originally known as the *York Street Wine Vaults*. As with other streets built from scratch in the eighteenth century, the houses at the end of York Street were built first to provide an imposing entrance, leaving the rest of the street to be added later. As a result, the *Alehouse* – four storeys high – was built with toothstones abutting the site of the house next door. Unfortunately, the builder of the next house opted for only two storeys, leaving the toothstones as a perpetual reminder of the piecemeal way the street was built.

The *York Street Wine Vaults* does not seem to have started off as a pub. The 1852 Directory lists the owner as Henry Dwyer, a spirit merchant. By 1888, however, the *Wine Vaults* had acquired a five motion beer engine, pewter beer measures, a rack of glasses, tables and chairs, and – a real giveaway that it was being used as a pub – "four spittoons and a brush."

As can be seen from the picture above, it once looked across to the old Bath Royal Literary & Scientific Institution which stood where Bog Island is today. Note also the old tramlines in the road.

A century ago, the *York Street Wine Vaults* was a free house. One of the city's smaller pubs, with just one bar, it was later renamed the *York Street Hotel*, before becoming the *Alehouse*. Some people still remember it as a cider house, but by the 1970s (by which time it had been taken over by Courage's) it was one of Bath's top real ale pubs. It has not appeared in the Good Beer Guide, however, for some time.

In July 1983 the pub was at the centre of a furore when the planning department and Bath Preservation Trust saw red after the top of the building was painted pink. Although this may seem like a bid to attract a particular clientele, a spokesman for Courage's said that it had only been painted pink because the council had not allowed it to be painted tangerine. A compromise was eventually reached.

If it were not for the cellar bar, which advertises some of the cheapest eats in the city, the *Alehouse* could well qualify as Bath's smallest pub. Its uncluttered, clear-glass windows and ever-open door give its punters an uninterrupted view of the open-topped buses queuing up to take visitors round the city. They also have the advantage of letting potential customers see what the pub is like before they go in.

ALL BAR ONE 10-11 High Street

Nothing exemplifies more clearly the contrast between the traditional pub and the modern bar than comparing the *Alehouse* with *All Bar One*. Even to the uninitiated, it is obvious that the *Alehouse* is a traditional public house. It says so on the wall outside. The *Alehouse* is not much bigger than a typical living room, with a few tables and chairs, a fruit machine, a telly, and blokes – almost invariably blokes – sitting on stools or standing at the bar. "Traditional" in this context, however, needs a bit of explanation. You will not find any olde worlde spittoons in the *Alehouse*, for example. And if you went back just 50 years, you would find a very different pub – no telly or jukebox, and a much more limited range of beers. There would be no draught lager – possibly no lager at all, and certainly not the range of chilled bottled beers you get today. Mackeson, brown or light ale, and similar delights, all served at room temperature, would be all you could expect. There would be a single brand of vodka, also served at room temperature, with ice if you fancied cooling it down. Instead of a rack of wine dispensers there would be a single bottle – or a couple of bottles if you were lucky – gathering dust somewhere behind the pickled eggs.

But, if the *Alehouse's* décor and drinks cannot be regarded as traditional, its appeal certainly is. If a regular from 50 years ago were to be rocketed forward in time to the twenty-first century *Alehouse*, he would find much to surprise him, but he would still manage to get a decent pint of bitter, and before long he would feel right at home, discussing football and generally putting the world to rights.

If he were plonked down in *All Bar One*, on the other hand, he would probably think he was on another planet. *All Bar One* is the antithesis of everything pubs like the *Alehouse* stand for. The *All Bar One* chain was the result of Bass's attempt to get more women into pubs. The bars were big and open-plan, with no hidden corners. There were no stools at the bar. You had to be over 21 to get in. They made a point of serving decent wines. They had large, uncluttered windows, so that potential customers could see inside as they walked past.* Nouvelle-cuisine-type menus, olives and magazines, all added up to an experience with a vaguely continental or transatlantic feel. It worked, and Bath's *All Bar One* is one of the most popular bars in the city – not only with women, but also (surprise, surprise) with blokes.

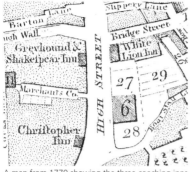

A map from 1779 showing the three coaching inns in the High Street – the *Christopher*, the *White Lion*, and the *Greyhound & Shakespeare*.

The fitting out of Bath's *All Bar One*, however, was at the expense of the remaining vestiges of Bath's oldest coaching inn. Two hundred years ago, there were three coaching inns in the High Street – the *Greyhound* (also known as the *Greyhound & Shakespeare*) near the corner of Upper Borough Walls, the *White Lion* on the corner of Bridge Street, and the *Christopher*. The first two have long gone, but the *Christopher* has become *All Bar One*, which, despite all appearances to the contrary, is a strong contender for the title of Bath's oldest pub.

Its original name was an inspired choice. As well as being the Patron Saint of Travellers, St Christopher was the Patron Saint of Weavers. As anybody familiar with Chaucer's Wife of Bath will know, the city was once one of Europe's top weaving centres.

The *Christopher* may date back to the days of Queen Elizabeth – there is even a legend that she once stayed there – but it was certainly an inn by 1644, when Simon Sloper, Richard Wakeman and George Chapman acquired the lease from the corporation.

An advertisement in the *Gloucester Journal* for 17 January 1738 gives us an idea of what the *Christopher* had to offer the weary traveller in the early eighteenth century:

> Henry Trinder, cook, from the Three Tuns in Stall Street, Bath, now keeps the *Christopher Inn* in the Market Place . . . where is kept a good ordinary every day at two o'clock; and where gentlemen may depend upon the civillest usage, and good entertainment – board and lodging – and all sorts of neat wines sold at the cheapest rates. He likewise dresses dinners at gentlemen's or ladies' houses or lodgings; and all sorts of soups, and made dishes drest.

Seven years later, the "Inn called the *Christopher* in the Market Place, late the estate of Thomas Penny, a Bankrupt," was advertised to let. It was taken by Mr Hadden, a staunch supporter of John Wesley. Wesley did not think much of Bath – he once referred to it as "that Sodom of our land" – but he liked the *Christopher* so much he stayed there over 80 times.

---

* As does the *Alehouse*, of course. The point is, though, that the *All Bar One* chain pioneered the plate-glass window approach, and many traditional pubs have since imitated it. The *Griffin* on Monmouth Street is another example. These are the exceptions. Traditionally, if the windows in a bar were low enough to see into or out of, frosted or stained glass was used to prevent people from doing so. If the budget did not run to special glass, curtains were put up instead, as in the *Volunteer Rifleman's Arms*. The glass bricks on the front of the *Livingstone* in Oldfield Park are a mid-twentieth-century example of this imperative to screen drinkers from the outside world. It was a policy that, until very recently, satisfied everybody. Temperance campaigners and guardians of the nation's morals wanted drinkers screened from the sight of respectable people, while drinkers cherished their secret boltholes, safe from the prying eyes of employers, police officers or irate wives.

After Mr Hadden's death in the 1770s, the *Christopher* maintained its connection with Methodism. Bath's Methodists were still holding dinners at the *Christopher* in 1799. Although it was not a temperance hotel, Mr Hadden and his successors took a principled stand on a variety of issues. Staff at the inn were given time off on Sunday, but only on the understanding that they attended church. Any who sloped off to a nearby alehouse or opted for a stroll along the river would soon have had their marching orders. Anything to do with gambling or riotous conduct was also frowned on. When the Bath Races were held in 1782, for example, the *Bath Chronicle* declared that "we have the honour to say that all the innkeepers have subscribed to the plates as usual, except the *Christopher Inn*."

In the nineteenth century, the *Christopher* consolidated its reputation as one of Bath's top inns. One of Bath's most famous MPs, the architect Sir William Tite, often stayed there when in the city. He regarded it "as widely known of good reputation and situated in the best part of town for a Hotel." Unlike many other inns, it successfully rode out the loss of business caused by the coming of the railway in 1841. In 1886 there were plans to completely rebuild the *Christopher*. The new building, which would have been set well back from the street, would have extended up the High Street as far as the Corridor and a considerable way along Cheap Street as well. These plans, however, came to nothing.

Many people will remember the Christopher's latter days as a hotel, when it boasted such delights as "Harry's Bar," the "Wig and Pen Lounge Bar," the "Judge's Chambers" and the "Coach House Restaurant & Bar." Today the hotel has closed and all the bars have gone – all, that is, bar one. Although gutted beyond all recognition, the Christopher is still open today. It has even kept its old name, high above the modern entrance.

ASSEMBLY INN   17 Alfred Street

Alfred Street was built by John Wood the Younger around 1773. The story of how the street got its name is a curious one.

One of the first people to move into it was the Reverend Dr Thomas Wilson, who lived in Alfred House at the far end of the street. Dr Wilson was a fervent admirer of the writer and historian Catherine Macaulay. Although almost totally forgotten today, in the 1770s she was one of the top celebrities in the country. Derby porcelain figurines of her were collector's items. Portraits of her were on every printseller's counter. When life-size waxworks of her and two top politicians were exhibited in London in 1772, hers was the one that everybody recognised.

Catherine Macaulay's great hero was King Alfred. Naturally, Dr Wilson shared her admiration for the Saxon monarch, and it is likely that, when he put down the money for John Wood the Younger to build him a house in this street (which still had not been named) he persuaded him to slap a bust of Alfred over the front door and name the street after him. A couple of years after Dr Wilson moved in, Catherine Macaulay joined him, although her stay proved to be a short one. She outraged Bath society by running off with a man 26 years her junior, leaving Dr Wilson to vent his spleen in the local paper. Despite this, the bust of Alfred stayed up over Dr Wilson's door and the street kept its name.

Originally, Alfred Street was publess. Like most of the houses in the street, No 17 started off as a lodging house for genteel visitors, a role it fulfilled for almost 150 years. After the First World War, however, it became the headquarters of the Somerset Mission to the Deaf & Dumb. Just before the Second World War, Sainsbury Bros. opened a wine merchants there.

After the war, the wine merchant's became the *Wine Vaults Public House*. By 1967, a bar had opened in the cellar. This was known as "The Teenagers' Tavern," and offered "guitar music" as well as "a large selection of drinks and snacks." In 1969 it was renamed the *Assembly Inn* after the nearby Assembly Rooms. Today it is a big double-barred pub, where Edwardiana rubs shoulders with Sky TV and the clink of pool balls echoes off the wood-panelled walls.

BARLEY 32 Bathwick Street

The *Barley* – originally known as the *Barley Mow* – opened as a beerhouse in the 1840s, when a new ground floor frontage was added to the stretch of Bathwick Street between Daniel Street and Daniel Mews.[*]

There were once two beerhouses along this short stretch. From the late 1850s to around 1872, a beerhouse called the *Sydney Porter Stores* (later the *Rifleman's Arms*) occupied what is now Bathwick Post Office and the launderette on the corner of Daniel Street. The *Barley Mow*, on the corner of Daniel Mews, has had somewhat better staying power.

When an inventory of the *Barley Mow* was drawn up in 1893, it had a five-motion beer engine in the bar, but no counter – unusual in a late-nineteenth-century town pub, although still common in the country. Instead, there was a serving door with a sliding sash over it. The bar also had a panelled settle and fixed seating around the walls. Beyond the bar was a tap room, and beyond that was a brewery, which closed in the mid-1920s.

---

[*] It is possible that this new frontage was a structural necessity. The row of houses running from Daniel Street to Sydney Place has, unlike most other terraces in the area, a wooden bressemer running along the front at first-floor level. This indicates that it was built on the cheap, with the frontage being only one course of stone thick. By the mid-nineteenth century, the addition of a new ground-floor frontage, extending outwards from the building, may have been necessary to act as a buttress and prevent the wall from collapsing.

When Fred Pearce visited the *Barley Mow* in 1976, it still had three bars – the public at the front, dominated by "noisy young drinkers in suits," a darts dominated smoking room, and a lounge reached via the yard at the back. Today the *Barley* has been knocked through and made-over inside, with sofas and imaginative décor, but the elaborate nineteenth-century sign bracket still hangs above the door.

The *Barley Mow* was – and still is – a common pub name, although Bath's two other *Barley Mows* – on St Margaret's Hill off the London Road and in Avon Street – have long since closed. A mow, incidentally, is a stack.

BATH TAP   19 St James's Parade

In 1765, the Corporation gave Richard Jones, Thomas Jelly and Henry Fisher the go-ahead "to pull down the Borough Walls next to the Ambury Gardens to build new houses there, the carriageway to be 30 feet wide and a footway either side to be three feet wide." St James's Parade (originally called Thomas Street) was the result. It was intended as a secluded backwater of genteel lodging houses, with no access to wheeled traffic – in other words, an eighteenth-century pedestrian precinct.

For a time, it attracted wealthy visitors. In 1774, for example, the great Catherine Macaulay stayed there. As she was often associated with Minerva, it is possible that the house she stayed in is the one with a bust of Minerva over the door. Unlike John Wood's Parades, however, which were raised high above the river, St James's Parade was regularly inundated by floods. It was probably the severe flood of 1774 that drove Catherine Macaulay out of St James's Parade and led to her ill-fated decision to move in with Dr Wilson in his house in Alfred Street. St James's Parade's reputation for dampness led to its speedy abandonment by fashionable society. By the early nineteenth century, it was home to a variety of small tradesmen, such as carpenters, tailors, plumbers, butchers and lamp sellers.

Thomas Hunt of Southstoke bought 19 St James's Parade in 1823. He seems to have done very little with it, and by 1848, when he leased it to one of his in-laws, George Love, it was more or less derelict. George Love already ran the *Devonshire Arms* on Wellsway, and when he opened 19 St James's Parade as a pub the following year, after an extensive refurbishment, and with a new brewery at the back, he decided to call it the *Devonshire Arms* as well.

In 1852, the comforts of the new *Devonshire Arms'* yard proved to be the undoing of one of the city's guardians. The Watch Committee reports for January of that year contain the following entry:

PC Cox is charged with being found asleep in a cart in a yard belonging to the Devonshire Arms Public House on the morning of the 20th instant at half past four instead of being on his beat, and the same being proved by Superintendent Frost, resolved that he be permitted to resign.

The concept of sleeping policemen clearly needed some refinement.

In 1853 Thomas Hunt died and George Love bought the freehold of the *Devonshire Arms* for £550. In 1897, it was acquired by Blake's Brewery of Union Street, Trowbridge. An inventory of the pub drawn up when Usher's took Blake's over in 1922 suggests that it was still very much a spit-and-sawdust cider house. Items listed include a sawdust holder, six iron spittoons, a table quoit board, and six two-handled cider mugs.

In 1990 the premises were revamped and reopened as the *Rugby Arms*, but since then have become the *Bath Tap*, one of Bath's top gay pubs. Hard to imagine what the regulars from 80-odd years ago would make of it if they came back today and found that, instead of quoits, a typical evening's entertainment consisted of male strippers, house DJs or drag-queen competitions.

BEAR 6-8 Wellsway

The old *Bear* around 1910

Most people, in search of Bath's historic pubs, would give the *Bear* on Wellsway no more than a fleeting glance before passing on. Its current appearance, however, belies a fascinating history. Nobody knows how long there has been an inn on this site, but as the *Bear* stands at the top of Holloway, one of the main routes into Bath from Roman times, it is possible that the building we see today stands on the site of a hostelry dating back to medieval times or even earlier. The first reference to it we have found, however, comes in 1786, when Robert Giles was the landlord.

Bears feature in many coats of arms, including that of the City of Bath. Many pubs called the *Bear* also take their name from the ancient sport of bear-baiting, once a highly respectable pastime, attended by civic dignitaries, and not finally outlawed until 1835. The *Bear* on Wellsway, however, has nothing to do with armorial bearings or ursine persecution, despite the Fox's Glacier Mascot above its entrance. In medieval times there was a village called Berwick (taking its name from the fields of barley round about) further up

Wellsway. There are still Berwicks in various parts of England (including three in Wiltshire), but the one near Bath disappeared in the late middle ages. It bequeathed its name, however, to Barrack Farm (the cottages of which still survive), Bear Flat and the *Bear Inn*.

In July 1793, "Mr Giles, master of the *Bear* at the top of Holloway, was thrown from his horse near his own door, whereby his hip bone was dislocated, and he was otherwise much bruised, but immediate assistance being had, he is in a fair way of recovery." He clearly did recover, for over a year later he placed an advertisement in the *Bath Chronicle*:

To be sold, four casks containing about 570 gallons each. Also a house to be let in Prospect Place.

Enquire of Mr Giles at the *Bear Inn*, Holloway, Bath.

The *Bear* was constantly busy with carriers and coaches travelling up and down Holloway, many of which needed an extra horse to pull them up the hill or extricate them from the mud. Across the road from the *Bear* was a large tract of open land which was used for regular horse and cattle sales and for the annual Holloway Fair, which took place in May and lasted for over a week. By the early nineteenth century, it had degenerated into a drunken revel, and, in 1835, a committee was set up to stop or regulate the Bath and Holloway Fairs "on the grounds of the inconvenience which they produced and the immorality which they encouraged." Four years later, however, it became clear that further measures to curb the excesses of Holloway Fair would not be needed, because it was so poorly attended that it was "only a shade above being no fair at all."

By 1846, however, the fair seems to have made something of a comeback. This was bad news for one local resident, whose novel way of raising a bit of extra beer money after visiting the fair ended up costing him more than he bargained for. This is the cautionary tale of John Bray, as it appeared in the *Bath Chronicle*:

George Knight, a sergeant of the 6th Royal Warwickshire Regiment, brought two recruits to be sworn before the magistrates. The men objected to their enlistment as illegal, because they were drunk at the time. The sergeant maintained that they were quite sober. John Bray, one of the recruits, a stripling in a smock coat, was the first who pleaded the objection. The sergeant, being sworn, stated that, on Friday evening, he was at the *Young Fox* public house in Holloway, when Bray came to him and asked to be enlisted, telling him he was "free, willing and able." The sergeant said he would take him, and he asked for half a crown, but the sergeant told him he should only give him the customary shilling. Bray was sober when he enlisted. This was confirmed by a private of the regiment, who saw him enlist and also by William Dick, the landlord of the *Smith's Arms*, Avon Street, at whose house Bray was billeted for the night, with two others. The recruit called several witnesses to prove the contrary, but they did not agree in their statements of some of the facts connected with his intoxicated state. They all concurred, however, in representing the occasion of his potations to be the annual fair held at Holloway, and the usual mockery of electing a Lord Mayor, which functionary they described as being carried in a procession on the shoulders of Bray and another man, who were so drunk that his Lordship was in great peril of losing the prop from under him, and exchanging his dignified elevation for an ignominious prostration on the stones. After a patient hearing of the evidence, the magistrates expressed themselves satisfied that the sobriety of Bray when he enlisted had been proved and ordered him to be sworn or pay the smart. He was not prepared for the latter, but his friends asked for time before he was sworn. It was agreed to give him till four o'clock.

Later in the century, after Holloway Fair was eventually outlawed, the eminently respectable Bath & West Show was held on the same site.

By 1816, the landlord of the *Bear* was Joseph Wilton, a member of the Bath Volunteer Regiment. In January 1817, the famous orator Henry Hunt held a mass rally in Bristol calling for parliamentary reform. The Bath Volunteers were called out and marched to Bristol on a bitterly cold and wet day. Despite the weather, their commanding officer told them that "he hoped they would not disgrace themselves by wearing their cloaks … The consequence was that [they] were soaked to the skin before they had got two miles on the road to Bristol. Their being kept in this woeful plight all day caused the death of two or three of them; Robert Ansty, a butcher, and Wilton, who kept the *Bear* at Holloway, never recovered from the effects of their trip to Bristol." After Joseph's untimely death, his widow, Rebecca kept the pub on for a while, but by 1819 Edward Davis had taken over. Three years later, Mr Davis fell victim to a con trick, but managed to have the last laugh, as the report in the *Bath Chronicle* explains:

> Saturday evening a man, apparently in a dying state, was found stretched upon the ground about 200 yards from the *Bear Inn* at the top of Holloway. Mr Davis, the landlord, with the greatest humanity, had brought him into his house and tried to force a little cordial into his mouth, but he appeared too far gone to take refreshment; the man was then carried to the Poor House, and medical advice immediately procured. Mr Crosby, on feeling his pulse and further examining him, pronounced that there was not anything the matter with him, and that he was an impostor. On hearing this the rascal quickly recovered his speech and legs, and admitted he was an impostor. He was on Monday taken before Sir Robert Baker, who committed him to the gaol at Shepton, to hard labour for two months. He called himself John Mobley. It is supposed that his object was to get accommodation for the night at the Bear Inn, for the purpose of robbing the house; a supposition which is greatly strengthened by the fact that the house was actually broken into the same night.

The Davis family were at the *Bear* for much of the nineteenth century. After Edward Davis died in the 1830s, his widow, Elizabeth Cottle Davis, continued to run the *Bear* with the help of her son, William Edward Davis. A newspaper report from 1841 indicates that she was a popular hostess:

> The annual carnation, picotee and gooseberry show [was held] at the *Bear Inn*, Holloway on Tuesday … The dinner on the occasion was served up at three o'clock in the large room which was tastefully decorated. Upwards of 60 gentlemen sat down to an excellent repast, the quality of which amply sustained the expectation which Mrs Davis has long since attained on account of her entertainments.

Not all her visitors were so respectable. In 1849, Mrs Davis was summoned for serving customers during divine service on Sunday. The men declared that they were travellers who had walked from Frome and "by their dirty shoes and gaiters she believed they had, and thought she was bound to serve them with refreshment as such." However, it transpired that they were locals and, therefore, not entitled to a drink. Such were the vagaries of the Sunday licensing laws in the mid-nineteenth century.* The Mayor, however, seems to have had it in for Mrs Davis:

• Sunday licensing laws had not changed almost half a century later when Mr Pooter fell foul of them in *Diary of a Nobody*: "At three o'clock Cummings and Gowing called for a good long walk over Hampstead and Finchley, and brought with them a friend named Stillbrook. We walked and chatted together, except Stillbrook, who was always a few yards behind us staring at the ground and cutting at the grass with his stick. As it was getting on for five, we four held a consultation, and Gowing suggested that we should make for the *Cow & Hedge* and get some tea. Stillbrook said a brandy and soda was good enough for him. I reminded them that all public houses were closed till six o'clock. Stillbrook said, 'that's all right – bona fide travellers.' We arrived; and as I was trying to pass, the man in charge of the gate said, 'where from?' I replied, 'Holloway.' He immediately put up his arm, and declined to let me pass. I turned back for a moment, when I saw Stillbrook, closely followed by Cummings and Gowing, make for the entrance. I watched them, and thought I would have a good laugh at their expense. I heard the porter say, 'where from?,' when to my surprise, in fact disgust, Stillbrook replied, 'Blackheath,' and the three were immediately admitted. Gowing called to me across the gate, and said, 'we shan't be a minute.' I waited for them the best part of an hour."

The Mayor said he had always heard Mrs Davis spoken of as a very respectable woman, but he had been frequently informed that on Sunday evenings her house was the resort of many domestic servants who sat there drinking instead of attending to something better.

As Sunday evening was probably one of the few times servants had to themselves, it would be interesting to know what the Mayor thought they ought to be doing. In her defence, Mrs Davis said that, "as her house was situated in a great public thoroughfare, do what she could, she could not prevent persons of objectionable character being there." She was fined 5/- and costs.

She also pointed out that she was in sole charge of the inn at the time because her son was meeting friends from London. One of them proved to be more than just a friend, however, and later that same year he married her at St Luke's Church, Chelsea – an event commemorated in the name he gave to the house he built at the back of the *Bear* – Chelsea Villa. The money to build such an imposing residence came not from the inn, but from the large brewery which William Davis had built next to it. A description of the brewery appeared in a book entitled *Ports of the Bristol Channel*, published in 1893:

This famous old brewery, which is undoubtedly one of the most noteworthy in the West of England, is an extension of an ancient hostelry, the *Bear Inn*, founded over a hundred years ago by the ancestors of Mr John Davis, one of the present proprietors. The inn was formerly well and favourably known among the country people round about, and being situated on the Wells Road, it was a favourite stopping place for farmers and others coming into Bath. The popularity of the house was great, and the first local dog-show was held here, while, during the show week of the Bath & West of England Society there have been as many as 200 horses at one time in the extensive stables and yards. The old inn was also the rendezvous of many clubs, and there may yet be seen the six large boilers or coppers which played such an important part in preparing the substantial repasts served here to large parties of hungry guests in the "good old days" of 50 or 60 years ago, before appetites went out of fashion. The *Bear Inn* still exists, but the large space once devoted to yards and stabling is now occupied by the brewery, a handsome and imposing structure built by Mr WE Davis , and extended in 1872 by his son, Mr J Davis. We ought to say that the old club rooms of the inn are still existent, though they are now use as hop stores. The fine old skittle alley also may yet be seen, fitted with all the conveniences beloved of our forefathers, and it is considered to be the best alley in Bath even to this day. As to the *Bear Brewery*, it is splendidly equipped with a large and highly efficient plant, and for many years it has maintained a wide reputation for the purity and fine quality of its beers. It has been built and arranged upon the most approved modern principles, and fitted with appliances of the most perfect character, so that every process of the industry is carried out under favourable conditions. The proprietors are thorough masters of the art of brewing, and their long experience and technical skill are well employed in the management of this substantial business, the whole of which comes under their immediate personal supervision. The products of the brewery are old and mild beer, bitter ales, and stout, and in all these a uniform standard of excellence is carefully preserved. Harvest and haying beers are also supplied, and a great reputation has been won for "home-brewed beers," which are a speciality of the *Bear Brewery* … A large and valuable family connection is maintained, both in and around Bath, and the brewery has always plenty of orders in hand. . . . The establishment is a prominent feature of the Wells Road, standing within a stone's throw of the old turnpike gate, and in the main elevation of the lofty brewery building there is a large clock, placed in position by Mr Davis' father, and greatly appreciated in the neighbourhood as a reliable recorder of the "time o'day."

In 1866, Ralph Shuttleworth Allen sold the freehold of the *Bear* (including the brewery) to a pair of bankers (Daniel Clutterbuck and Henry Tugwell).* In 1871, they sold it on to William Davis. A plan accompanying the deeds shows that the land he acquired included "Hay's Field" on the other side of the road, which later became Hayesfield Park.

It is at this stage that the story gets complicated. In 1884 the trustees of William Davis (deceased) leased the *Bear* estate to John Davis for 21 years at £141 per annum. In the same year John Davis and William Davis's widow leased the inn to Frederick Davis for £80 per annum. The lease also gave Frederick Davis "the right for himself, guests and customers to use the urinal in the small yard of the *Bear Brewery* between the brewery office and the inn."

The trustees also sold a malthouse at Sydney Wharf to Robert Bailey, a maltster from Hinton Charterhouse. Four years later, in 1888, they sold the rest of the estate, excluding Chelsea Villa and Hay's Field, to Robert Bailey for £4,000. In 1889, Robert Bailey mortgaged the *Bear* for £3,300. John Davis redeemed the mortgage the same year, but in 1891 he remortgaged the *Bear*, along with a number of other properties, including the *Porter Stores* (now the *Porter*) at 2 Miles' Buildings, and three lost pubs – the *Ambury Brewery* in Corn Street, the *John Bull* at Dunkerton and the *Beaufort Arms* in Princes Street.

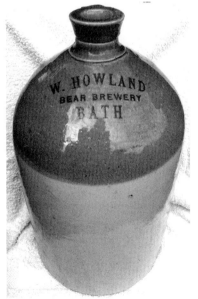

Two years later, in 1893, William Stoffell, having taken over the lease of the *Bear*, sublet it to Walter Barnard. The following year, William Barnard transferred the lease to Albert Harding. In 1895, William Howland took over the brewery. In 1896, Albert Harding transferred the lease of the inn to him as well.

In 1902 William Howland sold the estate to Wilkins Bros. & Hudson, Ltd., Brewers of Bradford on Avon, who closed the brewery down. They were themselves taken over by Usher's in 1920.

Before we come to the saddest episode in the history of the *Bear*, here are some letters published in the *Bath Journal* on 29 October 1898 which recall its finest hour. The first is from Mr F Curtis of Bridge Street:

A two-gallon jar from the *Bear Brewery* (c1895-1902).

I was one among about 600 eye-witnesses of the sparring match between Tom Sayers and John

---

* Ralph Shuttleworth Allen was an heir of Ralph Allen, who had not only owned the *Bear*, but much of the land around Bear Flat.

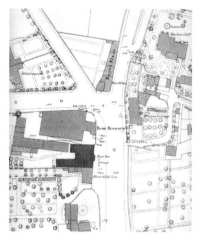

A map showing the *Bear Inn & Bear Brewery* in the late nineteenth century.

C Heenan from the United States at the back of the Bear Inn. The event took place some 38 years ago – I believe it was in the summer of 1860 – when they were on a tour in the provinces, a few months after their celebrated fight at Farnborough for the championship of England … The spot where the sparring took place was in the south-east corner of the grass enclosure then existing at the rear of the *Bear Inn* … The most striking features of the encounter … were, first, the two men perambulating the enclosure, smoking cigars, before the performance began, separated, though, from each other, but each one surrounded by a cluster of enthusiastic admirers. So closely were they invested that they had some difficulty in moving about, even slowly. They were patted and smoothed and almost smothered. They then appeared on the platform, or stage, raised about four feet above the ground, in the orthodox undress suitable for the business in hand, and exhibited their massive silver belts to the admiring crowd. Then the fun began: quite a unique and scientific exhibition of the noble art of self-defence. The disparity in size between the two men was remarkable. Sayers was rather below the middle height, but square and strongly built, with immense muscle, while Heenan was almost a giant, being about six feet two inches and of splendid physique, with weight and muscles to match. The sparring

The damage inflicted on the *Bear* by German bombers in April 1942

The same view today showing the modern *Bear*.

was fast and furious while it lasted, but of course there was no bag of gold appended to the result, though the blows appeared to be in earnest. The gloves used were proper boxing gloves, not reduced to 6oz or 4oz as at the present day.

Another correspondent, Mr R Hansford Mance, recalled that, "as a boy, I remember distinctly, Tom Sayers giving Mr Davis the proprietor's son and myself a lesson in boxing, when we were practising in the skittle alley at the back of the brewery." A third letter came from George Smith:

In those days [1860] and for years previous the Bear and grounds was next to the Sydney Gardens as a place of amusement. There was a long room behind the house and in this the coachmakers of Bath yearly held their "bean feast." Sometimes some of the newspaper offices would make

BATH PUBS

this the rendezvous for their annual "waygoose," and some of the Benefit Societies held their anniversary dinner here, for it was a hostelry famed not only for its genuine "Old English Ale," but also for its satisfactory accommodation. Under the long room was a well-kept skittle alley, which, especially during the summer months, was well patronised. Adjoining the alley was a closely mowed bowling green, which had to be kept closely cut with the scythe, for it was before the days of lawn-mowing machines. ... At the further or western end of this green the platform was erected on which the renowned boxers exhibited their skill ... The public were charged one shilling each for admission to witness the show, and the Yeomanry Band enlivened the proceedings.

In April 1942 the Bear Brewery was destroyed by enemy action. The inn was seriously damaged, and, although it could have been restored, it was decided to demolish it. After a lapse of several years (during which time there was a car showroom on the site) a new *Bear* opened in 1963. Its trademark polar bear – now one of Bath's best-known landmarks – was set up over the entrance at a cost of £350. The two-storey Bath Stone building's two large bars were knocked into one in 2002.

BELL 103 Walcot Street

The *Bell*, with an astonishing range of real ales and live music three times a week, is one of Bath's best-loved hostelries, its popularity underlined by being named Pub of the Year by *Venue Magazine* in 2002.

It is also very old. In 1587, the Corporation leased a "pasture ground" on "the way that leadeth to Walcot," with "the Parsonage Barn of Walcot on the north side" and "a lane called the new lane" on the west to a Mr John Wood. Whether this John Wood was any relation to the famous eighteenth century architect is not known, but he may have put up the building which later became the *Bell*, for by 1728, when Betty Hooper took over the lease, the pasture ground had become "a tenement and two orchards, between the way leading to Walcot on the east, the Parsonage Barn of Walcot on the north and New Lane on the west." This "tenement" was the *Bell*.

We do not know whether it has always been an inn, but it was certainly one by June 1763 when this item appeared in the *Bath Journal*:

On Saturday, John Harvey, Hostler to Mr Norris at the *Bell* at Walcot, carelessly riding a horse in field, unfortunately fell and fractured his skull. He died next morning in great agonies.

In the eighteenth and nineteenth centuries, the *Bell*'s address was 1 Cornwell Buildings. Cornwell Buildings were named after the Carn Well, fed by a spring which ran down from Lansdown past the *Bell*, turned south and followed the street for a short distance, before turning off and running down to the river. By the early eighteenth century, the spring had been culverted, but its course is still marked by the boundary between Walcot and St Michael's Parishes. The *Bell* stood just within the Parish of Walcot, and its name may derive, not from any association with the bells of Walcot Church, but because it stood near the parish bell-tree house where justice was doled out in medieval times. Its location just south of the old Walcot Parsonage Barn – likely to have been the bell-tree house – is further indication that this may have been the case.

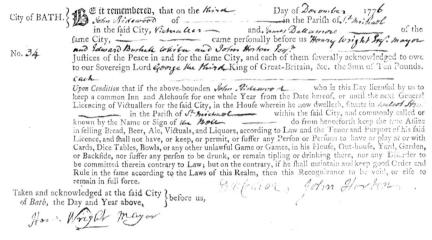

The licence granted to John Ridewood who held the tenancy of the *Bell* from Peter Hooper in 1776.

By the late eighteenth century, the *Bell* rather than the old Parsonage Barn was Walcot's chief meeting place. In 1778, for example, Messrs Shargood & Spackman, who ran a brewery "near Cornwall House" on Walcot Street, went bankrupt, and a meeting of their creditors was held in the *Bell*. In the early nineteenth century, a local friendly society, known as the Bath City Patriotic Benefit Society, used the *Bell* as their headquarters.

The Hooper family kept the lease of the *Bell* until the early nineteenth century. When Peter Hooper renewed the lease in 1790, the *Bell* was described as having a "garden ground, stables and other buildings." After his death in 1808 the Corporation instructed his trustees to "take down and set back the courtyard wall five feet to widen the turnpike road." By this time, the *Bell* was one of the busiest centres for carrier traffic in Bath, with regular services to Tormarton, Acton Turville, Malmesbury, Corsham, Melksham, Westbury, Trowbridge and Bradford on Avon. The concave front of the shop across the road from the *Bell* (which as once a pub as well) is a legacy of the days when carts and wagons needed a wide turning circle to enter the *Bell* yard. The steep slope into the yard was an added reason why they needed a good run up to it. A low wall running round the south-east corner of the *Bell*, which appears on a nineteenth century plan of the building, has, however, long gone. It protected the corner of the building and also spared pedestrians from one of the most common causes of death and serious injury around inn yards – being crushing against the wall by a passing wagon.

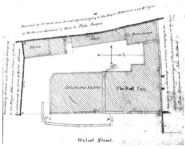

A plan of the *Bell* in 1829, showing the wall wrapped around the building to protect pedestrians – as well as the building – from carts turning into the yard.

BATH PUBS

The *Bell* was an eminently respectable and successful establishment, but had its share of "incidents." Take this bizarre report from 1846, for example:

Mary Marsh was summoned by Sarah Semper, wife of the landlord of the *Bell Inn*, Walcot Street, for using abusive and violent language towards her, whereby a crowd of people was collected near the premises, and the public peace endangered. The complainant stated that the conduct of the defendant arose from her refusal to draw beer for her son at 11.30 o'clock Wednesday night. The defendant was required to find bail to keep the peace.

In the mid nineteenth century an extra storey was added to the original two-storey building, almost certainly in connection with the brewery at the back. An extra storey was added to the *Crystal Palace* in Abbey Green at around the same time for the same reason. The *Crystal Palace's* top storey went when the brewery closed, but the *Bell's* is still there.

A fragment of a jar from the *Bell* dating from 1906.

An inventory of the *Bell* carried out in 1896 gives a vivid idea of what the pub was like over a century ago. The drinking area occupied only the right-hand part of the building (the left-hand part, at a slightly higher level, was originally the stables). As you walked through the front door you would have entered the main bar. This was flanked by two smoke rooms, with the left-hand smoke room leading through to a tap room.

The main bar had a six-motion beer engine, a set of four spirit crutches, a pewter-lined counter with "six sliding sashes" above it and "a half-glazed door and partition forming a bar enclosure." There were two mahogany drinking tables, a wall clock and eight spittoons. Over the mantelpiece were shelves with silvered glass backs. Lighting was provided by a gas pendant with two consumers. Drinking vessels included three two-handled quart cups, 14 two-handled pint-cups (four slightly damaged), seven two-handled half-pint cups, three small plain grogs, one large plain grog, two moulded beer glasses, five pewter quarts, 21 pewter pints, 16 claret glasses, five cut-glass pony glasses, 15 cut-glass spirit glasses and seven cut-glass beer glasses. There were seven decanters, four large plain sodas and one moulded soda.

The right-hand smoke room had seating with matchboard-back casing fixed around the walls, and a "dwarf partition with half glazed doors, rods and curtains" separating the bar from the parlour. The left-hand smoke room also had seating with matchboard-back casing, three drinking tables, two stools, a "panelled screen board with iron rod as fixed" and another eight spittoons. The tap room had fixed seating, two iron-bound drinking tables, a deal form and – inevitably – five spittoons. There were spittoons everywhere. You could hardly move for them. It makes you wonder what happened when they started to disappear. Was there was a Campaign for Real Spittoons, perhaps?

When the *Bell* was inspected by a council official in 1903, he found the premises "fair as to the front but . . . very dilapidated at the rear." This dilapidation included the brewery, the smoke from which was a regular source of irritation to residents in the Paragon until it closed in 1922. A century ago, the *Bell* was owned by the Old Market Brewery in Bristol. This was taken over by the Ashton Gate Brewery in 1911. In 1931, Ashton Gate was taken over by George's, which became part of Courage's in 1961.

It was also in 1961 that John Bradshaw took over the *Bell* and turned it into Bath's premier jazz pub. Although he has since moved to the *Old Farmhouse* (and taken the jazz with him), the *Bell* still has a reputation for the excellence of its music – not only jazz, but blues, ska, country, folk and world music, and a good deal else besides. The selection of beers is the best (and among the best-kept) in Bath. The *Bell* is a classic example of how a pub which, while being a world away from a traditional pub in terms of layout, entertainment, and decor, manages supremely well to keep a traditional pub atmosphere alive. And, as the epicentre of the annual Walcot Nation Day, it still stands firmly at the heart of the community. And if it gets too crowded inside, there's always the excellent beer garden in the old coachyard.

BELVEDERE WINE VAULTS 25 Belvedere, Lansdown Road

The *Belvedere Wine Vaults* was built around 1760 and had become an inn by 1792, with Isaac Stockwell as the landlord. It seems to have been an important commercial centre for the surrounding area. In 1795, for example, the following advertisement appeared in the *Bath Chronicle*:

> To be lett, a house, being No 22 in that delightful situation, Belvidere, lately occupied by Dr William Oliver. Enquire at the *Belvidere Inn*, opposite Camden Place.

Five years later, an important auction was held there:

> To be sold by auction at the *Belvidere Inn & Tavern* – the house adjoining Dash's Riding School (now John Howell's farriery) and the Tennis Court adjoining the riding school, opened about 20 years ago.[*]

The earliest reference to the "Belvedere Inn", from the *Bath Chronicle* of 14 May 1795.

In 1809, the *Belvedere Inn* was taken over by George Hulbert. By 1819, he had extended it into No 24 and renamed it the *Belvedere Private Hotel*. When he advertised it in that year's *Bath Directory*, he went to great lengths to stress the refined nature of his establishment:

---

[*] The Riding School has gone but the tennis court that adjoined it is now the Museum of Bath at Work.

BELVEDERE PRIVATE HOTEL

for Ladies, Gentlemen and Families of Distinction;

Most Delightfully Situated at No 24 and 25, Belvedere, Bath.

GJ Hulbert, Foreign Wine and Spirit Merchant,

begs leave to announce to the Nobility,

that he has fitted up the above House in a neat and commodious Style,

comprising every Accommodation of an Inn,

without any of its attendant Inconveniences.

This Establishment is unconnected with,

and entirely distinct from the Public Line,

by which Plan it has already received the Patronage and Support

of the first Ladies and Gentlemen of Distinction visiting Bath,

by whom it is allowed to stand unrivalled for its Neatness

as well as every Comfort, which will be always the

Study of the Proprietor to continue.

One is reminded of Alec Guinness as Canon D'Ascoyne in *Kind Hearts and Coronets*: "My west window has all the exuberance of Chaucer without, happily, any of the concomitant crudities of his period."

Despite George Hulbert's best efforts, the *Belvedere Private Hotel* was a fairly short-lived enterprise. When his widow took over from him in in 1829, she closed the hotel, let 24 Belvedere as lodgings, gave 25 Belvedere over to the wine and spirit trade, and renamed it the *Belvedere Wine Vaults*. Three years later she placed an advertisement in the *Bath Chronicle* to extol the virtues of its wares:

Belvedere Wine Vaults, near Camden Place.

Elizabeth E Hulbert is induced,

from the great importance of pure brandy in all cases,

but especially for medical purposes,

to solicit attention to her stock of fine and old cognac,

which will defy the most severe chemical tests,

and prove as unadulterated as imported.

Genuine wines and spirits of a superior character.

London bottled stout (in pints also),

and Scotch beer in the finest order for use.

BELVEDERE WINE CELLARS,

Near CAMDEN PLACE, BATH,

(Established by the late Mr. George J. Hulbert, 1809, and since 1829 conducted by the present Proprietor,)

HENRY PAYNE HULBERT,

Importer of Foreign Wines and Spirits,

AND DEALER IN THE BEST MALT LIQUORS,

IN WOOD AND IN BOTTLE.

Resident Families supplied in any quantity on the lowest wholesale terms.

Agent to the North British Fire and Life Insurance Company.

An 1848 advertisement for the *Belvedere Wine Vaults*.

Around 1840, her son, Henry Hulbert, built an extension on the corner of Morford Street and moved the wine merchant's into it. He also set about establishing outlets in the city centre. In 1843 he announced that he had "opened a receiving box for orders in Broad Street, under the Post Office, [with] stores for porter, ales, cider and perry."

By 1850, the city centre order office had moved to the north side of the Assembly Rooms. An advertisement in that year's *Postal Directory* shows that Henry had the Hulbert way with words:

The Proprietor is unwilling to hold out, as a decoy, an array of *Low Prices*, with which *Low Quality* is too frequently associated. A list of Prices and Samples may be had; and as Comparison is the test of CHEAPNESS, this he at all times respectfully invites, with an Assurance that every Article sold by him is of the purest character.

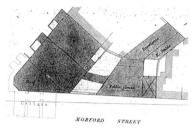

A plan of the *Belvedere Wine Vaults* in 1858, showing the newly-built extension on the corner of Morford Street and, below it, the *Bunch of Grapes*.

Henry Hulbert sold the *Belvedere Wine Vaults* (or the *Belvedere Wine Cellars* as it was sometimes known) in 1858. A plan of the property drawn up at the time shows that the layout was very different to that of today. The old public bar on the corner of Morford Street (currently closed to the public) was the wine merchant's. Below it, at 25 Morford Street, was a pub called the *Bunch of Grapes*. Originally this was the *Belvedere Tap*, provided for servants and coachmen of those staying at the *Belvedere Inn*. It had its own brewhouse and stable at the rear. After the inn closed, it stayed open and was licensed separately. It closed in 1907.

The 1903 report on the *Belvedere Wine Vaults* indicates that it still had some way to go before it became a pub:

> Business chiefly a wine and spirit merchant. Two entrances from Lansdown Road, one to order office with drinking counter and smoke room beyond and the other to office. Passage at rear of 25 with door into Morford Street, also yard at rear of 25 with another door further down street. Communication by steps from counting house to cellar and yard. Licence held by Edwin Young of London, policeman.

The *Belvedere Wine Vaults* was first recorded as a pub in the 1926 *Postal Directory*. Today, after many changes, it successfully combines the atmosphere of a traditional pub with the ambience of a wine bar. Accommodation is once again available and, as well as having a couple of well-kept real ales and good selection of wines, it is acquiring an enviable reputation for food. But there is an even more compelling reason to visit the *Belvedere*. During a recent refurbishment of the *Belvedere*, an eighteenth century frieze in the front room was uncovered and restored. Decorated with corkscrews and claret jugs, it is perhaps the earliest example of inn decoration in the city and a miraculous survival.

BELVOIR CASTLE
32-33 Victoria Buildings, Lower Bristol Road

The *Belvoir Castle* at 33 Victoria Buildings on the Lower Bristol Road opened around 1850. The building is older, but the single-storey extension fronting the Lower Bristol Road was added at this time. An inventory drawn up in 1862, when Joseph Sparks, who had worked at Bishop's Brewery in Weston, took over, gives us a good idea of what it was like in its early days. It had a bar, a parlour, a tap room, a skittle alley, and a brewery in the yard at the back. The bar, which was divided into two by a 56 foot partition, had a four-motion beer engine, a mahogany chiffonier for spirits, two cane seat chairs and a carpet on the floor. In the parlour were two mahogany tables, six Windsor chairs, a japanned pipe tray, a copper warmer and six iron spittoons.

Today the *Belvoir Castle*, full of cups and key rings, is in the vanguard of a movement to restore shove halfpenny to its rightful place as one of the Great British Pub Games, and represents Bath in the Anglo-Welsh Shove Halfpenny League. Externally, the pub has changed little since it opened in the 1850s. As far as we know, it is the only pub in the country called the *Belvoir Castle*. The origin of its name is unclear. Perhaps its first landlord came from near Belvoir Castle in Leicestershire. As Belvoir means "beautiful view," however, it is more likely that it got its name because it had one of the most splendid views in Bath, which disappeared when the Midland Railway built their line at the back of it in the late 1860s.

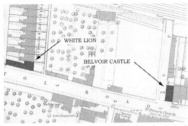

Although the *Belvoir Castle* is now something of an oasis as far as pubs are concerned, this was not always the case. A little further along the Lower Bristol Road, where Stones' Coach Depot is today, was Hopmead Buildings, with a beerhouse called the *White Lion* at No 1. This only lasted from around 1850 to 1870, but across the road – on St Peter's Terrace – were two pubs with much more staying power – the

A late-nineteenth-century map showing the *Belvoir Castle* and the *White Lion*.

Newbridge Inn, opened around 1840, and the *East Twerton Hotel*, opened in the 1870s. Both survived until 1971 when the City Engineer decided that they had to come down to improve the layout of the junction of Brougham Hayes and the Lower Bristol Road.

BLACK SWAN Broad Street

KING EDWARD'S SCHOOL   BLACK SWAN

The first thing to admit, of course, is that there is no *Black Swan* in Broad Street. But there was once, and – who knows? – there may yet be again. This is the story of a pub that refused to die.

Before we begin to unravel its history, however, we need to go back and look at the early days of one of Bath's most hallowed institutions. King Edward's School started off in a building which now lies under *Sam Weller's*. It was not there very long before it moved to the nave of a disused church – St Mary by the Northgate – which stood roughly where Bridge Street is today. This was very unsatisfactory, especially as the tower of the church was used as the city's gaol. The school had to put up with this because the Corporation, which had been entrusted with the estate that King Edward bequeathed to the school, had quietly absorbed it into their own portfolio. As a result, King Edward's, which should have been handsomely provided for, hardly had two groats to rub together. Eventually the headmaster of the school got fed up and threatened the Corporation with legal action. The Corporation, not wishing to have their affairs scrutinised too closely, offered to build a brand new school. The headmaster, bowled over by this act of generosity, dropped the threat of legal action. Sighs of relief were no doubt breathed a-plenty behind the Corporation's closed doors.

The spot chosen for the new school was that occupied by a seventeenth-century coaching inn with "good stabling, coach houses and a large yard" in Broad Street, known as the *Black Swan*. This inn, whose freehold was owned by the Corporation, dated back to at least 1607. In 1707, George Chambers signed a 99 year-lease on the property. After his death in 1729, this was transferred to his widow, Deborah.

In 1744, the Corporation decided "to apply for the purchase of the *Black Swan* in Broad Street as a place to build a free school." A month later, the Chamberlain was instructed "to contract with Mrs Deborah Chambers for the purchase of the house in Broad Street called the *Black Swan*, with appurtenances, at the price of £550, with the allowance of adding a life in a small tenement near without paying any fine." Although work on the school did not start for another eight years, the *Black Swan* was pulled down and Mrs Chambers moved into a new inn to the north of the school.

The new inn was a popular meeting place, especially for coachmen and chairmen. Behind it was Black Swan Court, consisting of "some twelve or fourteen little tenements with small garden plots in front of each, occupied chiefly by chairmen who stood on the Bladud and Edgar Buildings stands, and stablemen who were employed at the *York House* Yard." Around 1842 the *Black Swan* was renamed the *Post Office Tavern*, in honour of the Post Office (now the Bath Postal Museum) just down the street. The *Post Office Tavern* would have been handy for servants to nip into for a swift (or not so swift) drink when they were sent down to post their masters' or mistresses' letters. If questioned on their return as to the reason for their prolonged absence, they could reply, perfectly truthfully, that they had been held up at the Post Office.

The Post Office closed in 1854 and the *Post Office Tavern* went back to being the *Black Swan*. A visitor to the inn in the mid-nineteenth century would have found plenty of nooks and crannies to slip into for a quiet drink. As well as the main bar, there were two parlours and a panelled tap room. Upstairs were four bedrooms and a sitting room. There was also a brewery at the back. But its days were numbered. The Corporation, not content with having pulled the original *Black Swan* down, pulled the new one down in 1882 to redevelop the site.

So, the *Black Swan* passed into history. History, however, has a way of repeating itself – or at least of trying to.

By 1954, King Edward's had outgrown the old school building and got permission to knock it down and put up a new one. It is incredible what you could get away 50 years ago. However, it was decided to move the senior school out to a new site at North Road and keep the junior school in the old building. Eventually, the junior school moved out to North Road as well, and planning permission was granted to turn the school into offices. Nothing happened until 1997, when Samuel Smith Old Brewery (Tadcaster) Ltd., put in an application to turn it into a pub. The scheme was praised by English Heritage for its "imaginative and sensitive proposed re-use of the building," and planning permission was granted. However, the licensing authorities had other ideas. In July 1997, the *Bath Chronicle* reported that

> an appeal by Samuel Smith Brewery against refusal of permission for a superpub in King Edward Junior School, Broad Street, was dismissed by Bristol Crown Court on the grounds that first, there was no need for another licensed premises in the area, second that to grant a licence could only be detrimental to the maintenance of good public order and third, that it could not be in the public interest to grant it.

Since then, of course, two other superpubs have opened nearby – the *Slug & Lettuce* on George Street and the *Ha! Ha! Bar* in Walcot Street – but the old King Edward's School, built on the site of the old *Black Swan* stands forlorn and empty, high on English Heritage's at risk register. It would nice to think that after 250 years, the *Black Swan* could reopen on its original site, but there cannot be many people holding their breath.

Another solution could be for the building to be reclaimed from the brewery (who, one imagines, would be glad to see the back of it after all these years) and turned into that long-promised, long-awaited, and indefinitely deferred gap in the city's cultural and educational portfolio – a Museum of Bath.

It would be expensive, undoubtedly, to turn the old school into a twenty-first century showcase for the wealth of material currently squirreled away in vaults and store rooms all over the city, but there is surely no other project which has so much potential.

The important thing about this museum is that would not just be another showpiece for visitors – even though it is likely that it would become one of the city's top attractions. It would be a resource for the community – from schoolchildren eager to learn about how their ancestors lived, to older residents whose memories themselves form part of the city's heritage. And, far from robbing Bath's other museums of their visitors, a Museum of Bath would serve as a gateway to them, whetting the appetites of residents and visitors alike, making them aware of what lies behind doors they may never have thought of entering.

So much of the city's heritage provision focuses on the Romans and the Georgians that twenty-first century residents may be excused for thinking that, while history is all very well for visitors, it has nothing to do with them. The city's Roman and Georgian heritage are only two chapters in the story of Bath. That story is still unfolding, and decisions taken today – whether on bollards or on riverside redevelopment – shape our future. The problems of living in a World Heritage Site are complex and difficult. A Museum of Bath would provide a focus not only to raise our awareness of what we owe to the past but also to give us a clearer idea of where we go in the future.

BLADUD'S HEAD 1-3 Catsley Place, Lower Swainswick

On the edge of the city, with a brook burbling away on the other side of the road, the *Bladud's Head* is about the closest thing Bath has to a country pub. It was built in the late eighteenth or early nineteenth century as a row of three cottages. When the pub was first recorded in 1848, with John Cooper as the licensee, it occupied only the first cottage – No 1.

In the 1870s, another beer house, the *Waggon & Horses*, opened next door at No 2. It was absorbed into the *Bladud's Head* in 1890. In 1960, No 3 became part of the *Bladud's Head* as well. In 1984, the garage was turned into a children's room and in 1988 an extension was built at the back.

A century ago the *Bladud's Head* belonged to the Bath Brewery Company. The 1903 report on it reads as follows:

Side entrance on Rose Hill. Yard at back. Bar with serving window for jug & bottle. Arbour in front of premises. Small shop on side of bar for sale of sweets, bread, pickles and other provisions.

The *Bladud's Head*, still divided into public and lounge bars, has kept much of the atmosphere of a traditional country pub. Unfortunately, like many other country pubs, it would be worth much more as a private house. When the Trustees of St John's Hospital, who own the freehold of the *Bladud's Head*, applied to turn it into a residential property, 166 letters of protest were sent by local residents. The council's planning department initially recommended acceptance of the proposal for change of use, and for many months the fate of the *Bladud's Head* hung in the balance. However, wiser counsels prevailed. The *Bladud's Head* now has a new landlord, and its future is secure.

Bath has had other pubs named after its legendary founding father. The Sukhotai Restaurant in Walcot Street was a pub called the *Bladud's Head* from 1792 to 1934. Evan's Fish Restaurant in Abbeygate Street, which was a pub from sometime before 1759 to 1911, was known – briefly – as the *Bladud's Head*, and there was a beerhouse called the *Bladud's Head* in Weston High Street for about 20 years in the mid-nineteenth century.

Then there was the late lamented *Bladud's Arms* – up above the *Bladud's Head* on the Gloucester Road. This started off as a couple of cottages, one of which opened as a beerhouse around 1841. Eventually it took over the other cottage as well. Like the *Bladud's Head*, the freehold of the property belonged to the trustees of St John's Hospital. It closed in 1975, but was reopened the following year by Don Meylan, a real-ale fan. For many years it was one of Bath's top real-ale haunts, but sadly St John's got permission for change of use. It has now closed and been converted to housing.

BLATHWAYT ARMS Lansdown

The *Blathwayt Arms* (or the *Blathwayt* as it now seems to be known) is named after the family who built Dyrham Park. It may look like a typical twentieth-century roadside pub, but its present appearance belies its origin. Across the road from the pub is Chapel Farm, at the heart of which lies a medieval chapel and hospice – possibly dating from the twelfth century – used by pilgrims travelling to Glastonbury. Behind the farmhouse was a well dedicated to St Lawrence which was filled in in the 1940s. In 1304, Edward I granted a charter for an annual fair to be held across the road from Chapel Farm. All this suggests that there may have been a pub on the site of the *Blathwayt Arms* since medieval times. Its original name – the *Star* (referring to the Virgin Mary, and used by alehouses which had accommodation for pilgrims) – lends further credence to this theory.

In 1784, Bath Racecourse moved from Claverton to Lansdown, and in 1792, we find the first reference to the *Star* alehouse in the Weston licensing records, with William Sandy as landlord. It is possible that the *Star* opened at the same time as the racecourse, but it seems more likely that pilgrims, travellers and fairgoers had been enjoying its hospitality for centuries, possibly without the landlord bothering to apply for a licence. Such lapses were common in remote, lawless places such as Lansdown.

And, in case you are in any doubt about how lawless it was, take this fairly typical report from the *Gloucester Journal* of 4 July 1763:

> We have received the following particulars of a most audacious villain that has this week infested the road between this place and Bath. On Wednesday morning he attacked, near the Monument on Lansdown, two persons, whom he robbed of some small sums; and afterwards coming to the turnpike on this side the down, he found there a man who was paying for passing through; on which the highwayman ordered the turnpikeman to go into his house and shut the door, or he would blow his brains out, saying, "I'll receive the gentleman's money," and accordingly robbed the person of a considerable sum. He then came on to a little alehouse on the crossroad, where he put up his horse, and stayed half an hour; and having drank a quart of strong beer, and fed his horse, he told the landlord he should set off for Tetbury. Upon the road, near Petty France, he robbed a gentleman's servant of eight guineas; and soon after meeting with a man returning from Tetbury market, near Dunkirk, he demanded his money. The man, who had a little boy before him, told the villain that he had none. He then demanded his watch, and endeavoured to pull it out of his pocket by the string, which in the struggle broke; and the man refusing to give it him, he said, "Do you contest with me?" and immediately putting his pistol over the boy's shoulder fired it, and lodged three slugs in the poor man's breast, of which he died soon after. The villain was immediately pursued by some people who heard the report of the pistol, but got clear off. The landlord of the house where he baited says, he is a short young man, about 18, pitted much with the smallpox, well mounted on a dark brown mare, which is blind of one eye, and has a switch tail. One of his stirrups is new, the other an old one.

You literally took your life in your hands when you ventured into remote places such as Lansdown. Keepers of alehouses such as the *Star* had to be made of pretty stern stuff as well, with the ever-present threat of highwaymen and footpads nipping in for a few pints.

Until the early twentieth century the hospitality provided by the *Blathwayt Arms* was of a fairly basic kind. It was a small wayside beerhouse-cum-dairy, consisting of a bar and a tap room, neither of which had a serving counter. In 1908, however, William Hendy applied to have the licence transferred "to a certain house and premises about to be constructed upon a piece of land (now used as a garden) adjoining the *Blathwayt Arms* on the south side thereof and having a frontage to the Lansdown Road." And so the old *Star*, holding who knows what clues to its origins, slipped quietly into history.

BOATER 9 Argyle Street

Argyle Street was build by Thomas Baldwin in 1787. The *Boater*, at 9 Argyle Street, with its wonderful Georgian frontage, was first recorded as a wine and spirit merchants, belonging to Henry Morrish, in 1837. Later it was taken over by the Bath Brewery Company, who kept the wine merchant's going, turned part of the building into offices and built a bottling shed and a workshop at the back. After the Bath Brewery Company was absorbed by George's of Bristol in 1923, the wine merchant's was taken over by Smith Bros.

In 1976, when Fred Pearce dropped by, it was still called the *Argyle Wine Vaults* and had an atmosphere "more like a tea shoppe than a licensed premises." A quarter of a century on, it has been renamed the *Boater*. Any resemblance between it and a tea shoppe has long since gone. It is very lively, popular with students and visitors, as well as some regulars who were probably around when Fred looked in. The yard at the back, where the brewery's masons and carpenters once worked, is now a riverside beer garden.

BRAINS SURGERY 36-37 Dafford Street, Larkhall

Dafford Street is home to possibly the most incongruous street corner pub in Bath. Although a fine building in its own right, the *Brains Surgery* makes no concessions to the buildings around it. The *Marlborough Tavern* on the end of Marlborough Buildings is dwarfed by the row of buildings next to it. Here it is the other way around, as a late nineteenth century red-brick pub – which would fit quite happily into a northern industrial city – looms over a row of early nineteenth-century Bath stone cottages. How, you wonder, did it come to be built, even in the *laissez-faire* nineteenth century? This is its story.

Originally, Dafford Street did not end at No 37, as it does now, but at No 38. The

row of cottages continued through what is now the *Brains Surgery* and ended in the middle of the road. Around 1841, Charles Wheeler opened a grocery-cum-beershop in the end house, No 38. By the 1890s, it had been taken over by George Biggs of the Crown Brewery in New Orchard Street and called the *Royal Oak*. For the next chapter in the story, we need to turn to the licensing records for 1898, when George Biggs applied

for a full licence to sell at a new house and premises to be built on the site of the two houses known as 36 and 37 Dafford Street ... Mr Biggs was owner of No 38 Dafford Street, at present known as the *Royal Oak Inn*, and he wanted a full licence, instead of the beerhouse licence which attached to the premises at present ... Mr Biggs had recently become the owner of 36 and 37 Dafford Street, which lay immediately behind No 38. For some time the corporation had been anxious to widen a narrow channel that existed, and so make a road of something like uniform width running into Brooklyn Road. Mr Biggs had been able to acquire and was therefore in a position to allow the corporation to have the site of 38 to throw into the present roadway. It would be an enormous benefit to the inhabitants of the place.

It comes as no surprise to find that Mr Biggs's application for a full licence was granted, even though the members of the Corporation on the licensing board had to withdraw before the decision was taken. It is no surprise, either, that the *Rose & Crown* in Brougham Place, which applied for a full licence at the same time, was turned down and had to wait almost 60 years for one.

The *Royal Oak* is still open today, a well preserved example of a late nineteenth-century street corner pub, although, as Bath's only regular outlet for one of South Wales' most popular brews – Brains Bitter – it is now known as the *Brains Surgery.*

CASTLE Forester Avenue, Bathwick

This part of Bathwick was once known as Villa Fields after a gothic-style villa which stood here. Built in 1777 by James Ferry, who was also associated with Spring Gardens, it was surrounded by pleasure gardens which Fanny Burney described it as "very curious." Mr Ferry, she wrote, had made a "unsuccessful attempt at making something of nothing." His venture failed and in 1782 the gardens were auctioned off to a wine merchant called Mr Merrett. He reopened the gardens, placing advertisements in local papers to "inform the Nobility and Gentry and the public in general, that he has imported a stock of choice French wines." Concerts, fireworks and illuminations were laid on to encourage visitors, but to no avail. The gardens closed again in 1790.

However, they had a brief renaissance in the early 1840s when James Aust (probably a descendant of the Austs who built the *Star*, the Paragon and North Parade Bridge) opened "tea and pleasure gardens" there. The villa was demolished in 1897 and the pleasure gardens disappeared under houses.

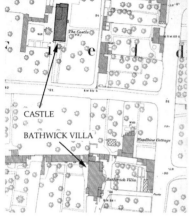

A late nineteenth-century map showing *Bathwick Villa* and the old *Castle Tavern*.

There was a pub on Villa Fields long before the villa disappeared, however. The *Castle Tavern* was recorded in the 1841 *Postal Directory* as the *Windsor Castle* and in the 1846 *Postal Directory* as the *Sham Castle Inn*. It was almost certainly opened by James Aust when he reopened Bathwick Villa, but we do not know if he used an existing building or built a new one. Unfortunately, we have little chance of establishing how old the building was, as it was pulled down and rebuilt in 1898. It has always been assumed that the pub took its name from the Sham Castle built for Ralph Allen in 1762. It may well have done, but there is another theory which, although seemingly far-fetched, offers another explanation for its name, and ties in very neatly with the date of its opening.

When the railway was driven through Sydney Gardens in 1840, many follies and diversions were destroyed. These included a labyrinth, a grotto – and a sham castle. This was described as "a facsimile of those ancient Baronial towers that served as strongholds for the heroes of the olden times." It was, in other words, a fairly substantial structure. Were the stones from that building used to build the *Castle Tavern*, thus giving it its name? It is an intriguing possibility, and one we can ponder over at leisure, sitting in the garden behind the *Castle* and studying the old stones that were incorporated into the present building when it was built in 1898.

CENTRAL WINE BAR 10 Upper Borough Walls

The *Central Wine Bar* on Upper Borough Walls has a licensed history going back over 200 years. It was originally called the *Royal Oak* and opened sometime before 1776. In 1812 it was rebuilt and the front was set back so that the street could be widened. In 1837, it was the setting for an uninspired bit of sharp practice:

> Ralph Whitehead and William Bibb were
> charged by James Peters with stealing his

jacket. It appears that Peters went into the *Royal Oak* and called for a pint of beer, and was shown into the tap room. The party there was just going to dance; Peters pulled off his jacket to join them, and gave it to Bibb to take care of for him. They did not dance; Peters then asked Bibb for his jacket, but he denied ever having seen it. Subsequently Whitehead was taken into custody in Westgate Street with the jacket in his possession, by a policeman whom Peters had informed of the robbery.

The *Royal Oak* was eventually taken over by Walcot Brewery. In the mid-nineteenth century it changed its name no less than three times. It was the *Half Moon* in 1841, the *New Moon* in 1849, and the *Owl's Nest* by the 1860s. The 1903 report on the *Owl's Nest* described it as having two entrances from Upper Borough Walls, a bar with a smoke room behind it and a brewhouse with a "concealed door" at the back. There was a urinal and WC on the stairs to the cellar which were described as "very dirty." It closed in 1907 and became a restaurant. Later it became a hairdressers, but today it has reverted to type as the *Central Wine Bar*. No trace of the old pub seems to survive, but the early twentieth century shopfront, similar in design to that of Shoon next door (with the sign of a new moon above its door), is a particularly attractive feature. Very popular, with an award-winning cocktail barman, good food and a pool table and Sky TV in a separate room, the *Central Wine Bar* is a much more pleasant place to pass the time than the *Owl's Nest* seems to have been.

Upper Borough Walls, whose only remaining pub is *Sam Weller's* (which we will come to later), was once lined with boozers. There was something of a celestial theme along here as well. At Nos 2-3 (now Brad Abraham's Opticians) was the *Seven Stars*, dating back to at least 1687, and closed in 1974. Across the road, where Dollond & Aitchison's Opticians is today, was the *Rainbow*, which closed in 1922. Add to that the *New Moon* and the *Full Moon* (the original name for *Sam Weller's*) and you have quite a celestial line-up. Further along, and breaking with the heavenly theme, were the *White Hart Vaults* (c1886-1919) at No 17 (now *Café Nero*) and *Fuller's Wine Vaults* (c1868-c1912) at No 18.

CENTURION Poolemead Road, Twerton

Given Bath's reliance on Roman remains to attract tourists, it is surprising that the only pub whose name recalls Aquae Sulis is one that few, if any, tourists will ever visit. On 10

April 1964, Leslie Lord was granted a licence for "permanent premises to be built on a site adjoining the eastern side of Poolemead Road, Twerton." The *Centurion* opened in December the following year.

When Fred Pearce visited in 1976, it had two bars – Buttery and Lounge – and he complained about the tables in the Buttery joined together in ranks like a school canteen. One particularly attractive feature of the *Centurion* is the lavish floral decorations which cover it every summer.

CHARMBURY ARMS 69-70 Brook Road

Sometimes you walk into a pub that you feel drinkers from a century or more ago would feel at home in. Not that the *Charmbury Arms* is stuck in a timewarp. If there was an award for the most vigorously knocked-through pub in Bath, the *Charmbury* would be a hot contender. Different coloured carpets signify where the rooms once were, a staircase runs up the back wall, and there is even a fireplace fitted into a free-standing pillar near

the front door. The fittings include what appears to be an old church pew in the pool area. But it is the people that make a pub, and here the *Charmbury* wins hands down. A relaxed atmosphere, with regulars constantly popping in and out and the feeling that, even if it has all been knocked through, the bar at the *Charmbury* really is somebody's front room rather than some marketing man's idea of what a pub should look like.

It has been a pub for over 120 years, first appearing in the 1882 *Postal* Directory with Will Slip as licensee. In 1976, when Fred Pearce visited, it was still a cider house, although the landlord said he only served cider to "certain people." It consisted of a small public bar and an even smaller smoking room. A few months after Fred's visit, Courage's decided to close the *Charmbury Arms* and put it up for sale for £14,950. Somehow, it managed to survive and today, knocked through and extended into the house next door, it is still going strong.

The *Charmbury* is just up the road from one of Bath's most recent alcoholic casualties, the *Royal Oak*, which opened as a beerhouse in the 1830s. In 1976, Fred Pearce described it as "an intimate and exceptionally pleasant well-kept house." In 1993, Courage's sold it to Moles Brewery (who also owned the *Hop Pole* and the *Old Crown* in Twerton). Sadly, although Moles is still going strong, the *Royal Oak* is not. The good news, however, is that plans by Jehovah's Witnesses to pull it down and build a meeting hall were turned down by the council in 2002. It may not reopen as a pub, but at least the building – a Twerton landmark for almost 200 years – seems likely to survive.

CHEQUERS 50 Rivers Street

The *Chequers*, on the corner of Rivers Street Mews, opened as the *New Inn* sometime before 1776 to serve the sedan chairmen who carried genteel visitors up to nearby lodging houses. As John Wood the Younger only built Russell Street in the early 1770s, the *New Inn* must have been a pub from the start. Situated on what were then the northern fringes of the city, it encouraged sedan chairmen to hang around rather than hare back down the hill after they had dropped customers off. Visitors who took lodgings nearby would, therefore, have had a reasonable chance of getting a chair into town when they wanted one. The last thing John Wood the Younger and the other developers wanted was for their expensive new lodgings to stand empty due to a

reputation for poor sedan-chair service. He need have had no worries. So popular was the *New Inn* with sedan chairmen, that, when the New Bath Loyal Society of Chairmen was founded in 1794, they chose it as their headquarters.

A century ago, when you entered the *New Inn*, you would have walked into a corridor with a bar on the right and a smoke room on the left. There was a glass room beyond the bar and a serving hatch in the corridor. There was a brewery at the back which closed around 1930. The *New Inn* was renamed the *Chequers* in the late 1950s. When Fred Pearce visited in 1976, it still had two bars – the Windsor and the Westminster – both decorated in "a rather fussy Regency style." Today, it is open plan, but a link with the past still survives at the back, where an old stable yard is an almost miraculously preserved bit of eighteenth century Bath that appears on few tourist itineraries.

Something else few tourists get to hear about are the *Chequers'* legendary Sunday roasts, although given the number of people who crowd in here every week that is probably just as well.

A half-gallon jar from the *New Inn* in Rivers Street dating from around 1882-96.

Although the *New Inn* was only renamed the *Chequers* in the 1950s, the name itself is one of the oldest pub names of all. In the eighteenth century, many pubs were called the *Chequers* when they first opened. There were at least than 24 *Chequers* in Bath at one time or another, although most of them were renamed after a couple of years. Both the *Old Crown* in Weston and the *Rummer*, for example, started life as the *Chequers*. It seems to have been a case of "if you can't think of a name for your pub, call it the *Chequers* until you can." There are various theories as to the origin of the name. Some say it indicated that a chequers or chess board was kept on the premises. Some say it indicated money-changing facilities (the word "exchequer" – as in "Chancellor of the" – comes from the word "chequers"). Others say it comes from the coat of arms of the Fitzwarren family, who licensed alehouses in the reign of Edward IV. There is another theory, however, that has nothing to do with chess boards, exchequers or coats of arms. The traditional way of indicating that a house served alcohol was to have the branch of a tree (known as an ale stake) sticking out above the front door. One of the most popular alcoholic beverages in medieval times was made from the fruit of the wild service tree.

The name of the tree may even have come from the Spanish word *cerevisia*, meaning "fermented drink." Not surprisingly, these trees were often to be seen growing in alehouse gardens – with their lopped boughs sticking out over the front door to tempt wayfarers inside. The fruits of the wild service tree, because of their chequered markings, are known as chequers. Hence, alehouses with wild service trees became known as "the chequers." Eventually, wild service brew fell out of favour, although by then the name "chequers" had become synonymous with alehouses. If nothing else, the theory is certainly worth debating over a few noggins of ale.

COEUR DE LION 17 Northumberland Place

Northumberland Place, leading off the High Street, was originally known as Marchant's Court and was described as "entirely new" by John Wood in 1749. Around 1866, a woodcarver called William Batt of 4 Northumberland Place (now one half of the Cancer Research Shop) obtained a licence to sell beer. A couple of years later he named his beerhouse the *Avondale Stores*, presumably because he got his supplies from the Avondale Brewery at Batheaston. Mr Batt left and was followed by a number of other licensees, none of whom stayed very long.

The *Avondale Stores* soon acquired a reputation as a rather insalubrious hostelry, and, before long, local residents were lobbying to have it shut down. In 1872, a petition was presented to the licensing magistrates, "praying them to discontinue granting the certificate to this house on account of urinal nuisance and harbouring suspicious characters, keeping open house after hours, etc." The magistrates responded by instructing the owner of the *Avondale Stores*, Frances Evill, to get rid of the licensee, William Hanks, and replace him with somebody else. Three months later the licence was transferred to Richard Osborne and the *Avondale Stores* began a slow return to respectability. Around 1880, it was renamed the *Coeur de Lion*. The choice of name is a puzzling one, and, as far as we know, it is the only pub called the *Coeur de Lion* in the country.

By this time, Stoffel & Co's grocery empire was slowly taking over more and more of Northumberland Place. In 1886, it owned Nos 1 and 2. Two years later, it had moved into a former jeweller's at No 3, a former trunkmaker's across the way at No 17, and the *Coeur* at No 4. Around 1890, the company decided that it made more sense to move the *Coeur* across to no 17 and expand the grocery into No 4.

The 1903 report on the new beerhouse described it as having a single bar with a "partitioned-off inner compartment." Although the partition has gone, the beerhouse, now with a full license, is still there today. If Devenish's had had their way, however, it would have been another of Bath's lost pubs. When the landlord, Dennis Thomas (who had previously kept the *Lamb* in Stall Street and the *Castle* in Forester Road), retired in 1987, Devenish's announced that they were "very conscious of the prices nearby properties have been fetching [and were] investigating the question of disposal." However, a new landlord, Stephen Shearing, was appointed and all seemed well until, three years later, Devenish's announced that the *Coeur de Lion* was to close. Regulars quickly got together a 1,800-signature petition. With the backing of local MP Chris Patten, the Bath Preservation Trust and the Georgian Society, the Council were persuaded to throw out plans to turn it into a shop.

The *Coeur de Lion*, Bath's smallest pub, is a gem, included in a CAMRA Guide to Britain's 100 top classic pubs, and little changed since it opened in the closing years of Victoria's reign. But appearances can be deceptive. One of its most striking features – the stained glass in the front-window – was made by John Hall & Sons of Bristol in the late 1950s. Ironically, Devenish's, who were thwarted in their attempt to close the *Coeur* but whose name is still immortalised in the stained glass, are no more, while the *Coeur* is still going strong.

CROSS KEYS Midford Road, Combe Down

On June 1718, Henry Palmer, a "Doctor of Physick," from Bath, leased "a new erected tenement or dwelling house called the *Cross Keys*, now a public house, on Odwood Down" from the Governors of Bruton Hospital. As well as being a pub, the *Cross Keys* was a farmhouse, standing in 80 acres of land. On Harcourt Master's 1787 Turnpike Map, it appears as Cross Keys Farm, suggesting that the public house side of the business was very much secondary.

Nevertheless, by the early nineteenth century, it was a stage for coaches to Salisbury and Southampton, and twice featured as such in the *Journal* of John Skinner, Rector of Camerton:

> Tuesday, 4 February 1823:
>
> I was up early to take leave of the boys, who went in the car to the *Cross Keys* to meet the Salisbury coach.
>
> Tuesday, 6 August 1823:
>
> We drove to Bath to my mother's. Joseph went early this morning in the car to meet the Southampton coach at the *Cross Keys*, in order to go to Romsey in his way to Twyford.

Despite being an inn, the *Cross Keys* also continued to be a farm for many years. As late as 1869, an inventory was drawn up of the "tillage and tenant's right together with live and dead farming stock, household furniture, brewing plant ... of the *Cross*

Keys and land connected with the same." One of the crops for which this area was noted until well into the twentieth century was watercress.

A painting of the *Cross Keys* dating from around 1853.

The *Cross Keys* in 1904, showing some of the watercress beds for which the area was noted.

Sometime in the early nineteenth century, the old three-storey farmhouse acquired a two-storey extension at the front, with a single-storey porch to one side. At the time of the 1903 report, the *Cross Keys* consisted of a bar with a parlour to one side and a tap room below. Today, its accommodation has been considerably extended, but it still preserves the character of a traditional wayside inn. The tap room has been converted into a restaurant reached by a flight of stairs from the right-hand bar, but the words "tap room" are still faintly visible above the door outside. A magnificent aviary in the garden, an impressive collection of cricketing memorabilia, framed ties in memory of former customers, an original fireplace, home-cooked food and an entry in the *Good Beer Guide*, all add up to a pub that is deservedly popular.

The sign of the *Cross Keys*, incidentally, refers to the emblem of St Peter, the keeper of the keys of heaven, and is generally displayed by houses owned by religious institutions dedicated to St Peter. The *Cross Keys* at Combe Down originally belonged to the Governors of Bruton Hospital, founded in 1638 by Hugh Sexey, but was sold to Oakhill Brewery in 1896.

CROWN 23 Bathwick Street, Bathwick

All manner of claims have been made for the *Crown* in Bathwick Street, including an association with a highwayman called Sixteen String Jack. The earliest landlord we can trace it back to is Thomas Bolwell, who was there in 1767. The Bolwell family stayed at the *Crown* until the early nineteenth century. They later became leading Chartists, and it is possible that that they established the tradition of radicalism which saw the *Crown* become one of the principal meeting places of JA Roebuck, Bath's famous liberal MP.

In 1848, William Hooper, a wood and coal dealer, was the landlord of the *Crown*. His sudden demise was reported in graphic detail in the *Bath Chronicle*:

On Friday last, Mr Hooper, landlord of the *Crown Inn*, Bathwick, having occasion to go into the *White Lion Tap*, Bridge Street, entered the parlour and sat upon the stool by the table, and having been served with a glass of ale, stood up for the purpose of drinking it. Having done so, he was on the act of resuming his seat when he fell backwards to the ground with great force and received a severe fracture of the skull. He was immediately conveyed home and medical aid procured, but it proved of no avail as he expired yesterday week.

In 1838, the *Crown* appeared in the pages of that most scurrilous of Bath's early newspapers, the *Figaro*. This was a cross between *Private Eye*, a student rag mag, and a political broadsheet. Its political sympathies were with the Chartists and local rallies were covered at great length. One aspect of Chartism which those who portrayed its followers as a drunken rabble chose to ignore was its links with the teetotal movement. Henry Vincent, who organised many Chartist rallies in the Bath area and who later settled in the city, was not only one of the most influential Chartist leaders but also a leading light of the teetotal movement. It is not surprising, therefore, that the *Figaro* aligned itself with the temperance movement, covering local meetings and lampooning those whose sobriety was not always conspicuous. The great and good of Bath must have loathed it, especially its Celebrated Untruths section, which contained entries such as:

> It is not true that Mr Andrews and Mr Keevil, on seeing their names in the *Figaro*, were so exasperated that the former gentleman drank a hogshead of Emerson's strong beer and the latter swallowed the barrel.

> It is not true that Jerry's master of the *Lion Tap*, and the Owl of the *White Hart* office, alias 50 Jemmy Page, with an ornamental character of the *York House* office known by the name of Cherry Checked Tommy went to the steeplechase in a short fishmonger's waggon and got turned over.

> It is not true that J . . n W . . t, butcher, intends having his whiskers cut off to stuff a cushion.

> It is not true that Mr B . . . n has lost his mistress, or that she left Bath with a certain banker's clerk of this city.

> It is not true that the Mayor's Officers are to wear green uniform; report says they are green enough already.

> It is not true that Mr Bennett got drunk at Mr Atkins' expense on brandy and water at the *Grapes Tavern*, Westgate Street.

> It is not true that the Butter-Man of Bath Street only escaped having his face scratched by a certain lady living in Balance Street, St Michael's Hill, for not taking her to London instead of his wife, to see the Queen go to Parliament, by promising to do so when he has packed off his better half to Torbay for the benefit of her health.

> It is not true that Inspector Norcross and PC 103 have applied to be removed from Bathwick Parish because the girls are so deeply in love with them.

The *Figaro* certainly gives us a different picture of early Victorian Bath than the one those who were so savagely lampooned by it tried to cultivate. Many of the "non-accusations" are still cringe-making today, even though the memory of those they were aimed at has long since faded. The point of some, however, has been entirely lost, such as this entry for 29 June 1838, which doubtless raised a few hackles at the time:

> It is not true that George Trimby and George Hill were engaged to play the pipes and violin to the skittle pins at the *Crown*, Bathwick, the last Gala Night.

Sadly, but perhaps inevitably, the *Figaro* folded after a couple of years. The great and good of Bath no doubt breathed a hearty sigh of relief at its passing. Perhaps, though, in our heritage-conscious age, it is time for it to be revived.

The old *Crown* survived until the end of the nineteenth century. Nobody knows how long it had been there and nobody bothered to find out. It was old, that was all that mattered, and being old it was best out of the way. And so, in September 1898, "Mr Ayton applied that the licence now held by Thomas James Maggs of the *Crown Inn*, Bathwick, might be granted to a new house it was proposed to build on the site of the present premises with No 21 Bathwick Street added. The Bath Brewery Company were lessees of this property. The application was granted."

This new pub is the one we see today. When built, it had a club room, a glass room, a jug & bottle department, a bar, a tap room and a skittle alley, with a lift from the skittle alley (in the basement) to the club room (on the first floor).

When the old inn was demolished, the following reminiscences of it appeared in the *Bath Journal*:

The removal of the *Crown Inn* at the end of Bathwick street removes the most ancient building in the parish. The removal of this yellow-washed old building reminds me that I owe your readers some remembrance of Bathwick of some years ago …

Collinson in his history says, "the population in Bathwick, in 1781, amounted to only 150 souls. It is difficult to point out a place in the kingdom which has improved so rapidly as this once quiet and retired village. About 90 years ago it consisted of an irregular street of about 45 houses, near the ancient village church. A stream of water, arising in Claverton Down, ran through the village in an open stone channel. Children sported in the meadows which lay between the village and the city, while crowds of visitors crossed the ferry, at the bottom of Boatstall Lane, to enjoy a ramble in the meadows. At this period, in addition to the mill, a broad-cloth factory stood near the river." Commenting on this, Mr Peach says, "it requires some stretch of imagination to realise that the foregoing passage contains a tolerably accurate description of Bathwick in 1780. We look in vain for the old fashioned irregular village, of which but one house (the *Crown Inn*) in Bathwick Street remains." And now we look in vain for that! … This inn was the birthplace of the notorious highwayman Jack Rann, better known by the sobriquet of "Sixteen String Jack," who, previous to adopting his nefarious occupation, was coachman to the Earl of Sandwich. The bunch of sixteen ribbons which he wore at his knee were supposed to have been some covert allusion to the number of times he had been tried and acquitted.

But let us picture the *Crown* in more recent times than the days of Jack Rann or the period given by Collinson. At galas, especially when the Oddfellows or Foresters perambulated the city in full regalia, with numerous banners, emblems and rich paraphernalia and marched in procession to the Sydney Gardens, when from four to five thousand people would pay for admission. At horticultural shows at these Gardens, when refreshments were provided for the gardeners and their assistants, this hostelry was the scene of an animation and bustle never witnessed at the present period. I allude to the time when it was occupied by Mr Vincent (1838), afterwards by Mr Hooper and his widow, then by Mr George Watts, who was for many years head cellarman at the old Northgate Brewery … The supplying of refreshments, etc., to the gardeners at the flower shows was divided between Mr Broad at the *Pulteney Arms* and mine host at the *Crown*, the lessee of the gardens and hotel having his hands quite full without this.

The reputation of the *Crown* as a place of entertainment was maintained after the rebuilding, and for several years there was a stage in the garden for pierrot concerts.

A salt glazed jug from Edward Manning of the *Crown* in Bathwick. He was licensee from around 1812 to 1819. This is probably the earliest surviving item from a pub still in business in Bath and was found during the dredging of the River Avon around Pulteney Weir.

Although Jack Rann, alias Sixteen-String Jack, was one of Bath's more disreputable sons, his career in the city was exemplary. While still a boy, he worked as a huckster, wandering around the city with a donkey, buying and selling whatever he could pick up. He was such a charmer that, within a short time, a lady of quality took him into her household, where he rapidly became a favourite both above and below stairs.

Before long, however, the bright lights beckoned, and he set off for London, working his way up to become coachman to several noblemen. He acquired a reputation for dressing flamboyantly, and, in particular, for the sixteen strings which he wore on his knee breeches. His employers spoke of him in glowing terms, but all the time his resentment at the unbridgeable gulf between his lifestyle and that of his employers grew, until, falling in with a bunch of ne'er-do-wells, he decided to take matters into his own hands and became a highwayman.

His career on the wrong side of the law soon brought him the riches he had dreamed of. It was not long, however, before he was caught and brought to trial. Here, though, his charm, wit, and cunning paid off, and he was acquitted on a technicality. Having outwitted the law, he was hailed as a hero, not only by his fellow criminals, but also by many in high society. Crime was, if anything, more glamorous in the eighteenth century than it is today. He was renowned as the man they could not hang, and, carried away by the adulation, he came to see himself as beyond the law. He turned up at pleasure gardens and race meetings, with doxies in tow, boasting about his exploits as a highwayman, gambling, drinking, fighting, and generally behaving like the aristocrats whose behaviour he had studied for so long.

It could not last. His exploits grew more reckless and daring as he struggled to fund his increasingly extravagant lifestyle. The authorities eventually caught up with him, produced a watertight case, and he was sentenced to death. He played the part of the gallant gentleman of fortune to the end. Seven women joined him in a farewell dinner the night before his execution, and, the following day, he approached the gallows without flinching.

Dr Johnson said later that "Gray's poetry towered above the ordinary run of verse as Sixteen-String Jack towered above the ordinary footpad." A more fitting tribute, perhaps, comes in the form of a pub named after him in Theydon Bois, Essex, the only known instance of someone from a pub in Bath having a pub named after them somewhere else. The *Crown*, on the other hand, is the most common pub name in Britain. Its sign swings outside no less than 704 pubs, well ahead of the *Red Lion*, which hangs outside a mere 668.

CROWN & ANCHOR 44 High Street, Upper Weston

The *Crown & Anchor*, with possibly the finest sign bracket in Bath – an anchor topped by a crown – was opened as a beerhouse around 1833 by a stonemason called Solomon Slingo. It has another masonic connection, for at one time a freemason's lodge met here. In the early twentieth century, a horse bus, stabled at the back, ran from the pub to the GWR station in Bath. It must have been a more welcome neighbour than the "White Ribbon Army" of temperance campaigners who met at a chapel behind the pub in the late nineteenth century. Today it is still a popular, traditional two-barred boozer with a potted history hanging on the wall in the public bar.

A late-nineteenth-century map showing: 1] the *Crown & Anchor* 2] the *King's Head* 3] the *Queen's Head*

The *Crown & Anchor* is only a stone's throw from the *King's Head*. A century ago, however, there was yet another pub within hailing distance. This was the *Queen's Head*, across the road from the *King's Head*, at 1 Trafalgar Place. It opened as a beerhouse around 1840 and carried on quite happily until 1914, when the magistrates decided that, with a pub for every 216 people in Weston, one of them had to go. Despite the landlord's plea that it was a well-conducted house, they were unmoved and the *Queen's Head* slipped quietly into history. The building is still there, in use as a flower shop.

CRYSTAL PALACE 10-11 Abbey Green

The *Crystal Palace* has only been a pub for just over 150 years. The building, however, dates from the early seventeenth century, and was originally used as lodgings for the *Three Tuns Inn* in Stall Street.

The *Three Tuns* started out in the late sixteenth century as an alehouse built up against the wall of the Abbey precincts – roughly where Swallow Street is today. The tenant of the house, Philip Sherwood, had "a post thrust out of the wall of the house and thereon a little sign of three tunns hanging, resembling the sign of an alehouse." In 1620, he obtained a licence from Sir Giles Mompesson to turn his alehouse into an inn, "whereupon he set a new fair sign of three tunnes, and fixed to support it two great posts in the street being the soil of the Mayor and Commonalty, which he could not do without their leave." No sooner had he started his expansion programme than the Corporation revoked his licence on a technicality. This may have been part of a campaign to suppress unnecessary drinking establishments, but is more likely to have been an attempt by the Chapman family, who not only owned Bath's biggest inns but were also influential councillors, to stifle competition.

Sherwood called the Corporation's bluff and "refused contemptuously to take down his sign." The Corporation sent the bailiffs round to remove it, only to be confronted by Sherwood's son "with a loaded weapon and a maidservant with gunpowder." When a crowd of around 300 people turned up to see what would happen next, the bailiffs withdrew, only to return when things had quietened down to complete their task.

The next day, Philip Sherwood put his sign back and filed a complaint with the Privy Council. Even though they upheld the Corporation's opposition to the inn and the "sundry disorders" that had occurred there, the *Three Tuns* stayed open. Its proximity to the King's Bath soon made it popular with those coming to immerse themselves in the waters. A diary from 1634, preserved in the British Museum, records the arrival of some officers from Wells:

> To this Citty we came late and wet and entred stumbling . . . over a fayre archt Bridge crossing Avon
> . . . and heere we billetted our Selves at the *3 Tuns* close by the King's Bath – And now prepared wee
> with the skillfull directions of our Ancient to take a Preparative to fit our jumbled weary Corps to
> enter and take refreshment in those admired, unparalelld medicinable sulphureous hot Bathes."

In 1632, Philip Sherwood was elected to the council and thereafter regularly supplied goods to the Corporation. In 1640, for example, he supplied a "pottle of sack which was brought to the hall." In the following year he provided the Recorder with "lodging, fier and beare." He had clearly patched up any disagreement with the Chapmans and during the Civil War served under Henry Chapman, the landlord of the *Sun* in the Market Place, as the Lieutenant of the Bath Trained Bands.

In 1666, the *Three Tuns* was leased from the Corporation by a Mr Smeaton. The lease passed to William Sherston in 1679 and to Richard Ford, an apothecary, in 1719. Its dimensions in 1719 were recorded as 18 feet 3 inches by 16 feet 4 inches. Clearly, this was just the original alehouse. When Philip Sherwood turned it into an inn, he had not expanded the original property, but acquired buildings nearby to use as lodgings and dining rooms. A new dining room was added around 1718, for in September that year, Dr Claver Morris of Wells recorded in his diary,

> We continued at Bath. I was called in to Mr Harington at Kelston. I got Mr Du Burg, Mr Shojan,
> Mr Walter, and Mr David Baswiwaldt to go with me. We dined there, and had a Consort of Musick.
> We returned to Bath in the evening, and I entertained them with 3 fowles and wine in the great new
> drawing room at the *Three Tuns*, where I had a performance of Musick by these extraordinary hands.

The adjacent buildings were still not formally regarded as part of the inn in the mid-eighteenth century, as an advertisement from the *Bath Journal* of 1748 indicates:

> The *Three Tuns Inn & Tavern* to be sold, in the city of Bath together with the coach houses and stables
> thereto belonging. And also a messuage called the *Three Tuns Lodgings*, and a House and Garden in the
> Abbey Green.

The property in Abbey Green later became the *Crystal Palace*. A further advertisement appeared on 10 October 1748:

> To be sold, an Inn called the *Three Tuns* in the City of Bath; together with the coach house and stables … in possession of Mr Joseph Phillott … also a Messuage call'd the *Three Tuns Lodging*, and also a messuage in the Abbey Green in the possession of Rebecca Salmon.

Joseph Phillott, the grandson of a French immigrant, was at the *Three Tuns* till 1767, when he left to take over the *Bear* in Cheap Street. His place was taken by Abraham Eve. The *Three Tuns* was a favourite meeting place for friendly and benevolent societies in the late eighteenth century. In 1778, for example, the Friendly Brothers of the Bath Knot and the Brothers of the Ancient & Most Benevolent Order of the Friendly Brothers of St Patrick used it as their headquarters.

In 1774, Henry Phillips from the *Saracen's Head* took over the *Three Tuns*. He, in turn was replaced by J Williams from Beckhampton in 1783. The following year, when the mailcoach service was introduced, the *Three Tuns* was chosen as its depot in Bath. On 4 August 1784, the *Bath Chronicle* reported that

> the new mail diligence set off from Bristol on Monday last for the first time at four o'clock and from the *Three Tuns* in this city at twenty minutes after five the same evening. From London it set out at eight on Monday evening and was in Bath by nine the next morning.

Shortly afterwards Joseph Dobson took over the *Three Tuns*. In 1789, he disposed of the Coach, Chaise and Stabling Business to Henry Phillips (who had been the landlord from 1774 to 1783), but kept the Inn and Tavern on. As coaching businesses mushroomed in size towards the end of the eighteenth century, there was an increasing tendency for them to be run and owned separately from the inns in which they had started off. At around this time, the *Three Tuns* increased its capacity by taking over the coachyard of the old *Bell Inn* in Bell Tree Lane.

In 1792, the *Three Tuns* was taken over by Henry Ballanger from the *Greyhound & Shakespeare* in the Market Place. Five years later he died and the business was carried on by his widow. Early in 1799 Elizabeth Ballanger married John Reidford. She kept her former name, however, and, on 5 April 1804, put a notice in the *Bath Chronicle*, thanking all those who had supported her "during fourteen years residence" at the *Three Tuns*, but adding that the inn was now closed. The *Three Tuns Inn*, set up over 170 years earlier in the teeth of official opposition, and the stopping place for the first mailcoaches through the city, had slipped quietly into history.

Eight years later, it was demolished. In 1812, Thomas Parfet, who was responsible for rebuilding much of Stall Street, leased "the plot of ground where the *Three Tuns* stands on the east side of Stall Street, [to] build three good stone messuages thereon, fronting Stall Street, and two fronting York Street. A licence to sell ale was not guaranteed." However, one of the buildings built on the site of the old *Three Tuns* did reopen as a pub, albeit briefly. In 1830, John Rudman was listed as the landlord of a new *Three Tuns* in Stall Street. The new inn was taken over by Joseph Claxton in 1839, but closed in the late 1840s.

Despite its early demise, in its heyday the *Three Tuns* was one of Bath's best-loved and most boisterous inns, as Smollett's description of an evening spent there in the company of the great Shakespearian actor James Quin (1693-1766) makes abundantly clear:

> I had hopes of seeing Quin in his hours of elevation at the tavern, which is the temple of mirth and good fellowship; where he, as priest of Comus, utters the inspirations of wit and humour. I have had that satisfaction. I have dined with him at his club at the *Three Tuns*, and had the honour to sit him out. At half an hour past eight in the evening, he was carried home with six good bottles of claret under his belt; and it being then Friday, he gave orders that he should not be disturbed till Sunday at noon. You must not imagine that this dose had any other effect upon his conversation, but that of making it more extravagantly entertaining. He had lost the use of his limbs, indeed, several hours before we parted, but he retained all his other faculties in perfection; and, as he gave vent to every whimsical idea as it rose, I was really astonished at the brilliancy of his thoughts, and the force of his expression.

The *Three Tuns* also played a minor part in one of eighteenth-century Bath's most shameful episodes. One night in 1778, the French Count and Countess du Barré, were playing cards with an Irish gentleman called Count Rice at their lodging in the Royal Crescent:

> At length a violent disagreement took place between the two Counts, and each being of an impetuous disposition, it was resolved that the dispute should terminate with the death of one or both. Accordingly, they left their abode about one o'clock in the morning, procured a coach from the *Three Tuns* in Stall Street; and provided with arms, seconds, and surgical assistance, reached Claverton Down long before daybreak. There they paced in sullen silence till dawn began to break, when their stations were taken. Count Rice fired but his ball did not take effect. Du Barré returned the fire, and the ball lodged in the groin of his antagonist, who fell; but raising himself immediately from the ground, he discharged his second pistol in a recumbent position, the contents of which penetrated the heart of the unfortunate Du Barré. The parties decamped, and the body of the deceased, Du Barré, was left on the field of battle for more than twenty-four hours, an object of curiosity to those who could patiently and calmly witness so horrid a spectacle. The wounded survivor was taken to the York House, and Monsieur Du Barré was afterwards buried at Bathampton, where a stone now marks the spot of his interment. Count Rice recovered, was tried at the Taunton assizes, in 1779, and acquitted.

The death of the Countess, 15 years later, was even more terrible. Arrested by the French revolutionary government for carrying a picture of Mr Pitt, the British Prime Minister, she was sentenced to the guillotine:

> On her passage to the scaffold, she leaned on the head of her attendant, and appeared almost dead; but when she reached the fatal spot, the sight of the instrument of death rallied her fainting spirits. Suddenly she rose up and rent the air with shrieks, her convulsed frame acquired most extraordinary strength; and, after a conflict with her executioners, at the relation of which humanity shudders, the fatal stroke released her from all her sufferings.

The *Crystal Palace* opened in the old lodging house of the *Three Tuns* in 1851 or 1852, its name commemorating the Great Exhibition held at the Crystal Palace. The wood panelling in the bar of No 10 (where Nelson is believed to have stayed) was salvaged from the old *Three Tuns* when it was demolished.

An old photograph on display inside the pub shows that at one time the *Crystal Palace* had three floors, the top one forming part of the brewery. Although the brewery closed around 1935 and the top floor was removed, its roof marks can still be seen on the gable end of the building next door. Legend has it that, while digging a well in the back yard to supply the brewery with water, workmen tapped into a hot spring, which was capped on the understanding that the Corporation would lay on a free supply of cold water.

The 1903 report on the *Crystal Palace* described it as having a glass room, a tap room and a drinks bar. At the back was a skittle alley and a private yard with a passage leading to Swallow Street.

In 1951 Bert Oliver, who had been a stocktaker at Fussell's Brewery in Frome, took over the licence. Food had been a staple of many pubs in the eighteenth and nineteenth centuries, but in the twentieth it had fallen by the wayside. Bert Oliver was one of the first publicans in Bath to start serving food again, rustling up delicacies such as fillet steak and chips for 5/6 (27.5p). When he left, Bass sold the pub to Eldridge Pope, the Dorchester Brewers, and Roy Wain became the new licensee. He soon became a celebrity when he uncovered several skeletons and a Roman mosaic in the cellar. It was decided not to try to move the mosaic, but to preserve it underneath a layer of polythene and sand, where it remains today.

Imaginatively revamped, with a Titchmarsh-inspired garden at the back, complete with decking, gazebo and cold-water fountain, the *Crystal Palace* is a popular oasis in the heart of the city.

CURFEW 11 Cleveland Place West, London Road

The *Curfew*, with its Cromwellian sign, wood-panelled interior and a wonderful warren of rooms on different levels, may give the impression of being one of Bath's oldest pubs. In fact, it is no such thing – even though it has been associated with the licensed trade for the best part of 150 years.

In the dim, distant past it was a bookshop, but by 1837 it had become John Snook's Wine & Spirit Merchants. Later, the business was taken over by the Edwards family. Although many wine merchant's did become pubs in the nineteenth century, this was not one of them. The 1903 report confirms that the premises were "used for wine merchant's business only – no drinking on premises." The Edwards family left in 1932, but it remained a wine merchant's, even after it was granted a full licence on 7 March 1956. It was known as the *Quadrant Wine & Spirit Merchants* until the late 1960s, when it was renamed the *Curfew*.

Henry Edmund Goodridge's design for the *Curfew*

A one-gallon salt-glazed jar bearing the name of John Snook, the first owner of the *Cleveland Wine Vaults*

With its Regency shopfront and magnificent ironwork, it is one of the finest looking pubs in Bath, hardly surprising as it was designed, in the 1820s, by the same architect who built Cleveland Bridge and Beckford's Tower, Henry Edmund Goodridge. The deeds of the property were signed at William Beckford's house, 20 Lansdown Crescent, in 1827, and bear the signatures of two of Beckford's servants as witnesses. This suggests that Beckford may have been involved in the development of Cleveland Place.

Next door but one to the *Curfew*, incidentally, at 9 Cleveland Place West, was one of Bath's earliest museums, opened in 1835 by Charles Empson. Admission was free, but there were "specimens" for sale, as well as models of the druidical remains on Jersey at one guinea each. In 1838, Barker's *Death of Haidée* was exhibited there, along with giant ox bones from Melksham, letters from Lord Nelson, Queen Victoria's signature and fake royal jewels. It was still there in 1841 but seems to have closed shortly afterwards.

Only open at night (except at weekends), the *Curfew*, with a garden tucked away at the back, and a game of chess or backgammon generally in progress at one of the large wooden tables near the window, is worth seeking out for its highly individualistic atmosphere.

DARK HORSE 4 Northampton Street

Once there were archery butts here and the area was known as Butt Hayes. Then in 1777 Charles Hamilton, who lived at Rock House in Lansdown Road, leased the land to create a landscape garden. This only lasted a short while, for in 1791, Thomas Baldwin, acting for William Johnstone Pulteney, bought it to build houses on. Northampton Street was planned as the central spine of a new development, with side roads leading off it and another street – Southampton Row – at the top.

A one-gallon jar from W Williams of the *White Horse* in Northampton Street (1862-67).

Within a couple of years, boom had turned to bust, Baldwin had gone bankrupt, and it was left to his assistant, John Pinch, to develop Northampton Street on more modest lines. Its houses bear a characteristic Pinch trademark – the extensive use of brick rather than stone for their lining, party and back walls.

The *Dark Horse*, originally known as the *White Horse*, opened as a beerhouse in the 1830s with Richard Hobley as the licensee. It was later acquired by George Biggs of the Crown Brewery in New Orchard Street. When an inventory was drawn up in 1897, it consisted of a bar, a smoking room, a tap room and a brewery. The bar had an oak-panelled, mahogany-topped counter with a half-glazed screen at the end, a five-motion beer engine, a matchboard partition dividing the bar from the smoking room (with a stained and diapered glass sash and fanlight), and a "dwarf partition with door and shelving at the side forming a bar enclosure." The 1903 report was more succinct. The property, it said, consisted of a "serving bar in passage with glass room at side and tap room beyond. Skittle alley at rear."

The *White Horse* was badly damaged in the Bath Blitz but was soon back in business, only to face the threat of demolition in the 1970s. Not only did it survive, but it also stayed open as a pub. The buildings below it have disappeared, however, and today it has gone from mid-terrace to end of terrace. One feature particularly worth noting is its nicely preserved Greek Revival porch.

For many years the *White Horse* was a noted cider house, with ginger and orange peel on the bar to tickle jaded taste buds. When Fred Pearce visited in 1976 he found the small public bar "very tatty indeed with just room for darts and fruit machine." There was a juke box in the back room annexe and custom was "young and sub-bohemian." Today, it has been knocked through, redecorated, and renamed the *Dark Horse*, but, although a good deal more sedate than it was when Fred passed through, it still has a highly individual character.

DELFTER KRUG Sawclose

Although not Bath's oldest pub by a long way (being licensed no earlier than the 1840s), the *Delfter Krug* on Sawclose occupies one of the oldest buildings in the city. Its rough grey lias walls stand in stark contrast to the smooth-cut Bath Stone all around and mark it out as one of the oldest buildings above ground in the centre of Bath. Try to imagine it standing in isolation from its neighbours, without all the bits that have been added on, and it is not difficult to see it as a plain but substantial farm building

dating from around 1636, which is when John Combe leased it, "lately erected," from the Corporation. Later leaseholders included William Bull, a farmer, who moved there in 1760 (when the city pound for stray animals lay outside its front door), and an early nineteenth-century carrier called Mr Cooper. A blocked-up window high on the south wall clearly indicates the building's early seventeenth-century pedigree.

Originally, the Sawclose was very much a working part of Bath. It was so called because wood was sawn in the timber yard there. It was also home to the city's rubbish dump and cattle market. By the early nineteenth century, when the theatre moved there, it was the hub of the city's nightlife. Take this report from 1825, for example:

> In St John's Court adjoining the Playhouse ... about ten o'clock on Tuesday night the 20th December, Louise Hulbert and Mary Ann ... [illegible] ... both of this city singlewomen (well known as common prostitutes and night walkers) were wandering abroad and making a great noise and disturbance, collecting a crowd around them and wantonly taking off the hats of the persons then and there passing and being; and were both intoxicated with liquor.

Clearly, wanton hat removal was a serious offence back in the early nineteenth century.

Sawclose was thick with pubs in the nineteenth century. In 1849, the overwhelming variety of tipples on offer proved too much for one visitor to the city, as this report from the *Bath Chronicle* records:

> Monday: A man, who gave his name as Hughes, was placed at the bar charged with being in a state of intoxication on the Sawclose, late on the previous evening. In explanation of his conduct, he said that he had walked from Bristol, at which place he had been staying some time. On arriving at Bath, he was induced to take a few glasses of beer, which in this city is superior to that in Bristol, and that it quite affected him. (A laugh)
>
> The Prisoner: Indeed, it's a fact.
>
> The Mayor: I think you are drunk now, or something else is the matter with you.
>
> The Prisoner: No, I ain't; and besides, the charge is false, for when I get a drop of beer, gentlemen, I am very circumspect, and walk in the middle of the road, so that I shan't tumble up against anybody. The Mayor, finding from the prisoner's manner and conversation that he was not quite recovered from a state of inebriety, ordered him to be taken away till he had become sober.
>
> The Prisoner: Oh no, I object to that, for I want to go.
>
> He was immediately removed, but brought up again at a subsequent period of the day, when it being found that he was still unfit properly to estimate his position, he was ordered to be taken back to the station house.

It was probably Edward Strange, a spring-van proprietor, who opened what is now the *Delfter Krug* as a beerhouse called the *Sawclose Tavern* in the 1840s. Its early history suggests that working there was not suited to those of a nervous disposition.

In 1852, Charles Henley, a labourer in its brewery, fell down a ladder and was seriously injured. In 1854, John Vaughan, who had workshops in the yard next door, was attacked by James Hucklebridge, a stableman at the *Sawclose Tavern*, when his

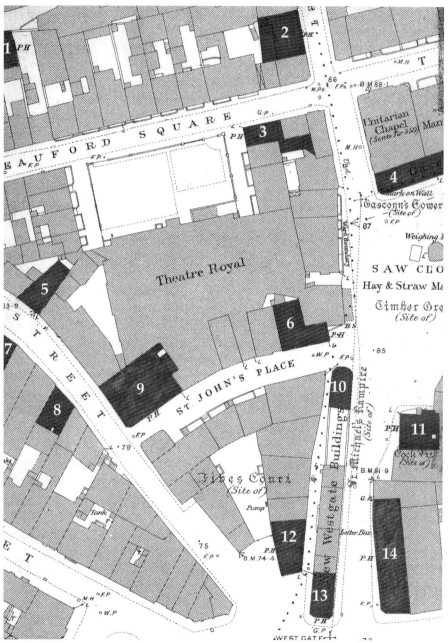

Pubs in the Sawclose area in the nineteenth century included:
1. the *Beaufort Arms*; 2. the *Queen Square Tavern*; 3. the *Prince Frederick*; 4. *Broadley's Wine Vaults*; 5. the *Bell*; 6. the *Garrick's Head*; 7. the *Times Tavern*; 8. the *Old Monmouth Arms*; 9. the *Theatre Tavern*; 10. the *Peep O'Day*; 11. the *Sawclose Tavern*; 12. the *Seven Dials*; 13. the *Westgate Tavern*; 14. the *County Wine Vaults* (now *Flan O'Briens*).

defences were down. He was sitting "in the watercloset [when] the defendant, whom he did not before know, forced open the door and began to drag him out and beat him." Hucklebridge was fined 10/- and costs.

In 1878 Mr Noad, who had taken the lease of the *Sawclose Tavern* ten years earlier, went bankrupt. His assets included "the machinery and plant with the hay, straw and corn at Sydney Wharf, Bath." The stables at the Sawclose contained "a grey cob, an aged grey horse, a brown horse, three cart wagons, a cart and a dilly." The tavern itself consisted of a bar, a tap room and a parlour.

In 1886 a music hall was built at the back of the *Sawclose Tavern,* and the pub was incorporated into it. Originally called the *Pavilion*, it was soon renamed the *Lyric*. The music hall had four bars of its own. The *Sawclose Tavern* was completely remodelled, acquiring a large oval bar, divided into four compartments, with a saloon bar at the back. It was the only pub in Bath owned by Bass, Ratcliff & Gretton of Burton on Trent. The *Lyric* later changed its name to the *Palace Theatre*. In 1957 it became the *Regency Ballroom* and the old *Sawclose Tavern* was renamed the *Regency Bar*.

In 1968 the *Regency Ballroom* became a bingo hall but the *Regency Bar* soldiered on. When Fred Pearce visited in 1976 he found that

> they certainly relish their image as a gay bar, though it's more a pose than a reality. The decor in the main bar is theatrical and Victorian warm and tactile; music is rock and soul records chosen by the butch barman ... the image is furthered by pictures of Ray Martine and Peter Wyngarde behind the bar. Theatre pictures from the old Palace Theatre (now the bingo hall next door) complete the scene.

The old *Sawclose Tavern* kept the name of the *Regency* for a while, but it has since embarked on a succession of name changes of which the *Delfter Krug* (a reference to a 1930s luxury liner) is the latest. Up close, it seems hemmed in by the buildings around it, but, in a city where long vistas are thin on the ground, it comes as something of a surprise to realise that the *Delfter Krug* closes one of the longest – from the Circus down Gay Street, through Queen Square and down Barton Street.

Inside, the ornate frieze of green men above the bar is said to date from the remodelling of the pub in 1886, but the bar counter was originally in the buffet at Green Park Station. Deep brown sofas and art-deco-inspired fittings create an easy-going ambience (so long as you do not mind the lack of real ale), while diners can watch their food being prepared on a range behind the bar. For those of a more energetic disposition there is music and a dance floor upstairs – where the luxury liner theme really takes off – with DJs most nights of the week. The extensive patio area outside is a great place to sit and watch the comings and goings in one of Bath's liveliest corners.

The *Sawclose Tavern* has come a long way from the days when its stablemen were dragged out of the outside toilets. Designed by Paul Jackson, who was also responsible for the *Clerkenwell House* bar in London, and Johnny East, its retro chic will also come as a surprise to those who remember the frenetic old *Loft* bar which occupied the building until recently. And, if you are heading west and want a *Delfter Krug* type ambience at the seaside, you will be pleased to know that Paul and Johnny have recently opened the *West Beach* bar at Woolacombe in Devon.

DEVONSHIRE ARMS 139 Wellsway

This big two-barred pub high in guest-house territory has quite a reputation for cheap eats, if the number of senior citizens who crowd into the lounge to take advantage of them is anything to go by. The public bar attracts a more sporty crowd.

The *Devonshire Arms* on Wellsway was first recorded in 1841 with George Love as landlord. It seems likely, however, that it was previously known as the *Wells Arms*, which featured in the *Bath Chronicle* on 11 July 1834, when "an attempt at robbery was made on the premises of Mrs Gingell, *Wells Arms*, Wells Road."

From the mid-1860s, James Rawlings was the landlord of the *Devonshire Arms*.

Around 1883, John Rawlings took over, and stayed till around 1918. A century ago, the *Devonshire Arms* had a bar with a bar parlour to the left of the entrance, a smoke room behind the bar, a small jug & bottle near the Wells Road entrance and a tap room opening off the passage. There was a brewery at the rear, which closed around 1914.

In 1920, considerable anxiety was expressed over a modification to the building which can still be seen. A window at the side of the building was converted to a doorway for loading and unloading lorries. As the door was two feet six inches above the pavement, it was considered that it might, if left accidentally unlocked, pose a danger to patrons looking for the gents. It was resolved, therefore, that, for safety reasons, the key of the door should be kept at the brewery and carried by the driver who brought the beer.

A one-gallon jar from J Rawlings & Son of the Devonshire Brewery.

DOLPHIN 103 Locksbrook Road, Lower Weston

The *Dolphin* in Lower Weston is one of the oldest pubs in Bath. Although we have not managed to trace it back further than 1786, when Leonard Lovenbury was the landlord, it probably dates back to the opening of the Avon Navigation in 1727. The pub stayed in the Lovenbury family from 1786 to around 1816, passing first to Leonard's widow, Elizabeth, and then to his son, Matthew. In the late 1840s, the landlord was George Griffin, who seems to have been keen on encouraging sporting fixtures at the pub. This

report, for example, appeared in the *Bath Chronicle* in August 1846:

> The game of fives – this game, so much in vogue years ago and until recently become almost obsolete, has been lately revived among the lovers of sport in Somerset and particularly in the neighbourhood of Bath. Several spirited matches have come off during the last month or two at the *Dolphin Inn* Fives Court, Weston, in which the players have exhibited the tactics of the game in an excellent style.

George Griffin stayed at the *Dolphin* until 1866. An inventory drawn up for William Slade, who took over from him, shows that the premises consisted of a bar (with a three-motion beer engine, a settle, a serving counter with a zinc drip, seven chairs and an oak table), a tap room, a club room and a tea room. The *Dolphin* was seriously damaged in the Bath Blitz, but soon rebuilt. Today, with one of the most enviable positions in Bath, it has been massively extended, and the long, low-ceilinged bar leads to a range of eating areas. It is very popular at lunchtimes and, with a garden alongside the canal, is a magnet for families on sunny weekends. Its name, incidentally, has nothing to do with sea creatures. In the eighteenth century a dolphin was a mooring post alongside a quay or wharf.

ENGLISHCOMBE INN   157 Englishcombe Lane

The *Englishcombe Inn*, despite its name, is nowhere near the village of Englishcombe, but on the lane leading to it. There was once a pub in Englishcombe, the *Grove Tavern* at Padley Bottom, a wonderful country pub with a green and gold sign, where they held the Harvest Supper and where, on Sundays, there was tea on the lawn. Just two small rooms, one of them filled with cases of stuffed birds and neither of them with a bar counter. It is the sort of country pub you always dream of finding. Unfortunately, it closed in the early 1950s.

The *Englishcombe Inn* was built to serve the housing estates that were built along Englishcombe Lane after the First World War. The pseudo-manorial Bath Stone building, set well back from the road, has a striking central bay which billows out at the top into a massive gable. Its opening, on 8 May 1934, was recorded in the *Bath Chronicle*:

> The ceremony of "drawing the first pint" was performed at Bath's new licensed house at Englishcombe Park on Saturday. This is the *Englishcombe Inn*, a fine, new building on absolutely modern lines and erected in conformity with the recommendations of the Licensing Committee. Sharp at 10.30am the doors were thrown open and in a few seconds "mine host," Mr Stroud Milsom, was drawing a pint for the first customer. Within a few minutes there

were a dozen visitors, all eager for the honour of having the inaugural drink, but they had been "beaten to it." There was no official opening ceremony, beyond the "christening" given by the first customers. Our representative was given an opportunity of inspecting the whole of the premises and it was obvious to him and to all the other visitors that neither pains nor money had been spared to render the inn attractive. The bars are light and airy, roomy and handsomely furnished, and upstairs, with a separate entrance, is an attractive tea-room. The building as a whole is in Bath stone and constructed on very pleasing lines, and with a spacious forecourt. Gardens and tennis courts are amenities which will be embarked upon in the near future.

The *Englishcombe's* most famous landlord was Graham Moffatt (1919-65), who, after appearing in a series of films (including *Oh! Mr Porter*) alongside Will Hay and Moore Marriott, decided on a change of career in the early 1940s. In 2003, the *Englishcombe* was closed for several weeks for a major refurbishment. Open plan, with a big telly, leather-look sofas, two pool tables and yellow walls, it has some splendid stained and leaded glass and a separate skittle alley up some steps at the back.

FAIRFIELD ARMS 1 Fairfield Park Road

Today, the *Fairfield Arms* is surrounded by houses. When it opened in 1888, however, it was, to all intents and purposes, in the country. Fairfield Park Road had just been constructed to link up with Charlcombe Lane, and the Bath Brewery Company were keen to get a pub in the area before any of their competitors did. They arranged for the licence to be transferred from the *Crown*, a tiny beerhouse on Tyning Lane, whose site is now occupied by the health centre.

The *Fairfield Arms* is still an old-fashioned community pub, open plan, with a small gravel garden at the front and splendid views to the southern hills of Bath.

FILOS 1 Beaufort West, London Road

This really is the last pub in Bath – unless you count those in Larkhall. Hence its original name – *First In, Last Out*. Two hundred years ago, however, there was another one further out, attached to some spectacularly unsuccessful pleasure gardens.

Too far out of town, too liable to flooding, Grosvenor Gardens were conceived at the height of a building boom. Hardly had they got off the ground, however, before the most spectacular slump in Bath's history put paid to the vaulting ambitions of their developer, John Eveleigh. Grosvenor Gardens struggled on for a while, but the loss of momentum transformed them from an exciting new enterprise into a partly-built white elephant. Like Bathwick New Town and John Wood's Forum, they are one of the tantalising might-have-beens of Bath's history.

The first stone of the hotel which formed the entrance to the gardens was laid on 24 June 1791, accompanied by "the firing of cannon and a liberal treat of beer." The following year, John Eveleigh took out a licence to serve alcohol at the hotel. At the end of May 1792, the Bath Chronicle announced that the gardens were "already in so forward a state that some idea may be formed of their future elegance and utility." By August 1792, pleasure boats were plying to the gardens from the *Rising Sun* in Grove Street, and "tea, wines, etc." were available for visitors. A year later, Eveleigh went bankrupt and the gardens were sold.

In 1794, John Townsend appeared in the licensing records as the landlord of the *Grosvenor Tap*, a pub for footmen and others not genteel enough to be admitted to the gardens. In April 1795, Mr Hewlett, a carpenter and property speculator, took over the gardens. He soon followed Eveleigh into bankruptcy and, in December 1795, the gardens were advertised to let again. A sad footnote to Mr Hewlett's brief tenure of the Gardens came two and half years later, when a Benefit Breakfast for Martha Hewlett, "whose husband [had] died under confinement," was held at Sydney Gardens.

In 1798, John Townsend left the *Grosvenor Tap* to take on the *Spring Gardens Tap*. The last record we have of the *Grosvenor Tap* comes in 1805 when Edward Jones was the landlord. The gardens, which had never fulfilled their early promise, closed around the same time, and now lie under a housing estate. All that remains to remind us of them is the hotel – the central building in Grosvenor Place – once a college, but long since converted to residential use. Almost 200 summers have passed since the Grosvenor Hotel closed its doors, but it still stands, frozen in time, its blank panels and uncarved garlands reminders of John Eveleigh's unrealised dream.

It was already a fading memory when Beaufort West was built around 1820. In 1858, Henry Burford opened a post office-cum-bakery there. A couple of years later, Frederick West took it over and turned it into a beerhouse. In 1894, Eliza West was running it as a wine merchant's, but around 1900 James Butcher, a carriage painter, reopened it as a pub called it the *First In Last Out*. At some stage during all these comings and goings, a single-storey extension – in an imposing Italianate style which made no concessions to the Georgian restraint of the original building – was added at the front.

A century ago, the *First In, Last Out* consisted of a bar in two compartments and a "small compartment for outside trade." It was a beerhouse until 1952 when it received a full licence. Today it has been officially renamed *FILOs*, the only pub in Bath to have an acronym for a name, and nothing whatsoever to do with Greek pastry. Any trace of its origins as a grocery-cum-beerhouse have disappeared under the retro chrome fittings, pool tables and karaoke machines of the modern pub.

FLAN O'BRIENS 21 Westgate Street

There was an old man of the Isles
Who suffered severely from pisles.
He couldn't sit down
Without a deep frown,
So he had to row standing for misles.

Words of wisdom from the great Irish writer, Myles na Gopaleen, aka Flann O'Brien. It is appropriate that, in a university city, a pub should be dedicated to this great philosopher of the public house (even if his name is spelt wrong). Here is Flann the Man on the beastly beatitudes of his own university career:

I paid no attention whatsoever to books or study and regarded lectures as a joke which, in fact, they were if you discern anything funny in mawkish, obtuse mumblings on subjects any intelligent person could master single-handed in a few months. The exams I found childish and in fact the whole university concept I found to be a sham. The only result my father got for his money was the certainty that his son had laid faultlessly the foundation of a system of heavy drinking and could always be relied upon to make a break of at least 25 even with a bad cue. I sincerely believe that if university education were universally available and availed of, the country would collapse in one generation.

The building which houses *Flan O'Brien's* represents the pinnacle of mid-nineteenth-century pub design in Bath, but it stands on a site whose licensed history goes back at least as far as the eighteenth century. In 1792, Robert Happerfield was the landlord of a pub here called the *Bird Cage*. It must have been quite a respectable

The original pub on the corner of Westgate Street, replaced by the present building in the mid-nineteenth century.

establishment, because the Royal Cumberland Masonic Lodge met there from 1799 to 1801. By 1822, James Grant Smith of the Southgate Brewery had taken it over and renamed it the *Falstaff Tavern*. When he renewed the lease in 1830 he changed its name to the *Bristol Tavern*. A few months later, he changed it again to the *Albion Tavern*. This period was characterised not only by frequent changes of name, but also by frequent changes of tenant. When one of them, Charles Bull of Clerkenwell, went bankrupt in 1832, the contents of the pub were auctioned off. The items up for sale included a beer engine, a spirit fountain, and mahogany tables and chairs.

In the mid-nineteenth century the *Albion Tavern* was acquired by the Oakhill Brewery,

A one-gallon jar from HC Lavington of the *County Wine Vaults*.

rebuilt in grand style and renamed the *County Wine Vaults*. Not only is the new building the most spectacular nineteenth-century public house in Bath, it is one of the best examples of Victorian architecture in the city. Its restrained Italianate symmetry, topped by overhanging eaves, with a spaciousness imparted by large plate-glass windows on the ground floor, give the building a lightness missing from so much Victorian architecture. It fits perfectly onto a somewhat restricted site, and uses the rising street level on the west side to dramatic effect. Details such as the intermittent sill band at second floor level, set off by the clock on the corner, and the bold horizontal mouldings on the ground floor, add to the effect of a building which combines function and ornament in a way Victorian buildings so often fail to do.

Although now open plan, the bar was originally in several compartments. There was one entrance from Westgate Street, one on the corner, and no less than four from the Sawclose – one to the bar, one to the office, one to the upstairs, and one "through the lavatory." The 1903 report on the premises went into great detail about this lavatory. The "urinal and closet" had a "penny in the slot system for the public." Brass tokens or "checks" were supplied to customers who wanted to use them. These bore a stern warning:

Westgate County Wine Vaults, HC Lavington: Any Persons Using this Check Otherwise than for the Urinal at the County Wine Vaults are Liable to Prosecution

Perhaps it is not surprising that the *County Wine Vaults* was affectionately known as *Lavy's*.

In 1990, Jack Charlton, the Irish soccer manager officially reopened the *County Wine Vaults* as an Irish theme pub called *Mulligan's*. Asked if it resembled a real Irish pub, he replied, in his rich Newcastle Brogue, "it's authentic in every way." Today it has been renamed once more – in honour of Flann "A Pint of Plain's Your Only Man" O'Brien. Despite – or perhaps because of – its Irishness, it is a fine example of a traditional city-centre boozer. Its website is also very entertaining, with an Agony Uncle page run by Myles, the landlord, and lists like this one of the Top Ten Famous People of all time:

Henrik Larsson	Tom Waits
Ken Livingstone	Martin O'Neill
Che Guevara	George Best
Kylie Minogue	Wolff Tong (shome mishtake, shurely? - Ed)
Bono	Father Ted

FORESTER'S ARMS   172 Bradford Road, Combe Down

An important function of pubs in the late eighteenth and nineteenth centuries was as the meeting places of friendly societies. A directory for 1819 lists no less than 28 of these organisations. The oldest was the Loyal Bathonian United Society, founded in 1749, which met at the *Rising Sun* in Grove Street. Some catered for specific trades, such as the Union Society of Carpenters and Joiners, which met at the old *Turk's Head* near the top of Broad Street, or the United Servants' Friendly Society which met at the *Marlborough Tavern*. Others, such as the Bath Independent Britons, which met at the *Rummer*, or St James's Patriotic Benefit Society, which met at *St James's Hotel* (now *St James's Wine Vaults*) had a wider appeal.

In the nineteenth century, small, independent friendly societies began to give way to nationally affiliated ones. The two main national organisations were the Oddfellows, founded in 1810, and the Foresters, founded in 1834. Both started off in the North of England, but soon expanded to cover the whole country. By the mid-nineteenth century there were no less than four pubs in Bath called the *Oddfellow's Arms* – in Avon Street, in Dolemeads, on Hedgemead, and near the *Hop Pole* on the Upper Bristol Road. There were also two *Forester's Arms* – one on Lower Borough Walls and one at Combe Down. All are long gone, the buildings they stood in demolished – all except for the *Forester's Arms* at Combe Down.

Lying to the west of the old village of Combe Down, it was opened as a beerhouse around 1870 by Thomas Bodman. A century ago it was owned by the Old Market Brewery in Bristol. The 1903 report on the *Forester's Arms* is unusually comprehensive and worth quoting in full:

> Premises rather dilapidated except skittle alley, which is very good. Serving bar on left of entrance with seats in room on right and tap room behind. Skittle alley at side of garden. Main entrance from Green Down Terrace. Door from tap room into old brewery. Exit through passage under brew house to garden at rear (shared with house next door). Stables and coach-house belonging to licensed premises at bottom of garden.

When it was offered for sale around 1909, however, there was – not surprisingly – no mention of dilapidation in the estate agent's blurb. It was described as

> a well-known, fully licensed house situated on a main road in a healthy village near Bath. Premises comprise: Serving bar, private bar, jug and bottle department, miniature shooting range, tap room, club room with bagatelle and billiard tables, private sitting room, kitchen, scullery and store room, ample cellerage, garden, stable, coach house, fowl houses, large garden, nice skittle alley, three nice bedrooms, WC, lavatory, etc.
>
> Rent £85 p.a. including cottage let off at 4/3 weekly, but ought to be 6/- and house adjoining let off at 7/- per week.

The licence was £17-5-3, and the rates were about £70. The pub had been in the Bodman family for over 50 years and monthly takings averaged between £55 and £60. The asking price was £250. However, when it was offered for sale again the following year, the price had leapt to £325.

There were no takers and in 1911 the Old Market Brewery, who owned it, was taken over by the Ashton Gate Brewery. Eventually, the *Forester's Arms* became part of the Courage estate. Today, no longer dilapidated, and boasting a mural of regulars in the games room, the *Forester's Arms* is as popular as ever.

FULL MOON Church Buildings, Twerton

With its venerable appearance and location next to Twerton church, it is tempting to think that the *Full Moon* is a very old inn. Unfortunately, it is not. In 1876, Mary Hicks moved from a beerhouse called the *Ring of Bells* at 4 Twerton High Street to open a new beerhouse near the church, which she called the *Full Moon*. The *Ring of Bells* closed in 1963 and has since been converted to flats, but the *Full Moon* is still going strong.

An early twentieth-century inventory of the *Full Moon* listed its accommodation as follows:

Bar with panelled oak counter with pewter top, old and new 5-motion beer engines;

Bar Parlour with antique sofa and four pictures in maple frames;

Tap Room with two cases of stuffed birds;

Garden with 33 foot long lean-to greenhouse;

Pleasure Lawn with 34 foot long lean-to summer house with corrugated iron roof, asphalt flooring fitted with seating and matchboard back casing, deal top drinking tables with turned legs, painted ornamental wooden partitions with trellis work end and gate forming enclosure to lawn and flag pole.

The *Full Moon* was granted a full licence in 1958 when the *Half Moon* and the *Angel Tavern* on Holloway closed.

The *Full Moon* is just the sort of pub you expect to find next to a church – a quiet two-barred local which looks as though it has not changed much for years. Sadly, though, most of the pleasure lawn and garden from a century ago has given way to a car park.

GARRICK'S HEAD 7-8 St John's Place

Thomas Greenway built the *Garrick's Head* for Beau Nash – on the site of the city's dunghill – around 1720. John Wood called it "the Palace of the King of Bath … the richest Sample of Building till then executed in the City," adding that it was "so profuse in ornament, that none but a mason, to shew his art, would have gone to the expence of those enrichments." By 1735, Nash had been forced to move to a smaller house

nearby (now Popjoy's Restaurant) when a change to the gaming laws cut off much of his income. His old house became a pub when the Theatre Royal moved from Old Orchard Street to its present site in 1805. Originally the main entrance to the theatre was in Beaufort Square, but, after a disastrous fire in 1862, a new entrance was built on the Sawclose, which took over much of the ground floor of the *Garrick's Head*.

Although called the *Garrick's Head* from the start, the bust of Garrick by Gahagan was only placed over the entrance in 1831. In the same year, the following advertisement appeared in the *Bath Chronicle*:

> To be lett . . . an old-established brewing public house . . . known by the sign of the *Garrick's Head*, adjoining the Theatre Royal. Applications to be made to Mr Hazard, the proprietor, who is about declining the above line, having occupied the house fourteen years."

In 1837, JA Roebuck, Bath's famous radical MP, held a meeting at the *Garrick's Head*. The *Bath Chronicle*, an implacable opponent of Roebuck, reported that

> it was his original intention to perch himself on the porch of the theatre to harangue the admiring multitude with which he expected the Sawclose would be filled. In his way, however, to the above public house, he found the space in front of the theatre was not occupied by friends. Those amid whom he passed hooted him thoroughly. So he remained in the house, where he delivered a most senseless and frothy speech, all about the Poor Laws, which was, as before, a miserable hobbling affair.

The roof onto which Roebuck decided not to climb was to prove the undoing of William Stiles, the landlord's son, 61 years later. In the early hours of a Friday morning, after spending the night at *Broadley's Wine Vaults*, he was found unconscious in the street outside the Circle entrance to the theatre and died in hospital shortly afterwards. His brother later explained that "he had known his brother get up over the railings by Trim Street Sunday School [now *Popjoy's*], pull himself up by a board onto the parapet, cross over the leads, and gain access to the house through the billiard-room windows." It was concluded that he had lost his footing and a verdict of accidental death was recorded.

An inventory of the *Garrick's Head* carried out in 1883 gives us an idea of its opulence. The "old bar and parlour" had a panelled partition, with two doors and six diapered glass panels separating the bar from the parlour. A match-board partition with a door hatch and three glazed sashes above it formed a private room at the end of the parlour. The "new bar" had a circular-fronted panelled counter with a mahogany top, a "centre brass ceiling ornament" and ten sporting pictures. An ornamental diapered glass sash separated the new bar from a private drinking bar. There was also a "large room" (with a square piano, four mahogany dining tables, 27 Windsor chairs, a japanned pipe tray, a mahogany sideboard, oil paintings and a brass tobacco box), a bagatelle room, a small sitting room (with a "draft board and men,"

City of Bath.} *At the General Annual Licensing Meeting of his Majesty's Justices of the Peace, acting in and for the City of Bath, in the County of Somerset, holden at the Guildhall, in the said City, on* Tuesday *the* 30th *day of* August *— in the Year* **One Thousand Eight Hundred and Thirty** One *for the purpose of granting Licenses to persons keeping Inns, Alehouses, and Victualling Houses, to sell Exciseable Liquors by Retail, to be drunk or consumed on their Premises,*

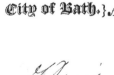

WE, being 4 of his Majesty's Justices of the Peace acting in and for the said City, and being the Majority of those assembled at the said Session, do hereby authorise and empower Robert Hazard now dwelling at Saint Johns Place in the parish of Walcot —————— and Keeping —————— an Inn, Alehouse, or Victualling House, at the Sign of the Garricks Head in the parish of Walcot —————— in the said City, to sell by Retail therein, and in the premises thereunto belonging, all such Exciseable Liquors as the said Robert Hazard shall be licensed and empowered to sell under the authority and permission of any Excise License, and to permit all such Liquors to be drunk or consumed in his said House, or in the Premises thereunto belonging provided that he do not fraudulently dilute or adulterate the same, or sell the same knowing them to have been fraudulently diluted or adulterated; and do not use in selling thereof any Weights or Measures that are not of the legal standard; and do not wilfully or knowingly permit Drunkenness or other disorderly conduct in his House or Premises; and do not knowingly suffer any unlawful Games or any Gaming whatsoever therein; and do not knowingly permit or suffer persons of notoriously bad character to assemble and meet together therein; and do not keep open h is House except for the Reception of Travellers, nor permit or suffer an Beer or other Exciseable Liquor to be conveyed from or out of his Premises during the usual hours of the Morning and Afternoon Divine Service in the Church or Chapel of the parish or place in which his House is situated, on Sundays, Christmas Day, or Good Friday, but do maintain Good Order and Rule therein; and this License shall continue in force from the tenth — day of October next until the Tenth day of October then next ensuing, and no longer, provided that the said Robert Hazard shall not in the mean time become a Sheriff's Officer, or Officer executing the Process of any Court of Justice, in either of which cases this License shall be void.

Given under our Hands and Seals on the day and at the place first above written

---

The licence granted to Robert Hazard of the *Garrick's Head* on 30 August 1831

On 7 July 1831, Robert Hazard advertised the *Garrick's Head* to let. He had had no takers by the end of August, when he renewed the licence. In October 1831, he eventually transferred it – along with the lease – to William Wood from the *King's Head* in Lilliput Alley.

23 "ovals of books," a Kidderminster carpet, a large map and antimacassered chairs), and eight bedrooms. At the back was a brewery, plus a malt room and cooperage. At the front of the building was a gas-star illumination, the bust of Garrick and two flags.

Today the *Garrick's Head* looks much as it must have done when Beau Nash lived there.

In the early 1970s, however, it was – from the outside at least – in a sorry state. In the *Bath Chronicle* of 9 October 1975 it was described as "standing out like a sore – actually black – thumb." Courage's took the hint and very soon scaffolding went up to clean the facade and replace the crumbling masonry.

There are at least seven other pubs named after David Garrick, the eighteenth-century actor manager – in Birkenhead, Bristol, Cheltenham, Hereford, Manchester, Stockton on Tees, and Stratford on Avon.

GOLDEN FLEECE 1-3 Avon Buildings, Twerton

Twerton grew up around the weaving trade, and so it is appropriate that one of its pubs should be called the *Golden Fleece*. It was first recorded in the 1848 *Postal Directory* with John Price as landlord. Until the 1870s it was simply known as the *Fleece*. Although the building's frontage, with its lettered and stained glass, is a well-preserved example of late-nineteenth-century pub design, the back of the building shows that part of it is much older.

The *Golden Fleece* is the only pub along this stretch of road today – but not that long ago there were four. On the opposite corner (now demolished) was the *Atlas Brewery*, which closed in 1962, next door was the *Seven Stars* (now the Trams Social Club), and a little further along, past Clark's Business Products, was the *Railway Inn*, which was destroyed in the Bath Blitz. At the back of the *Golden Fleece* was a huge malthouse belonging to JD Taylor & Sons, built in 1901 at a cost of £12,000 to replace one in Walcot Street which had been destroyed by fire two years earlier. In March 1915, the malthouse at the back of the *Golden Fleece* was also gutted by a fire described as the largest in Bath for several years, and malt to the value of £12,000 was lost.

When an inventory of the *Golden Fleece* was drawn up in 1901, weekly takings averaged around £35. The premises consisted of a bar, a glass room and a brewery. The bar fittings were as follows:

6 motion beer engine with piping and taps to cellar;

Mahogany-top painted oak panelled counter with return ends door and flaps and iron footrails;

Stained-glass sash with panelled door and partition forming jug & bottle entrance;

82

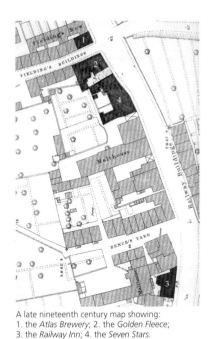

A late nineteenth century map showing:
1. the *Atlas Brewery*; 2. the *Golden Fleece*;
3. the *Railway Inn*; 4. the *Seven Stars*.

Spirit shelves with shelved glass panels at back;

Painted and glazed dwarf partition with door in front of counter as fitted with a mahogany seat on either side;

2 light gas pendant and 2 consumers;

3 gas pendants with 2 consumers;

Seating as fixed;

Wire blind as lettered and 4 brass guard bars;

3 roller blinds and fittings;

8 day deal clock;

11 spittoons, beer warmer and stand;

Turned leg drinking table;

Spring and straps to door;

Patent cork drawer;

Set of 5 china spirit barrels with taps;

2 engraved glass spirit barrels with taps;

Brass-bound pewter drip;

Set of pewter spirit measures and funnel;

3 pewter beer measures and tin funnel.

Until the 1960s there was a grocer's between the *Golden Fleece* and the *Seven Stars*, but this has now been incorporated into the *Golden Fleece*. The louvred window on the second floor of the extension at the back is a relic of the days when it had its own brewery.

GRAPES 14 Westgate Street

In 1749 John Wood wrote that Westgate Street was "adorned with a capital messuage, that looks like a palace without, besides five or six other houses, which seem more like mansions for persons of rank and fortune, than for common town dwellings" The "capital messuage" was probably the building now occupied partly by the *Grapes* and partly by the charity shop next door. It is a very old building. Parts of it may even date from the sixteenth century. There is also a wonderful ceiling on the first floor (not accessible to the public and visible only when the curtains at the front of the building are left undrawn), but perhaps the most wonderful thing about it is that nobody knows when it was done or why. Jean Manco sums up speculation on its origins as follows:

The centrepiece includes the double-headed eagle, famous as the symbol of the Holy Roman Empire. This has generated speculation that the house was used by Charles Granville, 2nd Earl of Bath, who became a Count of the Holy Roman Empire in 1684. But that

BATH PUBS

date is far too late for the style of the ceiling. The house was leased in 1620 to Richard Gay, three times Mayor of Bath. It seems that he sublet it to Dr John Ostendorph, a physician from Germany who had settled in Bath by 1637. Ostendorph's widow certainly lived there after his death. The double-headed eagle could have been a patriotic gesture by a man far from the land of his birth.

There is also some seventeenth-century panelling and a small blocked-in window from around the same time on the second floor. The present frontage was probably added around 1720. The three tiers of columns forming the centrepiece of the building, in Doric, Ionic and Corinthian style, predate John Wood's use of the same arrangement in the Circus by at least 30 years. Only in a city like Bath, with its wealth of architectural treasures, could a building as monumental in conception, with such splendid internal features, be so overlooked. Yet overlooked it has been for two centuries or more. How many people have noticed, for example, not only that its frontage is one of the finest in Bath but that its back wall, visible from St Michael's Court, is built of brick?

Today, the *Grapes* occupies half of what was designed as a single building. It seems to have vacillated between one and two buildings for most of its history. In 1620, when Richard Gay leased it from St John's Hospital, it was a "dwellinge house and garden which formerly have bin demised as two tenements." By 1665, when the lease passed to Tobias Rustatt, it was two tenements. In 1728, John Billing, a vintner, moved in, and once again it became one tenement. However, when Robert Hayward, a maltster, took the lease in 1760, it was back to two tenements. Robert Hayward leased both parts of the building, however, as did all subsequent lessees until 1831, when Henry Perry took over the half that is now the *Grapes*. It is probable that its name dates from John Billing's tenure in the early eighteenth century, although it is likely that he ran it as a wine merchant's rather than a tavern. Many eighteenth century wine merchants traded under the sign of the *Bunch of Grapes* (or the *Grapes*) and most pubs with this name started out as wine merchant's.

In 1823, the following advertisement appeared in the Bath Chronicle:

MOST ELIGIBLE OPPORTUNITY

TO BE SOLD

That Capital FREE PUBLIC HOUSE called

"THE BUNCH OF GRAPES"

now in full trade, centrally situate in WESTGATE STREET

in the City of Bath, with a most convenient and compact

BEER AND ALE BREWERY

attached, fitted up with horse malt mill ... force pump

and every apparatus for common brewing under the most approved

principles, and which has been carried on for many years with

considerable success. There is an excellent WINE AND SPIRIT TRADE

combined with the retail business, which has been established

as a public house of the first respectability for nearly

thirty years.

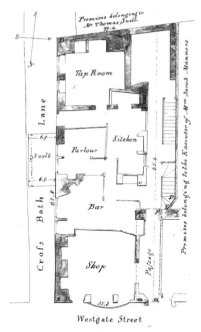

A plan of the Grapes in 1831.

Although the *Bunch of Grapes* appears in the licensing records for 1776, it is clear from this advertisement that it was exclusively a wine merchant's until around 1794. The description of it as "of the first respectability" may have been wide of the mark, however, for, less than 30 years later, the *Grapes* was one of seven pubs in Bath which the police wanted to close on the grounds that the "keepers of these houses, after repeated cautions, had some of them kept open their houses on Sunday mornings, and others allowed prostitutes and other bad characters to resort to them."

The problem dated back at least as far as 1839, when this report appeared in the *Bath Chronicle*:

> On Friday last, Mrs Smith of the *Bunch of Grapes*, Westgate Street, was summoned to answer a charge of keeping a disorderly house. In addition to instances of disorderly conduct in the house, the police had frequently been called to quell disturbances. Mr Smith, who appeared for his mother, said it was impossible to pay constant attention to the tap room, and that parties were constantly coming in without his knowledge.

By the end of the nineteenth century, things seemed to have improved somewhat. The Anglo-Bavarian Brewery took over the lease and the 1903 report on the premises described them as "good." In the mid-1930s, however, the *Grapes* almost disappeared in the name of road widening. Its reprieve was announced in the *Bath Chronicle* on 2 November, 1937:

> This fine house was scheduled for destruction, but will probably be preserved under the new Act, since the introduction of one-way traffic has eased the situation in that direction.

After bemoaning the recent demolition of "another fine house in that street" (No 19, further down towards Westgate Buildings) the paper's correspondent made a heartfelt plea on behalf of Bath's Georgian buildings:

> One is getting very weary of the endless repetition of pseudo-Georgian motifs in place of original work.
>
> However, it is no use crying over spilt milk, and all we can do is preserve to the utmost what is left.

What he would have said of the wholesale redevelopments of the 1960s and 1970s – or of the mock-Georgian pastiches that pass for architecture today – is anybody's guess.

Happily, the *Grapes*, making up half of one of the most interesting yet most overlooked buildings in Bath, survives to this day. In 1966 it closed for several weeks for renovation. This included the removal of multiple layers of paint from the first-floor ceiling. At one time the curtains on the first floor were left undrawn and the lights left on to show it off. Unfortunately, at the time of writing this is not the case. One day perhaps the room will be opened to the public – perhaps as a restaurant. Failing that, readopting the practice of leaving the curtains open at night would at least give visitors a glimpse of one of Bath's hidden showpieces.

Finally, an historical footnote. In 1994 the landlord of the *Grapes* was banned from putting up signs outside the pub describing its history. Gus Astley, a senior conservation officer with Bath City Council, said that, "if every trader in the city wanted to write a bit about the history of his building and put it on a board we would be in a bit of trouble. We don't want to set a precedent." So the pub's history was painted on a beam in the bar, where it can still be seen today. And, in case you are wondering where its confident assertion that the building dates from around 1302 comes from, the answer lies in an ancient corporation deed dated circa 1302-3:

> Grant by Robert, son and heir of Thomas de Cellario, for 17 shillings, to Adam Fullo, of an annual rent of two shillings which Robert ought to take in respect of Adam's tenement, which said tenement lies in the West Street, between the tenement of Richard, son of the aforesaid Adam, on the west, and the way which goes towards the Cross Bath on the east.

How much of that early fourteenth century building is left, and how old it was when Adam Fullo took the lease, is something we will probably never know.

GRAPPA BAR   3 Belvedere, Lansdown Road

The *Grappa Wine Bar* opened in 2002. Many people still associate No 3 Belvedere, however, with the pub that was there for around 170 years – the *Beehive*. Belvedere was built in the mid-eighteenth century and the *Beehive* opened in the early 1830s. When an inventory was carried out in 1897, the *Beehive* consisted of:

> a wine & spirit department, with a wire protection frame on the window, a lettered and embossed glass blind, a red curtain, two spittoons, five stools, several spirit casks, a "new union bitter ale tap" and pictures on the walls;
>
> a bar, with an eight-motion beer engine, ornamental fittings behind the bar and engravings on the wall;
>
> a smoking room, with sporting prints and a fly catcher.

There were two front entrances but no exit from the yard at the back. The yard contained a brewery and a "wall used as a urinal."

In 1976 Fred Pearce described the *Beehive* as "one of those traditional working class pubs, full of flat cap characters that middle class sociologists love so much." It was Bath's last cider house and Fred was particularly taken with the fact that the locals had their own mugs hanging above the bar. At the time of his visit it still had three separate bars.

Three years later, in 1979, it became something of a cause célèbre when Courage's tried to close it down and turn it into a shop. A campaign was launched to save it. The licensee, Eric Kesterton, said that "public opinion requires it to remain as a pub. This is the last pub of its kind in Bath, a true cider house, which plays its part as a tourist attraction ... The *Beehive* is one of the most famous pubs in England. Courage's tell me they cannot make money out of it, but I feel if I were free of the brewery I may be able to make a living."

Bath students organised a boycott of Courage pubs and on 2 May, the Council met to determine the *Beehive's* fate. The *Bath Chronicle* takes up the story:

The toast at the *Beehive* public house, Lansdown Road, last night was "Bath City Council," after the planning authority had rejected Courage's application for permission to turn the cider house into a shop. Twenty-four members of the city council voted against the brewers' proposal, although the planning committee chairman, Councillor Ian Dewey, thought grounds for such action did not stand up.

A petition signed by 2,100 and put in by the landlord objected to the application and asked for the pub to be retained as a cider house. A burst of clapping in the public gallery greeted the council's decision. Councillor Laurie Coombs, who moved rejection of the shop plan, said the *Beehive* was a pub of character with an international reputation. If the application to convert it to a shop were granted, it would mean a serious loss of amenity to local residents, which he described as a perfectly valid planning reason. As a second reason he claimed that such a change would be detrimental to the area's character. His fellow ward representative, Councillor Elgar Jenkins, said it would be catastrophic for a West Country council to close down the only remaining cider house in the city. Councillor Michael Cheek said that if the pub closed and cider was so important to residents, some other licensed houses would soon take up the sale of cider. Councillor Jeff Higgins interjected, "Not on Abbey ward." Councillor Cheek introduced a little spirit into the occasion. He said it had been suggested that the ghost, reputed to be a feature of the Beehive, would be driven away if it became a shop. He felt that may not happen. It would probably like the new customers. He contended that there were no good planning grounds for refusing the application for change of use. He was in no doubt that, if there was an appeal, the brewers would be successful ... The planning committee chairman, Councillor Ian Dewey, sympathised with the 2,100 objectors, but he saw no grounds to support refusal. They were talking about a drink amenity rather than an environmental one.

The *Beehive* landlord, Mr Eric Kesterton, who attended the council meeting, said today that his supporters filled three-quarters of the public gallery. After the meeting he had treated them to a glass of cider. "We were delighted with the outcome – we felt it was the right decision," he said. Asked how he viewed the future of the pub, Mr Kesterton said it was a difficult question. The ball was now in the brewers' court. "I hope," he said, "they will give me the first option as I cannot see the brewers keeping it on themselves. I have made an offer to get things started. The *Beehive* will never be a goldmine, but it provides me with a roof over my head and enables me to carry on."

And carry on the *Beehive* did, consolidating its reputation as one of Bath's most atmospheric and colourful pubs, until one day in 2001, when the doors closed – allegedly – because the landlord suspected certain of his customers weren't just smiling like that because of the cider. The *Beehive* was left, like the *Marie Celeste*, with the dust slowly settling and the clink of glasses heard no more, until it was tidied up, made over and relaunched as the *Grappa Wine Bar*.

GREEN PARK TAVERN 45 Lower Bristol Road

The *Green Park Tavern* on the Lower Bristol Road was built around 1813 as a private house. Five years later, the following advertisement appeared in the *Bath Chronicle*:

> To be sold ... Green Park Cottage, situated in the Lower Bristol Road, and exactly opposite Green Park Place, Bath. This pleasant residence has been built about five years and contains two parlours, two best bedrooms and a servant's ditto ... The above dwelling house [is] fit for the immediate reception of a small genteel family.

In the 1840s it became a pub called the *Green Park Tavern*. In its early years, you could walk across the road and catch a ferry over to Green Park. The road that led down to the ferry – Riverside Road – is still there, but the ferry stopped running over a century ago. The large villas that once lined the river bank (with names like Sydenham Villa, Netley Villa, and Green Park Villa) have also disappeared and their place is now filled by the Renault Garage.

Today, the *Green Park Tavern* is the first pub you come to as you walk along the Lower Bristol Road. Back in the nineteenth century, if you had stopped at every pub on the way out of town, the chances are you would never have got as far as the *Green Park Tavern*. Even if you had, you would probably have been in no state to appreciate its finer points. The first pub you would have come to – on the north side of the road near where the pelican crossing is today – was the *Engineer's Arms* (c1866-1901). Over the road, on the other side of the alleyway from the building which has recently been restored, was the *Lower Bristol Road Tavern* (c1876-1931). Just beyond it, where the Esso Garage stands today, was the *Angel & Crown*. This opened in the 1850s and lasted only a few years. Then, just before you got to Oak Street, you would have found the *Gardener's Arms* (c1840-1940). The next pub – the *Bell* – was on the opposite side of the road, facing the entrance to Oak Street. It opened around 1837 and was so badly damaged in the terrible floods of 1894 that it closed. Finally, after braving the delights of these five pubs, you would have reached the *Green Park Tavern*.

A late nineteenth-century map showing the *Green Park Tavern* and the buildings that once stood across the road.

Green Park Ferry in the mid nineteenth-century.

When an inventory of the *Green Park Tavern* was drawn up in 1902, it consisted of a club room, a glass room, a bagatelle room, a jug & bottle, a bar, a tap room, a skittle alley and a stable. The bar had a panelled counter with a matchboard partition, two embossed panelled doors and a partition at the side forming the jug & bottle department, and a diapered glass panelled door with a serving flap for the tap room.

The report prepared a year later was very uncomplimentary about the premises. Their general condition was described as "poor" and the sanitary arrangements "very defective." It noted, however, that plans for alterations had been submitted but not yet approved. Happily, whatever upset the inspector has long been put right, and it is difficult to see any connection between the pub of 1903 and the large open-plan pub of 2003. Today, this popular wooden-ceiling pub, with its pool players, cocktail menu, and strategically-placed sofas breaking its open-plan layout up into separate drinking areas, has a vaguely American feel. Go there on Bluegrass Night and the illusion is complete – even though you can still get a decent pint of 6X. Imaginatively decorated, with the skittle alley converted to a dining area, and with no pubs anywhere near, the *Green Park Tavern* is a popular hangout for young and old alike. Plans to extend the pub into the old clubhouse next door, which will increase the area available for entertainment, seem likely to turn the *Green Park Tavern* into one of the city's top music spots.

GRIFFIN Monmouth Street

The *Griffin* can only be traced back as far as 1776, when William Pomeroy held the licence. However, it may have opened when the street was built in the 1730s, taking its name from one of Bath's latest tourist attractions, the impressive griffin on top of the Lansdown Monument, erected in 1727.

When the 1903 report on the property was prepared, the public entrance was in Beaufort Street. There was a bar and three small rooms on the ground floor. A club room upstairs was used occasionally for smoking concerts. Around 1906, the *Griffin* was offered for sale (together with the adjoining house, which was let for lodgings) for £170. The annual rent of the two properties was £35 a year and the *Griffin* was tied to the Anglo-Bavarian Brewery of Shepton Mallet.

The *Griffin* is very much an old-time local, busy most of the time, with a loyal crowd of regulars, and with its layout hardly changed in the last 100 years.

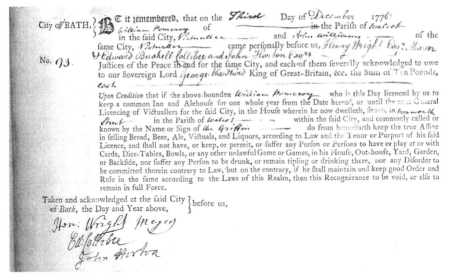

The licence granted to William Pomeroy of the *Griffin* in 1776.

HADLEY ARMS North Road, Combe Down

The *Hadley Arms*, on the corner of the Avenue, was built in the Italianate style in the 1840s by a quarrymaster called Samuel Spence. What better place for him to pay his men – and to ensure that their wages found their way back into his pocket – especially when quarrying was such thirsty work? There were even underground entrances to the Firs Quarry at the back of the pub, so that no time need be lost getting to the bar.

The *Hadley Arms* was not the only pub in Combe Down with an entrance into the Firs Quarry. At the end of Rock Lane is the old *Rock* beerhouse, dating from the early nineteenth century. It was more commonly known as *Davidge's*, after the landlord, George Davidge, who was also a quarrymaster. The entrance to the quarry was at the back, and the story goes that, on Sundays, drinkers retreated into the quarry with their beer if there was any danger of a visit from the local constabulary.

When an inventory of the *Hadley Arms* was drawn up in 1900, it had a smoking room with a bagatelle table, a bar, a tap room, a club room with piano, a skittle alley, and a "pleasure lawn," with a rockery, tables and chairs, and a "fowls' run." The Victoria Rooms, running along North Road at the back of the pub, was at one time a barracks. The pub was named after the Hadley family who owned land hereabouts in the early nineteenth century.

A curious story from 1915 indicates that, even after all the bad publicity gin received in the eighteenth and nineteenth centuries, some people in the early twentieth century still regarded it as medicinal – or expected others to believe they did:

PC Oliver Butt stated that [at 10.30pm on 9 February 1915], he saw a man who later proved to be Mr Simmonds coming up the Avenue towards the *Hadley Arms*. He went to the front door of the hotel and knocked. The door was answered by Mrs Flower, [the landlord's] wife, who asked 'Who is there?' Mr Simmonds replied, 'I am the new postmaster. I want a pint of Hollands gin; I have a cold on my kidneys.' The door was immediately opened and Mr Simmonds walked into the hotel and the door was shut. Witness went and pushed at the door. In two minutes or less the landlord and Mr Simmonds came out. Witness said to Simmonds, 'I heard you just now ask for a pint of Hollands gin.' He replied, 'Yes, I did. I had a cold on my kidneys and someone told me it was a good thing for it.' Witness said, 'it is an hour after time, and only in extreme cases can you get spirits for illness.' Mr Simmonds then produced a bottle of Hollands gin, properly labelled and sealed and stated that he had paid 3/6 for it. The landlord said, 'that's quite right. I let him have it.' The Postmaster said, 'I have been working late at the post office tonight, so I could not come for it before … Mr Glover [who appeared for the Licensed Victuallers' Association] said he did not dispute the facts or raise any question over PC Butt's evidence. Mr and Mrs Flower . . . were extremely respectable people who had kept this highly respectable house, where meetings and suppers were held, for 14 or 15 years, not only without conviction, but without complaint of any sort. Before going there, Mrs Flower had a house on the main road at Swinford. . . . After the bench had discussed the case in their private room, the Chairman said, 'We are unanimously of the opinion that there should be no conviction in this case whatsoever. Evidently it is only a technical error, if it is an error at all.

The *Hadley Arms* has one of Bath's longest-serving landlords – Graham Barnard, who took over in 1977. One of the features Mr Barnard has introduced is a three-lane skittle alley. The entrance from the Firs Quarry is also still there.

HA! HA! BAR Beehive Yard, Walcot Street

It is hard to ignore the *Ha! Ha! Bar*, housed as it is in the most prominent redbrick building in Bath. Just as Westward Ho! is the only British town with an exclamation mark after it, so the *Ha! Ha! Bar* (or the *Ha! Ha! Bar & Canteen* to give it its full title) is the only pub in Bath with two exclamation marks. Whether the exclamation marks are there for the same reason is unknown.

Although it only opened in 2002, its site has alcoholic connections going back to the eighteenth century, when James Racey established a brewery there. When this closed in the early nineteenth century, the malthouse stayed open. The old brewery yard was leased for a time by Henry Hunt, the famous orator and political agitator. In 1817, it was the venue for a mass demonstration which had to be transferred to the Orange Grove when the crowds grew too large for the yard.

The malthouse was eventually demolished to make way for the Tramshed in 1903. This was the main depot, powerhouse, workshop and administrative centre of the Bath & District Light Railway. Bath was never really suitable for trams. They were all right trundling along the London Road or out to Twerton, but when it came to climbing hills it was a different matter. Runaways and collisions were common, and most Bathonians probably breathed a sigh of relief when they were withdrawn in 1939.

The old tramshed was put to a variety of uses, most recently as an antiques market. However, in the late 1990s, the whole site was redeveloped. Bath Archaeological Trust was able to carry out extensive excavations, which revealed significant Roman remains on the site. The tramshed itself was converted to provide industrial and commercial units, as well as apartments and a large bar on the ground floor. The conversion has won praise as a strikingly successful application of modern design to an old industrial building.

There are 13 other Ha! Ha! Bars in other towns and cities throughout the country, all owned by Yates Group PLC. This company started off in Oldham in 1884 where the first Yates's Wine Lodge opened. Yates's also has a place in history as the company that first introduced Australian wine to this country, during World War Two. Although there are still over 120 Yates's Wine Lodges, the company is keen to expand the Ha! Ha! side of its business, and has identified 50 other towns and cities as possible sites for future Ha! Ha! Bars.

The name of the yard in which Bath's *Ha! Ha! Bar* stands – Beehive Yard – recalls a pub called the *Beehive* which stood at the entrance to the yard at 66 Walcot Street (part of which is now occupied by Domino's Pizzas). It opened in the 1840s and, although it closed in the 1950s, its sign bracket can still be seen on the wall of the building.

HARE & HOUNDS Lansdown

Although the *Hare & Hounds* appears relatively modern, eighteenth, nineteenth and twentieth additions conceal what was originally a seventeenth-century alehouse. The earliest surviving licence for an alehouse in Charlcombe dates from 1695. The licensee was Jane Wait, and as there seems never to have been another alehouse in Charlcombe, it is fairly safe to assume that she was the landlady of the *Hare & Hounds*.

For much of the eighteenth century, the licence of the *Hare & Hounds* was held by the Lansdown family. For brief periods in the mid-eighteenth century, however, Ambrose Hulance (or Hewlins) and James Greenaway took over. By the early nineteenth century, the *Hare & Hounds* had been taken over by the Anchor Brewery in Southgate Street. In 1819, Pierce Egan, in his *Walks Through Bath*, advised thirsty ramblers heading up Lansdown that, "a little beyond the first milestone on the right stands a small public house known by the sign of the *Hare & Hounds.*"

As can be seen from Thorpe's map of 1742, the original alehouse was much smaller than it is today. Over the years, cottages and outbuildings were built around it, and sometime in the late nineteenth century these were incorporated into the pub. It is still possible, however, looking at the pub from the road, to make out the original alehouse, hemmed in and almost swamped by later additions. Inside, the layout is even clearer, and visitors can still sit in the old alehouse, with its original hearth. A cupboard staircase also survives, although this is in part of the pub not open to the public. Another relic of the distant past is the faint outline of words on the lintel above the window closest to the city on Lansdown Road. This dates from the time when the window was the main door into the pub. The writing, which can only be seen when the sun is shining full on it, carries the names of long-dead licensees.

In December 1967, a fire broke out in the *Hare & Hounds* after the landlord and his family had gone to bed. The alarm was raised by a Jack Russell terrier and, although the bar was extensively damaged, the fire brigade arrived in time to save the building. The *Hare & Hounds* has seen many changes over the years, and has many attractive features – the nineteenth-century porch being particularly fine – as well as an unrivalled view over the valley below.

HAT & FEATHER 14 London Street

Much of London Street, including the *Hat & Feather*, was rebuilt at the beginning of the twentieth century in order to widen the road. The original *Hat & Feather* dated back to at least 1752 when the following advertisement appeared in the *Bath Journal*:

> To be lett … a house called the *Hat & Feather*, at Walcot; and the stock and brewing utensils, together with a horse, a staunch pointer, a bullet gun, and three shot guns, to be sold. – Enquire of John Flower, Baker, in Broad Street, Bath.

However, a token, dated 1667, bearing the emblem of a hat with feathers in it, and the name "Richard Pitcher in Bath," suggests that the *Hat & Feather* may be much older. The sign of the hat and feathers was a reference to the distinctive broad-brimmed hats, replete with ostrich feathers, worn by Royalist officers in the Civil War. The date, just after the Restoration, would tie in with this. Innkeepers could not have got away with such a sign during the Puritan interregnum, even though Royalist sympathisers may have met there, but, after Charles II's return such a sign would have not only been a declaration of patriotic sentiment but also a reminder that the flame of Royalist sentiment had been kept burning during the years of Cromwellian rule. Naming a pub the *Hat & Feather* in the mid-eighteenth century would have been an anachronism, as fashions – and patriotic emblems – had moved on. All of which suggests – even though we cannot prove it – that the *Hat & Feather* has been there for around three and a half centuries.

Such a theory becomes even more plausible when we consider its location. In

To be Lett,
And Enter'd upon immediately,
A HOUSE, call'd the H AT and F EATHER, at WALCOT: And the Stock and Brewing Utensils, together with a Horse, a staunch Pointer, a Bullet-Gun, and three Shot-Guns, to be Sold.———☞ Enquire of JOHN FLOWER, Baker, in BROAD-STREET, BATH.——And all Persons indebted to the late THOMAS FLOWER, are desired to pay it to JOHN FLOWER by the 1st of November next, or they will be prosecuted without further Notice.

The *Hat & Feather* advertised to let in 1752.

the late sixteenth century, a charter granted by Queen Elizabeth extended the city boundaries to take in part of Walcot Parish. Walcot "In" Parish, as it was known, ended at the northern end of Walcot Churchyard. This meant that, until the city boundaries were extended to take in Walcot "Out" Parish in 1832, the *Hat & Feather* was the first pub outside the jurisdiction of the city. Pubs outside cities were subject to far less control and scrutiny than those within. They were also notorious as the rendezvous of criminals and those unhappy with the status quo. As the *Hat & Feather* lay on the most important route into or out of the city, it would have been an ideal place for disaffected Royalists to meet during the years of Puritan rule.

Whatever its genesis, by the middle of the nineteenth century the *Hat & Feather* was notorious, not as the haunt of disaffected Royalists, but because it stood at the entrance to one of the roughest yards in Bath, known, appropriately enough, as Hat & Feather Yard. At one stage it even looked as though it might get its own police station. In 1841 "certain inhabitants of the neighbourhood of Hat & Feather Court" complained to the Watch Committee "of the disorderly state of the residents in that court and suggesting the removal of the Brunswick station to that quarter."

A somewhat Pooterish letter to the *Bath Chronicle* on 22 July 1869 gave an eye-witness account of a ritual kept alive by some of these disorderly residents:

Sir, As I was passing near Walcot Church on Monday evening [9 July] I found the street full of people in an excited state, and on enquiring the cause, was informed by one of the bystanders that it was 'Cuckoo Revel.' I waited some few minutes when there emerged from *Hat and Feather* Yard a company of about a dozen labouring men carrying on their shoulders a grotesquely dressed, masked individual, with a 'short churchwarden' in his mouth, seated in a kind of bower of evergreens. They were accompanied by two or three men at liberty, whose continual cry was 'Holler, boys, holler.' As may be expected, the small boys, most of whom carried thistles which they unceremoniously thrust in the faces of any smaller urchin not similarly armed, when thus appealed to did 'holler,' much to the annoyance of the respectable residents of the locality. Thus surrounded, this curious and fantastic cortege proceeded to an adjacent 'public' where both outers, bearers and figure were regaled with 'good home-brewed' that did not, according to the testimony of a bystander, 'taste copperish.' They then proceeded to another 'public,' where the scene was repeated, and this appeared to be the aim of the expedition, the end being that both figure and bearers were in danger of coming to mother earth. Seeing an old gentleman near whose bowed figure betokened that, if not the most talked-of 'oldest inhabitant,' he was at least a veritable 'book of reference' on parochial, and, no doubt, other matters, I accosted him, and learnt that, in former years this 'cuckoo revel' was kept in much greater splendour than at present, the figure being splendidly apparelled and wearing a large pair of gilt horns. It was borne aloft in a bower of evergreens, and, numerously accompanied, proceeded through the leading thoroughfares of the parish, levying 'blackmail' on those individuals who during the previous twelve-month had been guilty of conduct similar to that now referred to the court presided over by Lord

Penzance.*The proceedings were then wound up with a capital supper, so that if they did not commence as merrily as a marriage bell they ended in conviviality and good fellowship. My informant added that he had seen the windows broken in cases where the 'blackmail' was refused, and also that no class was held exempt from this visitation.

I have no doubt that this absurd and not very reputable exhibition, which lasted more than two hours, had its commencement in the church revel, the present commodious parish church, rebuilt in 1777, being dedicated to St Swithin; but I would respectfully ask the question, whether, having fallen into its present condition, the powers that be had not better prohibit its annual celebration? As a self-elected court for the trial of certain causes it had a use, perhaps not very agreeable to offenders; but at present it is simply a nuisance, which, like the turnpike gates around our fair city, 'if missed would not be wanted.' I do not think it capable of renovation, though I see no real reason why a few of the leading parishioners at least should not meet in commemoration of the anniversary of the dedication of their original parish church, but that I may never again witness the spectacle of Monday night is the hope of

Yours truly

An Artisan

Perhaps he's why they call Walcot Street Bath's Artisan Quarter.

The 1903 report on the *Hat & Feather*, shortly after it had been rebuilt, found it "very good indeed." At that time the bar was "in several compartments," with "a good bar parlour behind." Despite several changes, many of the splendid decorative features incorporated into the rebuilding of the *Hat & Feather* a century ago are still to be seen today, painted in a vibrant colour scheme in which deep red, blue and gold predominate. The *Hat* (as it is known to regulars) is a very lively pub, with a strong emphasis on music, ranging from acoustic sessions to computer beats and from kora players to the legendary DJ Derek, possibly the oldest DJ in the business. It bills itself as "Bath's original underground hangout – not a style bar, more a way of life – the kind of pub legends are made of – or at least tall stories." It is, however, unlikely that you will meet many Royalists there today.

HATCHETT'S 6-7 Queen Street

Hatchett's – at the sign of the raven – has a complicated history (and so does the raven, but we will come to that later). Queen Street and Quiet Street were laid out by John Wood around 1730 on part of the Rivers Estate. However, most of the buildings in Queen Street, including *Hatchett's*, date from around 1780 and were designed by Thomas Baldwin.

Around 1837, James Collins opened a beerhouse in 6 Queen Street. Collins soon moved on and the beerhouse closed. Then, in the 1860s, a wine merchant called

---

* The divorce court. This makes it clear that the innocent-sounding Cuckoo Revels were originally "Cuckold Revels," a rough and ready process of naming and shaming that was no doubt acceptable to the church authorities. The word "cuckold" is derived from the word "cuckoo," due to the cuckoo's habit of laying its eggs in other birds' nests. Cuckoo Fairs are still held annually in many English towns and villages – Downton in Wiltshire, Heathfield in Sussex, Poughill in Cornwall and Tenbury in Worcestershire to name but a few. It is not known whether these were originally "cuckold fairs" or, as the organisers prefer to believe, rustic festivities to celebrate the return of the cuckoo.

Thomas Toleman, who was already operating from the Bazaar in Quiet Street (now the *Eastern Eye Restaurant*), took over the premises on the corner of Quiet Street (No 12) and Queen Street (No 7). In the 1880s he moved into 6 Queen Street as well.

Around 1900, the property was renamed *Fullers' Wine Vaults* and became a pub. The entrance, on the corner of Quiet Street and Queen Street, led to a bar in three compartments with a smoke room behind. By 1914, it had been taken over by Applegate & Sons and renamed the *Quiet Street Wine Vaults*. Usher's took over in 1935. It only held a beer and wine licence until 1955, when a full licence was transferred from the *Norfolk Arms* on the Upper Bristol Road (the *Norfolk Arms*, incidentally, now lies under the Vauxhall Garage). At this time the *Wine Vaults* only occupied the building on the corner of Quiet Street, No 12. It was renamed *Hatchett's* in 1961 after a former landlord and subsequently moved from 12 Quiet Street (which then became an estate agent's), into 6 & 7 Queen Street.

Hatchett's is a fiercely individualistic pub, as far away from the blandness of your average theme pub as it is possible to imagine, and there is no doubt that its loyal band of customers would have it no other way. Its website is superb, billing the pub as "a relic from a time before men in suits decided beer had to get served in funny shaped bottles," and "not so much a public house as a refuge for a group of people who find themselves strangely out of step with modern attitudes." It is also disarmingly honest about its furniture, which it describes as "crap."

Now, about that raven. There was once a pub called the *Raven* just across the road from *Hatchett's* on the north side of Quiet Street. That was not where it started off, though.

As long ago as 1585 – the year that Sir Walter Raleigh established the first English colony in the New World – there was a pub called the *Raven* in Cheap Street, on the corner of Cock Lane (now known as Union Passage). It was later renamed the *Three Goats* and the name of the *Raven* was transferred to a new inn in Abbey Green, built around 1631, which today houses Evans Fish Restaurant. Although we know when the building dates from, however, we have no record of it being an inn before 1759, when the *Bath Journal* advertised a "genteel four-wheel post chaise" for sale "at the sign of the *Raven* in the Abbey Green." This was a fairly substantial establishment, "with convenient stables and a remarkably healthy cellar room, sufficient to contain one hundred buts of beer."

In 1778, John Fox the landlord of the *Raven* in Abbey Green, left to open a new pub at 4 Quiet Street. He was so attached to the sign outside his old pub, however, that he took it with him. He called his new pub the *Raven*, while the old one embarked on a series of name changes – including the *Druid's Head*, the *Bladud's Head*, and finally the *Freemason's Tavern*. The new *Raven* closed in the 1850s and the block in which it stood was refronted in 1871, so that nothing of it now remains – except, of course, for the memory of its name, preserved in the sign outside *Hatchett's*.

HOBGOBLIN 47 St James's Parade

The *Hobgoblin* is one of two Bath pubs named after a beer – in this case one brewed by Wychwood Brewery, established in Witney in Oxfordshire in 1983. When the pub opened around 1830, it was known as the *Green Tree*. It changed its name to the *Talbot* in 1893, had a brief spell as the *Hot Tub Pub* in the 1980s (with a sign based on Botticelli's *Birth of Venus*), before becoming the *Hobgoblin*. An inventory from 1870 paints a tantalising picture of its smoking room – Kidderminster carpet, three mahogany drinking tables, sofa, easy chairs, and (the ultimate sign that its clientele could be relied upon to behave themselves) ornaments. There was also a bar (part of which was partitioned off to form a bar parlour), a tap room and a brewery. By the time of the 1903 report there was a large club room upstairs and six bedrooms to let. The brewery closed around 1921.

In 1976, when Fred Pearce stopped by, the *Talbot* still had "two very pleasant bars – a small panelled lounge [and] and a large street corner public." Today it has all been knocked through into one and the cellar has

been opened up, but the pub's original name is recalled by a green tree growing out of a tuba on the stairs. The rest of what looks like an entire brass section is plastered around the walls, along with posters for BB King and Dog's Bollocks Beer. Dark wood, high-backed settles, student discounts, anaglypta ceiling, chip butties that run those in the *Pulteney Arms* a close second, and bubble-gum-flavoured vodka all add up to a very distinctive and eclectic town-centre boozer, popular with students. There is live music on a regular basis, as well as theme nights and fancy-dress parties. The single-storey Victorian extension on the street corner, although totally out of keeping with the late eighteenth century elegance of the rest of the building, is a very effective addition.

A one-gallon jar from EA Ditte, who ran the *Talbot* on St James's Parade in the early twentieth century.

HOP POLE 7 Albion Buildings, Upper Bristol Road

The *Hop Pole* was first recorded in 1826 with Mr P Haselwood as the licensee. John Seaborne, who ran it in the 1870s, also had a cooper's business there. By 1903, it had acquired a single-storey extension to the right of the main entrance. It had two other front entrances and an exit to the river at the back which was kept locked. There was a bar with a small room behind, a large smoke room beyond that, another room with a bagatelle table, and a skittle alley. As late as 1976 it still had three bars – a darts-dominated public bar, a lounge bar and a quiet back room. After a spell under the ownership of Moles' Brewery, the *Hop Pole* – now one big bar with a skittle alley and magnificent patio at the back – is owned and run by Bath Ales. A pity the old partitions had to go, but the new *Hop Pole* does have a good deal of mock-Victorian character (albeit of a slightly whimsical variety), and, of course, it's always worth trekking out to for the beer. It has also built up an awesome reputation for food (featuring in the Saturday *Guardian* no less), while retaining the atmosphere of a traditional local. Past winner of Bath CAMRA Pub of the Year and named by the *Bristol Evening Post* as having the best pub food in Bath, it hardly needs any further recommendation. And you will be pleased to learn that the exit to the river at the back is now kept unlocked.

HORSESHOE 1 Raby Place, North Road, Combe Down

Pubs called the *Horseshoe* generally started off with a smithy at the back and the *Horseshoe* in Combe Down was no exception. William Brooks was first listed as a blacksmith and beer retailer at 1 Laburnum Place (the original name of Raby Place) in 1875. However, the *Horseshoe* is almost certainly older than that. In 1848, a Mr Brooks, whose address was just given as "Combe Down," was listed as a blacksmith and beer retailer. It is likely that he was operating from what later became known as the *Horseshoe*. There was a blacksmith's forge at the back of the *Horseshoe* until the Second World War, run by a Mr Daniels.

The *Horseshoe* received a full licence in 1951 and is still open today. Originally it consisted of three bars and, although it has been knocked through into one, still retains its old layout.

HUNTSMAN 1 Terrace Walk

The *Huntsman*, originally the *Parade Coffee House*, stands at the end of the raised terrace where visitors promenaded on sunny afternoons, exchanging polite (and impolite) conversation, catching up on the latest gossip and devising stratagems for that evening's ball. The *Huntsman* is chiefly notable for having the earliest surviving shop front in Bath. The building has been attributed – wrongly – to John Wood. In fact, John Wood was very unhappy when it went up in the 1740s. It not only scuppered his plans to extend Terrace Walk but also blocked the view from Ralph Allen's Town House.

An advertisement for the *Parade Coffee House* appeared in the *Bath Journal* for 19 September 1754 showing that even then it was cheaper to get a take-away:

> HARTSHORN JELLIES fresh made every day At the *Parade Coffee House*. Four pence per glass in the coffee room and three pence per glass out of doors. (Money to be left for the "Glasses" till return'd.)*

For several years in the late eighteenth century, the *Parade Coffee House* was run by Meshach Pritchard (who also held the license of Spring Gardens). An advertisement from 1781 indicates that, although the *Parade Coffee House* was very far from being your average pub, it did at least serve alcohol:

BATH, *May* 12, 1755.

The PARADE COFFEE-HOUSE
Is KEPT by
Richard Stephens, WINE-MERCHANT,
Where the NOBILITY and GENTRY may be assur'd to be accommodated in the best and genteelest Manner,
By their most obedient humble Servant,
RICHARD STEPHENS.

☞ Of whom may be had WINES of the best Growth ; also ARRACK, RUM, BRANDY, SHRUB, all Sorts of CORDIALS ; and JELLIES Fresh every Day, at Four-Pence at the Coffee-House, Three-Pence without Doors.
₊ Sells also MINERAL WATERS, in the greatest Perfection, viz. Pyrmont, German Spaw, Seltzers, Bourne, Scarborough, and Bristol.

A 1755 advertisement for the *Parade Coffee House.*

> To be let, the *Parade Coffee House* with the lodging house there belonging, the goods, fixtures and stock of liquors. Contact Mr Pritchard.

However, Mr Pritchard decided to stay, and, on 17 September 1791 another advertisement appeared, notifying the public that he had "agreed a further lease with Mr Ferry." (This was the Mr Ferry who lived at Bathwick Villa and had opened Pleasure Gardens there in 1783.) Meshach Pritchard finally gave up the lease around 1798.

In the early nineteenth century the *Parade Coffee House* became a wine merchant's. It was renamed the *Institution Wine Vaults*, after the Bath Royal Literary and Scientific Institute which stood where the disused toilets in the middle of Bog Island stand today. In 1837, JK Welch & Co., who had tried to dispose of the business on account of "being engaged in a wholesale business in London which required

---

* For those eager for a taste of the eighteenth-century, the recipe for Hartshorn Jelly is as follows: "Boil half a pound of hartshorn in three quarts of water over a gentle fire till it becomes a jelly; when a little hangs on a spoon it is done enough. Strain it hot, put it into a well-tinned saucepan, and add to it half a pint of Rhenish wine, and a quarter of a pound of loaf sugar. Beat the whites of four eggs or more to a froth, stir it sufficiently for the whites to mix well with the jelly, and pour it as if cooling it. Boil it two or three minutes, then put in the juice of four lemons, and let it boil two minutes longer. When it is finely curdled and of a pure white, pour it into a swan-skin jelly bag over a China basin, and pour it back again until it becomes as clear as rock water; set a very clean China basin under, fill the glasses, put some thin lemon rind into the basin, and when the jelly is all run out of the bag, with a clean spoon fill the rest of the glasses, and they will look of a fine amber colour. Put in lemon and sugar agreeable to the palate." "

their full attention ... but not succeeding in meeting with a successor upon the desired terms, and unwilling to part with their highly respectable connection, ... determined upon continuing the wine trade [at the *Institution Wine Vaults*] upon an enlarged and more liberal scale, under the superintendence of Mr Richard Cowley Polhill, a gentleman whose many years experience and long connection with one of the first rate London houses, shipping from Oporto and Cadiz, render well qualified to receive and execute the orders of their friends and the public." At this time, the *Institution Wine Vaults* was also an agency for the Argus Life Assurance Company and for "Schweppes' Celebrated Soda Water, and Aerated Lemonade."

In 1898, Eldridge Pope, the Dorchester Brewers, took over the *Institution Wine Vaults*. In 1968, they renamed it the *Huntsman,* after one of their beers. In 1976, when Fred Pearce visited, it had four separate bars – public, buffet, lounge and cellar. The cellar bar, "all wood beams and flagstones and a well in the middle," was open in the evening at weekends with "young local groups playing live." The "star feature" was Royal Oak beer (ABV 5%) straight from the barrel at 28p a pint.

Photographs from the early twentieth century show that the front door was not in the centre of the building as it is today, but in the right-hand arch (looking from the street). The nineteenth-century side door into Lilliput Alley with its elaborate lamp bracket is also worthy of note. Today, the *Huntsman* is chiefly famous as the starting point for the nightly ramble round Bath known as Bizarre Bath. If you thought stand-up comedians only appear on stage, turn up here one summer evening at 8pm and prepare to be proved wrong.

That is not the full history of the *Huntsman*, however. If you walk down Lilliput Alley, past the ornate nineteenth-century side entrance, you will come to a much older, gabled building which now forms the back of the *Huntsman*. This is about 120 years older than the rest of the pub, having been built (like Sally Lunn's next door) in the

1620s.* It opened as a pub called the *Star & Garter* sometime before 1776. It changed its name to the *Prince of Wales* around 1785, but quickly reverted to the *Star & Garter*.

The history of the buildings on the north side of Lilliput Alley is a fascinating one. Lilliput Alley was originally known as Segar's Alley, then as Evelyn Street. There was even an attempt to call it Abbey Green Street. Today it is officially known as North Parade Passage – but it is not all it seems. For a start, the level of the pavement is much higher than it once was – so much so, in fact, that what is now the ground floor of the houses on the north side was once the first floor.

---

* The date of 1482 on the plaque fixed to the wall of Sally Lunn's is a red herring, as Sally Lunn's own website makes clear. There have been buildings around here since Roman times, but the present ones date from around 1622 when John Hall was granted a building lease.

"All publicity is good publicity" – an announcement by the landlord of the *Star & Garter* in 1780.

What is more, they were once the other way round – or, to be more precise, what are now their back entrances were once at the front. It is hard to imagine, picking your way down the grubby alley at the side of the *Huntsman*, that this was once the front way into Sally Lunn's and the buildings on either side of it, but one look at the architectural embellishments and ashlar blocks on this side (as opposed to the rubble stone on the Lilliput Alley side) should provide ample confirmation. And, if more evidence is needed, it is provided by a 1725 map of the Duke of Kingston's Estate in Bath, which shows that, at the time, these buildings looked across a bowling green to the Orange Grove.

In 1780, the landlord of the *Star & Garter* was a John Peterswald, who was forced, rather shamefacedly, to put this notice in the *Bath Journal*:

> Whereas I have been lately robbed by a servant of about £5, which he took out of a till; and having very unjustly charged John Lansdown, chairman, with committing the said offence, I do hereby declare the said John Lansdown's innocence.
>
> John Peterswald.

But Mr Peterswald was determined to have the last word, and under the above notice he added the terse comment:

> Beef Alamode every evening at eight o'clock.

Under Mr Peterswald's management, the *Star & Garter* seems to have been quite an upmarket establishment. A couple of months later he placed another notice in the *Bath Journal*, advertising "mock turtle soup," as well as "Burton Ale, London Porter and Dorsetshire Beer in draft or in bottles."

By 1824 it seems to have gone down in the world, as this story of sharp practice from the Vagrancy Records shows:

> The information of Elijah Gold of the Parish of Chilcompton in the County of Somerset, labourer, taken on oath this third day of July 1824 before me one of His Majesty's Justices of the Peace – Who on his oath saith that this afternoon about two o'clock as he was coming up Horse Street [Southgate Street] he was accosted by a stranger (whose name he has since learnt to be William Humphries) who inquired of deponent if he was a farmer. Deponent replied that he was not, but that he was a labourer. Said William Humphries then invited him to take a glass of beer, and he took deponent to a public house called the *Star & Garter* in Lilliput Alley . . . where they drank a pint of porter which deponent paid for. Whilst they were drinking the beer a stranger came in and joined them and he appeared to be acquainted with the said William Humphries – deponent has since heard that the stranger's name is William Trueman, who, soon after he entered the room where they were sitting, pulled out of his pocket a pack of cards and offered to bet deponent and Humphries a guinea each that neither of them could take out of the pack a spade by drawing three times. Deponent refused to bet, but said Humphries strongly persuaded him to try and after some further hesitation he agreed to put down a guinea, which deponent did, and said Humphries put down a one pound bank note, which, with deponent's guinea, the said William Trueman took up and put into his pocket. Humphries shuffled the cards, and Trueman drew for the spade for deponent and the attempt was unsuccessful

and immediately afterwards deponent and Humphries left the room and went to the street door together, leaving Trueman behind. Deponent went up Lilliput Alley, believing Humphries was behind him, but upon turning round to look for him he found that he had left him. Deponent returned to the public house but could not find them there. Soon afterwards a man met him and informed him that Humphries with whom he had seen deponent was a rascal and a great swindler, and he inquired of deponent if he had been gaming with him, and if he had lost anything. Deponent replied he had and that he had lost a guinea. They then procured a constable, who went in search of Humphries and apprehended him. Deponent saw the constable search Humphries and find on his person the guinea he had lost at the public house aforesaid. Deponent verily believes that the said William Humphries and William Trueman are well acquainted with each other, and that they used together the above subtle means to deceive and impose upon him. Wherefore he prays that they may be dealt with according to law.

Around 1826, the *Star & Garter* changed its name to the *Duke of Wellington*. The last we hear of it is in a newspaper report from 1849:

William Edwards, an Irishman evidently a man of some education, though his appearance was against him, was committed for trial on two charges – the first was that of having stolen a set of bagatelle balls from a beerhouse kept by a person called Parfitt [the *Woodman* at 9 Gallaway's Buildings], and which he subsequently disposed of at the shop of Mr John Ford, turner, John Street, for ten shillings; and the second of having stolen from the *Duke of Wellington* Public House a Meerschaum pipe and a brass candlestick, which were found in his possession when taken into custody.

Shortly afterwards, the *Duke of Wellington* closed and was absorbed into the *Institution Wine Vaults*. Although today the back room of the *Huntsman* may be a rather overlooked part of Bath's pub scene, it must be a contender for the title of Bath's oldest pub. And, as one of the few early seventeenth century buildings in the city to have survived in anything like its original form, it certainly deserves to be better known.

JUBILEE 91 Whiteway Hill, Twerton

The *Jubilee* on Whiteway Hill (originally the *Jubilee House*) was named in honour of Queen Victoria's Golden Jubilee in 1887. George White built it in 1888, having arranged a loan of £1,000 with Spencer's Brewery of Bradford on Avon. South of the pub, strung out along the main road, was a lawn, a yard with stables and a brewhouse, and four small cottages. Today the old pub has been swamped by massive modern extensions which cover the site of the old yard and cottages.

KING'S ARMS 1 Monmouth Place, Upper Bristol Road

The *King's Arms* can be traced back to at least 1776, but is probably much older. The frontage is remarkably well preserved, indicating its origins as an early eighteenth or late seventeenth century inn with local coaching and carrier trade. A little further along

the Upper Bristol Road, there is evidence of early seventeenth century building, which suggests that that the *King's Arms* may date back earlier still.

The coat of arms above the door is particularly fine, as is the restored sign board on the wall in the courtyard. The *King's Arms* may never have been in the first or even the second rank of Bath's coaching inns, but it seems to have provided several of its landlords with a step up the ladder to a prosperous career in the coaching trade. In 1792, for example, the landlord was William Springford, who, less than ten years later, moved to the much more prestigious *Elephant & Castle Inn* in Monmouth Street. Because it was never one of Bath's more fashionable inns, and was well out of the city centre, it has survived more or less intact, at least externally, while the inns in the centre have either gone or been changed beyond all recognition.

A half-gallon jar bearing the name of William Osborne who was landlord of the *King's Arms* from 1855 to 1890.

Just like them, however, the *King's Arms* suffered when the railway came. By the end of the nineteenth century, it was clear that it had seen better days. The 1903 report stated that it had "three beds to let, but not often occupied." It still had its moments of glory, though. In January 1900, 46 volunteers for the North Somerset Yeomanry were examined and enlisted at the *King's Arms* before being sent off to fight the Boers.

A few months later the *King's Arms* was in the news for a less auspicious reason. The landlord, a Mr Coles, had gone bankrupt, and Oakhill Brewery put in Henry Trude to run the pub. They forgot, however, to apply for a licence transfer. The police got to hear of this and went round to make further enquiries, only to be greeted by a torrent of abuse, followed by a volley of punches. Mr Trude certainly knew how to make a drama out of a crisis. He was fined £12 with costs.

An inventory from 1890 gives a good idea of what the old *King's Arms* was like. It still had a brewery. There was a bar, a smoking room, a club room, a tap room, a dining room, and – luxury beyond imagining in those dark days – a bathroom with a fixed bath, a bidet and a chamber pedestal. In the yard was "an old phaeton, a heavy spring cart, a crank axle cart and a bay gelding."

Today, with its old courtyard miraculously preserved, it is one of Bath's top music venues with a lively clientele, instruments ranged round the walls and Nipper on high looking into his horn.

KING'S HEAD 40 High Street, Upper Weston

The early history of the *King's Head* is somewhat problematic. Licensing records go back to 1779, when Betty Crew was the licensee. In 1786 John Crew took over. By 1792 he had been replaced by Martha Crew. So far so good. In 1794, however, Elizabeth Thompson was recorded as the licensee of the *Old King's Head*. By 1798 Thomas Fennell held the lease of the *Old King's Head* and Joseph Lockyer held the lease of the *New King's Head*. The *Old King's Head* closed around 1808, while the *New King's Head* (which soon dropped the "new" from its name) kept going. So far, it has proved impossible to determine precisely what was going on here. One possibility is that the two *King's Heads* were next door to each other, and eventually merged into one. The *King's Head* today is an amalgamation of at least two buildings – a modest two-storey cottage and an imposing three-storey structure. The large building dates from the early eighteenth century, if not before, but the small building may date from around 1800. It is difficult to be certain, but this may suggest one possible explanation for the existence of two *King's Heads* in Weston for around ten years at the beginning of the nineteenth century.

The *King's Head's* most celebrated landlord was Robert Snow, who was there from around 1821 to 1847. During the reign of William IV, he changed the name of the pub to the *William IV*, but later changed it back again. He eventually handed over to Arthur Snow, a fly proprietor, who stayed there till around 1855. Arthur Snow, in turn, handed over to George Snow, who left in 1859.

The *King's Head* was a popular venue for local events. Take this report of a dahlia show in 1837:

> The room was thrown open to the visitors at two o'clock, and for the next two hours filled by a fashionable company, amongst whom were nearly all the fashionable families of Weston and its neighbourhood.

Far more spectacular, however, was an event which took place in 1834, in response to the ceremonials in Bath to celebrate the passing of the Municipal Act. The Act brought Widcombe, Bathwick and much of Walcot under the jurisdiction of Bath Corporation. Weston, however, was not included (it did not become part of Bath until 1951), and held its own festivities to celebrate:

> The annual inauguration of the municipal officers of the ancient Corporation of Weston took place on

Tuesday last, on which occasion a most numerous and highly respectable assemblage met, invited by his Worship to partake of a repast as good as the most exquisite of Corporations could desire. The choice variety of viands, the superiority displayed in the cookery, and the quality of the wines, furnished proof that Mr Snow, the caterer, was not praised above his deserts. It was all against the Bath Guildhall cookery – a line-of-battle ship to a nutshell. After dinner, the installation of the officers for the year ensuing took place. Most persons are acquainted with the forms made use of in our city and at Bristol upon similar occasions; but I believe few are aware of those attached to the civic election of Weston, which have improved upon them, as must naturally be the case under any circumstances. Weston was anciently titled "The City of the Seven Streams." The Mayor entered the Hall preceded by

Two Mace Bearers

Champion in complete armour

Champion's Esquire in panoply, bearing the Knight's Coat of Arms,

with Banner Bearers on either side

Officers of Court in full costume

Members of the Common Council in robes

Servants in full livery

Two Sheriffs

Twelve Aldermen in robes

Mayor's own Servants in livery

THE MAYOR

splendidly attired in robes and cap,

with plume of feathers,

glittering with jewels

WESTON ARMS: Motto, Loyal au Mort

MAYOR'S ARMS: Motto, Pro Rege et Populo

Officers and Banners

Town Clerk's Secretary, bearing Records

Town Clerk in splendid robes, with the Wisdom Wig

Recorder

Commander of the Forces

Lord High Admiral

Ambassadors splendidly attired, with their suites

Cardinal Boniface, with scarlet hat and robes

Turkish Ambassador, splendidly attired

Dutch Burgomaster, in costume

Other Officers and Functionaries, etc., etc.

The whole flanked with a numerous array of Officers,

Banner Bearers, etc., and accompanied by a

Band of first-rate Musicians

To have an idea of the effect of this procession – the glittering of armour that sword had never dented, the gorgeous banners, guiltless of waving save in the steam of savoury viands – is impossible. The Mayor, having taken his seat, the Town Clerk administered the oath to him, by which he swears to protect, to the best of his power, the rights, privileges, luxuries, profits, and comforts of the lieges of the ancient

Corporation of Weston, and to maintain peace between the said Corporation and the Township of Twerton, and all Foreign Countries; to protect all the watercourses, and steal water, if needful, from anybody, for Corporation purposes; to keep up all landmarks by which anything is to be put into the pockets of the Civic Dignitaries; and to make use of this authority exclusively for the benefit of the said Corporation. Upon this the Champion arose, threw down his gauntlet, and defied to mortal combat any person or persons … who might dispute the authority of the Mayor of the ancient City of the Seven Streams. The Sheriffs and other officers were then sworn in. The Town Clerk afterwards read the Records of the City, in which are traced the existence of a Charter to the remotest period of British antiquity, before King Lud was in being. The learned gentleman corroborated these records by the production of an original document, in the handwriting of Julius Caesar, granting a charter to the Mayor for his good services in providing billets for his soldiers at the time of their encampment on Lansdown. This document has but lately been found, and is generally understood to have been concealed in a stone in the old church, and discovered during the time of the late repairs. The learned gentleman argued most powerfully for the ancient consequence of the City of the Severn Streams, clearly shewing that Bath had usurped a consequence and power which of right appertained to Weston, even with regard to its sanatory springs, as it had been proved that a gentleman then living, who had been afflicted with rheumatic gout, in passing over the stream at Weston, accidentally fell into it, was fortunately rescued from his perilous situation before life had fled, and has never felt a touch of the rheumatism since.

And so it went on. The description ended with the following observation:

There have been only two cases of repletion reported by the medical men; both will recover. This is something after our rivals in Bath.

The celebrations were repeated, although with somewhat less pomp, at least once, in 1839, when the scurrilous *Bath Figaro* used them as the pretext for two of its Celebrated Untruths:

It is not true that William Short, Jr, of Gloucester Street attempted to sing the "Old English Gentleman" at the Mayor's Dinner, Weston, but failed owing to having eaten so much turkey.

It is not true that Mr Pr . . ce of the Dolphin was found swimming in the mud in Weston Lane after coming from the Mayor's Feast on Tuesday evening. Nor is it true he macadamised the lane with his nose.

Life in Weston was not one long picnic, however. In 1830, for example, Robert Snow, the landlord of the *King's Head*, was involved in a tragic incident at Foulkes' Brewery in Weston:

A large store piece or cask had been taken to pieces a few weeks since, and thoroughly scoured and cleaned … As soon as it was refitted, a small quantity of beer grounds were put into it to prevent it from getting musty. Between nine and ten o'clock on Wednesday morning last, Mr Foulkes, being desirous to prepare the cask for the reception of new beer, desired the men to take out these grounds, but particularly mentioned that they were not to descend into the vat, until he had procured a rope ladder. One of the men, namely Few, observed to his fellow workman, Little, that the precaution was proper, as he considered there was some danger, but the latter observed that he was too timid, and that he himself should descend without further scruple or delay. When Mr Foulkes returned with the rope ladder, finding neither of the men there, he called out to them in the vat, and receiving no reply, became greatly agitated and alarmed, and immediately sent down to Mr Snow, the landlord of the *King's Head*, for assistance. Mr Snow instantly repaired to the spot, accompanied by a man named

Miles, in his employ, and Mr Foulkes, having taken the precaution to place a rope around his own body, desired Miles to hold it while he descended to see what had become of the two men. Miles being well acquainted with the business and aware of the danger, called out to Mr Foulkes about half a minute after he had descended, and receiving no answer, immediately drew him up, and found the body bent double, the head hanging on one side, and animation suspended. Restoratives being however expeditiously applied, Mr Foulkes soon after revived. The two other bodies being then drawn up were found quite dead from the effects of the foul air in the cask. The jury having heard the evidence, found a verdict of accidental death. The deceased were both favourite servants of Mr Foulkes and had been many years in his employ. Their ages were between 30 and 40, and Little has left a wife and three children. Few has left a wife but no child. The sad event has been a source of deep regret to Mr Foulkes, and of general commiseration throughout the village.

In 1882, William Deverall, from the *Queen's Head* in Twerton, moved to the *King's Arms*. At the time he took over, the premises consisted of a bar, a glass room, a parlour, a tap room, a club room (with oil paintings, stuffed birds, a model of a ship and a five-volume encyclopaedia), and five bedrooms. Almost a century later, in 1976, Fred Pearce visited and left this report:

> The large public bar is like a working men's club – a totally male preserve … Lots of smoke and chalk dust from the dart board, football rosettes, dirty postcards, dominoes, shove ha'penny, colour TV, table skittles, Sun racing pages, fivers changing hands discreetly in the corner … The "garden with aviary" we had been promised turned out to be a few seats in the back yard next to a couple of parrots in a cage.

There's just no pleasing some people! Today the *King's Head* is a beamed, lively, barn-like boozer, with its own Druid's Corner. It is a very old, if much extended, building – and it is worth going round the back, not to look at the parrots, but to see the range of different building styles. Although it does not make a song and dance about it, the *King's Head* is one of the most historic pubs in the Bath area.

KING WILLIAM   36 Thomas Street, London Road

Of all the monarchs immortalised on pub signs, King William IV is by far the most popular, simply because he happened to be on the throne when the Duke of Wellington's Beer Act was passed in 1830. There was even a song about him:

> So "Long," we'll sing,
> "Live Billy the King,
> Who 'bated the tax upon beer."

The tenant of 36 Thomas Street, like hundreds of others up and down the country, must have felt in a particularly patriotic frame of mind when he coughed up his two guineas for a licence to run a beer house. He could just as easily have plumped for the name that hundreds of others chose – the *Duke of Wellington*. It is a curious quirk of history that the Iron Duke, whose posthumous fame has been considerably enhanced by the number of pubs signs he features on, owes this extensive coverage not to his victory at Waterloo but to the passing of a rather dubious act of parliament.

The *King William* seems always to have been a lively pub. In its early years, Bath's radical MP, JA Roebuck, held regular public meetings and election rallies there. Although this sounds eminently respectable – as, of course, it would be today – it is likely to have been anything but in the bad old nineteenth century. Pubs played a major part in early nineteenth-century election campaigns. In an election in Horsham in Sussex in 1844, for example, "every public house and beershop in the Parish was secured by one side or other as an electioneering stronghold … If a voter wanted a drink he could go into any public house and obtain any kind of refreshment without being asked for payment. The labourer whose taste was usually satisfied with small beer was now in a position to discover and indulge his taste for more aristocratic beverages … It is not too much to say that most of the male population of Horsham were frequently drunk, many were continually drunk and some were continuously drunk for the whole six weeks preceding election day." The Bath Election of 1841 has gone down in history as the "drunken election," and when Roebuck lost his seat six years later a large mob went on the rampage, smashing the windows of anybody who had supported the Tory candidate. Roebuck himself was no stranger to physical violence, having smacked his political opponent in the mouth when he bumped into him in the polling booth in Sydney Gardens in 1832.

The *King William* is remarkably well-preserved, a rare survival of a nineteenth-century two-room, street-corner boozer. But, as a measure of how much it has changed internally, we are lucky to have two inventories – one from 1886 and the other from 1953.

In 1883, the bar had a "sweep-fronted counter" with a matchboard front and a fixed till. At the end of the counter was a matchboard screen. There were red curtains at the windows. The back room had a bagatelle table and six large pictures on the wall. These included two views of Chicago in Flames, one of Bermuda Floating Dock, one of the Oxford and Cambridge Boat Race, a deerstalking scene and one entitled "There's Life in the Old Boy Yet."

In 1953, the furnishings included an upright antique barometer in a mahogany frame, a Bissett automatic dart-scoring apparatus, a shove-halfpenny slate, a decorated jardinière on a stand, an upright piano in a rosewood case, and three group photographs of football teams.

There was once another pub on the opposite corner of Thomas Street. This opened at around the same time as the *King William*, and was called the *Queen Adelaide* after William's queen. It lasted for only about ten years, closing around 1841.

The *King William*, on the other hand, is still going strong – an unlikely survival, perhaps, given its location – well out of the city centre – and its size. Such places are as much a part of our heritage as Royal Crescent and Beckford's Tower. Go there any Tuesday night, when a group of musicians crams into the back bar and consider how lucky the residents of Thomas Street are to have a pub like this on the corner.

POSTSCRIPT: Since writing the above, the *King William* has closed, hopefully only temporarily

KING WILLIAM IV 54 Combe Road, Combe Down

King William is also commemorated in a pub at Combe Down which was opened in October 1830 by a Mr Brookes. In 1848, the landlord was Thomas Hine, who also ran the Combe Down Brewery at the back. The 1903 report on the property described it as follows:

> Stone tables in front of house with seats – said to be seldom used for drinking. Exit from bar to garden, also porched entrance to same garden from large private house occupied by licensee.

The *King William IV* is still there today, a well-proportioned early nineteenth century building with a wonderful porch, and much of the brewery still standing. It would not look out of place in the market square of a small country town, or as a

COMBE DOWN BREWERY, NEAR BATH.

THOMAS HINE,
MALTSTER AND HOP MERCHANT.
STRONG BEER, ALE, PORTER, AND TABLE BEER.
Brewed from Pure Spring Water. *Recommended by the Faculty.*
Orders received by Mr. Morrish, Wine Merchant, 3, Argyle Street, Bath.

In this advertisement from 1864, the *King William IV* can be sen behind Thomas Hine's Combe Down Brewery The brewery closed after it was acquired by the Limpley Stoke Brewery in the 1880s, but much of the building is still standing.

backdrop to a remake of the *Mayor of Casterbridge*. Instead, it is tucked away down a cul-de-sac in a little known corner of a little known part of Bath, looking out over the green hills of Somerset. It is a friendly local, with a busy social calendar and a constantly changing selection of real ales.

Its asymmetrical front, with one set of windows to the left of the entrance and two sets on the right, suggests that the original building was extended when the brewery was added at the back. Evidence of this can be seen in the stonework between the two sets of windows on the right.

LAMB & LION 15 Lower Borough Walls

The *Lamb & Lion* stands on the site once occupied by the stables of one of Bath's biggest coaching inns, the *Lamb*, which stood on Stall Street, midway between Lower Borough Walls and Beau Street. We know that the *Lamb* was an inn by 1718, but it was probably open at least a century earlier. In 1721, when the stables were leased to Mary Chapman (who also held the lease of the *Lamb*), they were described as lying "between a barton of the inn on the east, the way leading by the Borough Walls south, and a house and garden of Mary Chapman on the north, and opening into Bimbury Lane on the west."

By the mid-eighteenth century, the *Lamb* was the starting point for coaches to Devon and Cornwall. In 1766, the Rev. John Penrose wrote to his daughter in Cornwall:

So this morning away trudged Fanny and I to the *Lamb Inn* in Staul Street, a little below Abbey Lane, the other side of the way, where the Exeter machine puts up, and took places for Monday the second of June.

In October 1767 the *Lamb* was advertised to let, as the licensee, William Angell intended "quitting that way of business and going into the cabinet trade." It was taken by Edward Shaw, who in September 1773 advertised "an ordinary each day of the races at 1/6 a head" and "London porter at 5d a quart." Before the end of the year, however, due to ill health, Mr Shaw put the lease of the *Lamb* up for auction. There were 12 years left on the lease and the advertisement stated that the inn had stabling for over 100 horses.

The lease was taken by John Dover from the *Coach & Horses* near the Cross Bath, but he died a few weeks later. His widow, Elizabeth, carried on the business with the assistance of her son, also called John. John Dover Jr kept the *Lamb* for over 25 years, eventually handing over to Benjamin Banks sometime between 1800 and 1805.

In 1812, the *Lamb* was the scene of great excitement when Wellington's victory at Salamanca "was announced by Lord Clinton as he passed through this city, bearing the official dispatches, with two French eagles, and six standards of colours. The stay of his Lordship was necessarily short, yet while a carriage and horses were preparing, an immense crowd gathered round the *Lamb Inn*, for the pleasure of interrogating him, and viewing the trophies of that glorious victory."

Even wilder celebrations occurred two years later, in June 1814, when peace broke out:

Tuesday morning the bustle of preparation was again seen in the streets; and anxious crowds assembled to witness the approach of the London mails, containing the proclamation of peace. Additional horses, richly caparisoned, had been sent out to be harnessed to the mails at Walcot; but nothing could withstand the enthusiasm of the populace, who insisted they would themselves perform that office. Some considerable time was occupied in arranging the procession; when about midday, it moved forward in a style of regularity worthy the importance of such a cause. Thousands of men and boys led the van, spontaneously formed in regular sections, linked together arm in arm, and proceeded, amid loud huzzas and the waving of handkerchiefs from every window and roof, down Milsom Street, New Bond Street, High Street, and from thence to the Lamb Inn, Stall Street (at that time the rendezvous for mail coaches).

The same year, George Cruikshank visited and wrote that "the city is well furnished with inns. The *White Lion* and the *White Hart* are the two principal, but for attention, neatness and reasonable charges, none are more conspicuous than the *Lamb* in Stall Street."

This was to prove the high point of the *Lamb's* fortunes. In 1822 a fulsome and verbose advertisement – yet one with a sting in its tail – appeared in the *Bath Chronicle*:

MESSRS. ENGLISH, ENGLISH and BECKS
announce to the Public that they are commissioned to LET for any term of years, that valuable and

spacious premises, known by the name of the LAMB INN, and situated in STALL STREET in the City of BATH.

This capital Hotel possesses the advantages of local situation, with an extensive modern elevation of a superior description, united with totally new and convenient internal arrangements corresponding with the same, and in every respect finished in a suitable and expressive manner, so as to render it perfectly calculated for the purposes for which it was originally designed. The bedrooms are excellent and extend to thirty-seven in number; the other apartments and sitting rooms are equally good; the coffee room is commodious; the bar, larder and coach office are similar in point of effect and convenience. Situated in the great thoroughfare to the western counties, and its long-established reputation as an inn are strong and obvious circumstances in its favour; whilst the rapid increase and improvements in the city and its vicinity form also many and considerable advantages.

The TAP, which makes a uniform part of the buildings, is of a very superior description and is now occupied by a yearly tenant.

The STABLING is spacious and compact, and well calculated for an extensive Posting Concern; and the Cellaring particularly good and adapted for a Wine Trade to a very extensive degree.

The Proprietors, wishing to exercise the greatest candour and liberality, have no hesitation in observing that the business, in some departments, has been suffered to decline; they also wish to add that this valuable concern is now offered under the impression that by the management of a skilful conductor, and the easy and liberal terms by which he might enter on the same; there is no doubt but it will prove an important acquisition, and secure a speedy and ample remuneration.

Estate agency blurbs were no less upbeat in 1822 than they are today, and back then they could risk not only economy with the truth but total avoidance of it. For Messrs English, English & Becks to admit that "some departments have been suffered to decline," the *Lamb* must have been in a sorry state indeed.

The tenancy was taken by Thomas Hobbs, who sublet the tap to George Lumley in 1825. The tap, which George Lumley renamed the *Lamb & Lark*, was south of the inn on Stall Street. By all accounts it was a pretty desperate place. In 1831, for example, a regular called John Edmunds drank himself to death there. At the subsequent inquest, witnesses declared that he had been "so drunk he could hardly move." Since this was nothing out of the ordinary, they only started to get worried when he stopped moving altogether. Five years later, by which time the tap had been renamed the *Lamb & Cottage*, a group of hardened drinkers were reduced to such dire straits by a marathon drinking session that they agreed unanimously to sign the pledge. They had, they admitted later, been "carousing for a fortnight at the *Lamb & Cottage* in Stall Street."

Despite Thomas Hobbs subletting the tap, it soon became apparent he was not going to make a go of the business. Things went from bad to worse, and one night in 1826, with debts mounting around him, he gave up the struggle and swallowed a lethal dose of arsenic.

The *Lamb* was taken by William Crisp. He left in 1832, and it was advertised for sale again:

For sale … a large and commodious inn … consisting of a well fitted-up coffee room, six sitting rooms of different dimensions, 15 best bedrooms, ten servants bedrooms, large bar, immediately fronting the entrance … The stables afford accommodation for about 24 horses, with excellent coach houses for the standing of about eight carriages, harness rooms, lofts, and a good paved yard, with a dwelling house … for the residence of the ostler. Also a large piece of void ground immediately adjoining the stables, on which may be erected additional stables and coach houses or other buildings. The whole of the premises are well supplied with water. A cistern is fitted in the upper part of the inn, which is supplied with water by a force pump in the yard.

The entrance to the *Lamb's* yard was on Lower Borough Walls, to the right of what is now the *Lamb & Lion*. It was here that tragedy struck in November 1832:

Yesterday as a wagon loaded with hay was entering the yard of the *Lamb Inn*, Stall Street, it struck against the course of the wall, which fell down and killed on the spot, a boy about nine years of age who was standing near. The boy's father is a carrier of Trowbridge and had left him to look after his cart and horses.

LAMB INN COMMERCIAL AND FAMILY HOTEL,

STALL STREET, BATH.

———

T. ENDICOTT,

GRATEFULLY impressed with a sense of past favours, begs to return his acknowledgments to his Friends, and to assure them of his earnest endeavour to merit their future patronage.

Private Families, Commercial Gentlemen, Agriculturists, and Others, will find that the Accommodations afforded at this Inn are not inferior to those of any Establishment in the Kingdom; it being T. E.'s determination to omit nothing that can add to the comfort and convenience of all who may honour him with their support.

To the Stabling Department, which is extensive and highly commodious, the best attention is devoted. Experienced Ostlers are employed, and the greatest care observed in the selection of Hay, Corn, &c.

———

Wines, Spirits, &c., of the first Quality.

Coaches to all Parts of England Daily, and to Bristol every Hour.

Excellent Lock-up Coach-Houses.

HORSES TAKEN IN AT LIVERY.

An 1837 advertisement for the *Lamb Inn* in Stall Street.

Eventually, the *Lamb* was taken by Thomas Endicott, who had been running the *Lamb & Cottage* next door since 1830. A little while later he announced that he had "reopened the above old-fashioned inn, every department of which has undergone extensive alterations and improvements."

The *Lamb* struggled on for a while, but the knockout blow came in 1841 with the opening of the railway from London to Bath. The coaching trade which the *Lamb* and other inns relied upon disappeared almost overnight. Two years after the arrival of the railway, the *Lamb* was advertised for sale again. Prospective purchasers were advised that "if the premises are considered too large for an inn, a portion thereof may at no great expense, be converted into dwelling houses and shops." This, not surprisingly, is what happened.

When we next hear of the *Lamb*, in 1861, its public accommodation had shrunk to just three rooms – a bar, a bar parlour, and a tap room – quite a change from the "large and commodious" premises of thirty years earlier. It still had a brewery at the back, which closed around 1895, but the pub stayed open, a pale shadow of its former self, until the 1970s. It now houses the Halifax Building Society.

After the inn was broken up in the 1840s, the *Lamb's* stables were rebuilt as the *Lamb & Lion*. This opened around 1852 with a Mr J Neil as landlord. Until the early twentieth century the *Lamb & Lion* had its own stables and brewery at the back, where the sun-trap beer garden is now. The *Lamb & Lion* is, incidentally, a very rare pub name, the only other known examples being at Hambridge in Somerset and Exeter.

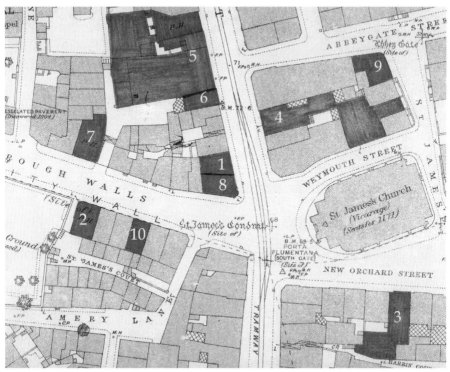

The nineteenth-century drinker had a prodigious choice of pubs to choose from in the St James's Church area. They included: 1 the *Chequers*; 2 the *Bell*; 3 the *Crown Brewery*; 4 the *Golden Lion*; 5 the *Lamb Inn* (eventually reduced to the northernmost part of the building shown); 6 the *Lamb & Lark* (aka the *Lamb & Cottage*); 7 the *Lamb & Lion*; 8 the *Royal Oak*; 9 the *Talbot*; 10 the *Forester's Arms*. The *Lamb & Lion* is the only one left.

LAMBRETTA'S 8-10 North Parade

North Parade, originally called Grand Parade, was begun by John Wood in 1740. Although not traditionally pub territory, *Lambretta's* (with a lavishly festooned scooter serving for a pub sign) now occupies the ground floor of the former *Grosvenor Hotel*, which up until the First World War was a lodging house. Today it is the *Parade Park Hotel*. The building is Grade 1 Listed and the wood-panelling inside *Lambretta's* is still intact, although much of it is hidden by the collection of Lambretta-related memorabilia.

Lambretta's is perhaps Bath's most unlikely pub to be included in the *Good Beer Guide*. Its one large bar, with a pool table in one corner, attracts a loyal crowd of regulars, and the tables on the pavement outside are another great place to sit and watch the tour buses go by.

LARKHALL INN St Saviour's Road, Larkhall

Not many people know that Larkhall takes its name from the *Larkhall Inn*, which started life as a country residence within easy reach of Bath. An announcement in the *Bath Journal* in 1773 painted an idyllic picture of it:

> To lett ready furnish'd for the summer season, a pleasant house called Lark Hall, with a garden well stock'd with fruit, situated in a retired vale, within a short walk of Bath. Enquire of Mr Hayward, Clerk of the New Rooms.

It is believed to have become an inn in 1784, although the licensing records only go back to 1822, when Thomas Kidman was the landlord. It must have been an inn before that, however, because there is a record of an auction being held at the *Lark Hall Tavern* at Lambridge in 1812. This was no average auction. On offer were the estates of R Hewlett and J Shipp, bankrupts, consisting of five unfinished houses (Nos 30, 31, 36, 39 and 40 Grosvenor Place) and the foundations of 42 Grosvenor Place.

> To be LETT READY-FURNISHED,
> For the SUMMER SEASON,
> A Pleasant HOUSE called LARK-HALL,
> with a Garden well stocked with Fruit,
> situated in a retired Vale, within a short Walk of
> Bath.——Enquire of Mr. Hayward, Clerk of the
> New-Rooms.

Lark Hall advertised to be let in 1773

By 1829, the *Larkhall Inn* had become the *Larkhall Inn & Pleasure Gardens*. It seems to have been a hotbed of radicalism, for in 1838 several Chartist ladies' meetings were held in the gardens, one of which was addressed by the great Chartist leader, Henry Vincent. His incarceration in Monmouth Gaol the following year was the catalyst for the Newport Rising.

Other groups using the *Larkhall Inn* were less controversial. In the mid-nineteenth century, the Larkhall Benefit Club met there. Every Whitsun, as a participant later recalled, the members of the club marched around the village, each one "wearing a large rosette or ribbon on his breast, or at the side of his high black beaver-stiffened, chimney-pot hat, and carrying his club stick on his shoulder, with either a brass emblem at the top or a gilded ornamental head. On these occasions scenes of merriment, dancing and joviality were participated in at the Larkhall Gardens, concluding with a display of fireworks."

A less welcome procession, which has already trundled through our pages, also turned up at the *Larkhall Inn* every St Swithin's Day, according to a report in the *Bath Journal* for 29 January 1898:

> Walcot or "Cuckoo" revel, with its rowdiness, drunkenness and rough horse-play, disturbed the peace of the whole neighbourhood from the *Star* public house at the bottom of Guinea Lane to the *Larkhall Inn*. The chief character in this ceremony was an individual masked and got up, smoking a long clay pipe, and seated in an armchair surrounded with evergreens. Two poles were secured under the bottom, or fastened to the sides of the chair with pieces of cord, the chair was hoisted, and the poles rested on the shoulders of four stalwart fellows, and in this fashion the occupant of the chair was borne, followed by crowds of rough men and boys armed with stalks of wild thistles, which they

wielded in all directions, inflicting severe punishment on many … The places of call, of course, for these rowdies were the numerous public houses in this neighbourhood, where they were given beer, not only by the publicans, but oftentimes by customers also, and by the time the circuit of these houses had been made the figure in the chair could no longer hold his "alderman" or sit upright; and the bearers made circuitous steps with their human burden, for the potations at the numerous houses of call had produced a be-muddled state of the "mob," and the bearers could with great difficulty scarcely keep their equilibrium. The last man that was carried round in this fashion many years ago is still alive, and he well remembers the occasion, for the powers that be sent him to gaol for 14 days for obstructing the thoroughfare and causing disturbance.

An edited version of an inventory from 1894 shows that the *Larkhall Inn* was a fairly opulent establishment. It reads as follows:

Five bedrooms;

Club room with bagatelle board;

Drawing room;

Smoking room, with 4 colour prints – "Herring's Stable Scenes";

Glass department;

Bar, with pitch-pine panelled counter with mahogany top, glazed sashes and framing over, 3 glass screens on counter, 6 motion beer engine with extra piping taps, matchboard partition with door sash at side forming passage to smoking room, 6 plated spirit taps, 2 sliding gas pendants and consumers, 2 glass door cupboards in recess, chimney glass in black and gold frame, 2 majolica flower vases, 4 cut decanters;

Tap room, with seating as fixed and 2 screen boards, 3 iron bound drinking tables, 2 deal forms, bell pull;

Coach house, with hurdle dog cart in varnished oak with lamps and cushions, blue and yellow painted 4 wheel gadabout with cushions, crank axle cart (medium size), four-year-old chestnut horse;

Skittle alley;

Pleasure gardens, with fixed seating, 2 drinking tables, 2 forms, pair of old brewers' trucks, corrugated iron shed, 30 head poultry;

Brewery.

The 1903 report goes into more detail on the layout of the premises:

Entrance from St Saviour's Road and side entrances from same road. Side entrance for private purposes from Brookleaze Buildings. Very large yard at rear, with large gates to St Saviour's Road. Bar in 4 and glass room beyond. Brewery at rear and skittle alley on one side of yard.

In 1959 the Bath Health Committee accepted the landlord's offer to erect the old drinking fountain from Larkhall Square (which had been pulled down to build toilets) in his garden, on condition that he return it to the Corporation if requested. In 1978, Courage's awarded the *Larkhall Inn* an accolade for the best pub garden in the West of England. It was a well-earned award, as the landlord, Doug Wooten, admitted spending up to 40 hours a week working in the garden. He also ripped out gas fires in the pub, replacing them with stone fireplaces, and installed two beer engines dating from 1887. When Fred Pearce visited in 1976 he found the *Larkhall Inn* "satisfyingly cluttered with a piano, table football, old photos of Larkhall, several 'no under 18' notices, model ships, two wooden alligators (or were they crocodiles), TV, signs advertising their pizzas (30p) and dog hairs."

The *Larkhall Inn* had its partitions ripped out years ago, but that is about as far as modernisation of the rambling old place has got. Apart from the obligatory fruit machine, you could almost be back in the days when Minnie Caldwell supped milk stout with Ena Sharples, Stanley Matthews was in long pants, Acker was high in the charts and Cliff was young. Pictures of prize pigeons hang on the wall, a Dennis the Menace glove puppet sits on the pumps, illuminated signs for Wills Whiffs and Guinea Light twinkle behind the bar and, in summer, award-winning floral displays bedeck the outside of this venerable Larkhall institution.

LITTEN TREE 23 Milsom Street

Most of Milsom Street dates from the 1760s, but there were many changes in the nineteenth century, most notably the building of two banks at the northern end. Regardless of their architectural merit, they are so out of scale with the rest of the street that they effectively destroy the harmonious arrangement which the Georgian builders had taken great pains to achieve. They were both built by William John Willcox and both have now found other uses – the former National Westminster Bank, dating from 1865, is now a fish restaurant, while the former Lloyd's Bank, dating from 1875, is now the *Litten Tree*. A litten, incidentally, is a churchyard, but forget any idea that the pub got its name because it is on the site of an old churchyard. The Litten Tree chain covers much of the country, and is owned by the same company (SFI) that owns the *Slug & Lettuce*. They have pioneered the concept of the "chameleon" bar. This does not mean that they cater for insectivores with opposable toes, independently rotating eyes, and long tongues, but to find out what it does mean you will have to skip to the entry on the *Slug & Lettuce*.

LIVINGSTONE 24-25 Moorland Road, Oldfield Park

The present *Livingstone Hotel* before it became a pub.

David Livingstone went to Africa and named a waterfall after Queen Victoria. Oldfield Park reciprocated by calling a road and then a pub after him (they also called a pub after Queen Victoria, but we will come to that later). The *Livingstone Hotel*, opened by WG Reynolds in the 1880s, is the only pub on Oldfield Park's main shopping street. Originally it was at 32 Moorland Road, on the corner of Livingstone Road, and had a bar, a private parlour, a smoking room, a tap room and a club room. No good looking for them now, for the pub was so badly bombed in the Bath Blitz that the licence was transferred – temporarily – to 24 & 25 Moorland Road (previously a post office and stationer's). The pub stayed at its new address, and the licence transfer was eventually made

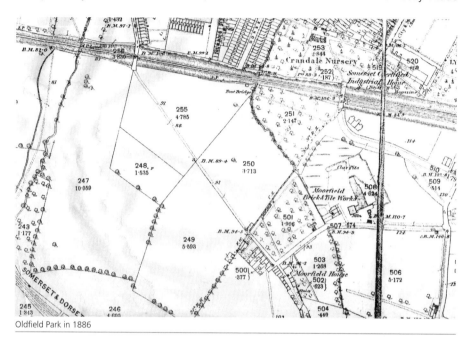

Oldfield Park in 1886

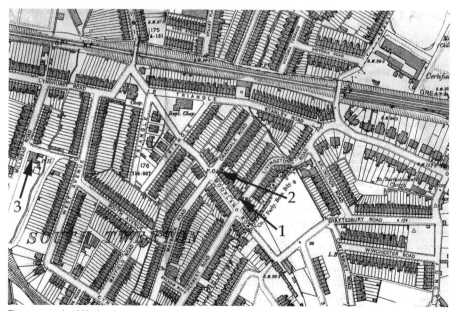

The same area in 1903, showing:
1 the original site of the Livingstone Hotel; 2 the present site of the Livingstone Hotel; 3 the Victoria Hotel.

permanent. With its unusual glass-brick frontage, it is a bustling, street corner local with a small public bar and smaller lounge which manages to appeal to all age groups.

LONG ACRE TAVERN 4 Long Acre, London Road

Although the *Long Acre Tavern* is a modern building, there has been a pub on this site since the 1840s, when Joseph Langdon opened a pub called the *Hole in the Wall* here. Around 1850, it was taken over by Robert Ridout and renamed the *Long Acre Tavern*. In 1851 Mr Ridout was summoned "for keeping his house open during divine service. His plea of ignorance of the law was dismissed on the grounds that he had been in the police." It was also recorded that he "had been repeatedly cautioned against allowing bad characters in his house." He was fined 40/- with costs.

The *Long Acre Tavern* later passed to John Cole, a plasterer, who issued tokens which still carried the name of the *Hole in the Wall*. When he died, in 1864, it passed to his sons, John and James Cole, who were also painters and decorators. However, their address was Long Acre House, Napier Street, Melbourne, Australia. Not wishing to abandon life down under, they put the *Long Acre Tavern* up for sale. The sale particulars described

it as "a most commodious Home-brewed House, with Spirit Licence attached, in a populous neighbourhood." There was "ample cellarage, well arranged Brewery, Malt Room, Back Yard, Skittle Alley, and every convenience for the trade of a publican." The "dwelling house" was also "very capacious and convenient." The tenancy was held by William Tutton, who paid £30 rent a year.

The freehold was bought by George Northmore, a saddler. William Tutton, who held on to the tenancy, was a member of one of the most influential families on the Bath pub scene in the second half of the nineteenth century. An earlier William Tutton, possibly his grandfather, had been the first licensee of the *Rising Sun* in Grove Street in the 1780s. His father, John Tutton, was a brewer in Bristol. In 1858 William, then aged 23, married Ann Crocker, three years

his elder, in the Catholic Chapel in Trenchard Street, Bristol, before moving to Bath and setting up in business at Sydney Wharf. Nine months later his only son, John William Tutton, was born. As well as the *Long Acre Tavern*, William Tutton was involved with

The *Long Acre Tavern* advertised for sale in 1864. Appropriately the sale was held at another pub, the *Porter Butt* the *Rainbow* on the Upper Borough Walls, the *Bath Arms* in Kingsmead Street, the *Barley Mow* (now the *Barley*) on Bathwick Street, the *Chandos Arms* in Chandos Buildings, and the *Bunch of Grapes* in Morford Street. William Tutton died in 1905 and the tenancy of the *Long Acre Tavern* passed to his son, who ran it until his death in 1914. His widow ran it for a further five years, before it was taken over by Mr Withers of the County Brewery at Batheaston.

The *Long Acre Tavern* has a special place in the history of brewing in Bath, as an extract from the *Bath Chronicle* of 14 January 1956 indicates:

> At the weekend, the *Long Acre Tavern* on the main London Road at Walcot is changing hands and this will not only mean the end of a long connection between the Withers family and this establishment, but also will mark the end of "home brewing" in the city – the *Long Acre Tavern* is believed to be the only house in the city still producing its own beer. Ever since 1919, when the Withers family took over, "home brewed" has been available to patrons. Mrs EG Withers, who has been in charge since her husband died, is leaving and the tavern is being taken over by Wadworth & Co, Ltd, brewers, who will bring their own beer from Devizes.

The closure of the *Long Acre* brewery marked the end of brewing in Bath. A craft which almost certainly predated the Roman settlement, and which had been one of the city's main industries in the eighteenth and nineteenth centuries, was no more. It would be another 41 years before the city's drinkers could once again down a pint brewed in Bath.

Unfortunately, the old *Long Acre Tavern* was demolished in the late 1960s (a picture of it appears on page 86 of Peter Coard's *Vanishing Bath*). It was rebuilt and is still open today, an immaculately-preserved piece of 1960s design. The lounge has a clubbish feel, and the bar, with Scandinavian-inspired light wood open beams, seems hardly to have changed since it was built. A telly, constantly on, sits on high, competing with the juke box and the fruit machine. There used to be thousands of pubs like this, but most have changed almost beyond recognition. This one has been cared for with rare dedication. Twenty years hence, heritage buffs will be slapping preservation orders on survivals like this, just as they have stuck one on the *Old Green Tree's* vintage 1920's wood panelling. Is it too much to hope that the *Long Acre Tavern* may survive as a classic example of a style which, although not popular at the moment, will surely become so before too long?

Finally, it is worth pointing out that the *Long Acre Tavern* has not one, but two, international connections. As well as Long Acre House in Melbourne, there is a biker's pub called the *Long Acre Tavern* in Minneapolis.

MANDALYN'S 13 Fountain Buildings, Lansdown Road

The old *Lansdown Arms* at the bottom of Lansdown Road has had a bewildering variety of names in recent years (including the *Black Sheep*, the *Sticky Wicket* and the *New Lansdown*) but today it is firmly established as *Mandalyn's* (an amalgamation of the names of its two licensees).

Its early history is somewhat obscure, but it seems to have opened in the 1770s as the *York House Hotel's* original tap. Although the *York House* was some way away,

some of its stables were right behind the pub. *Mandalyn's* predates the *York House Hotel* by some years, however, and its early-eighteenth century rusticity stands in glaring contrast to the grand buildings around it, which were built much later. Originally, this substantial hipped-roof building would have stood in open countryside, at the side of the road leading up to Lansdown, and with wonderful views over the city.

Around 1805, a new tap for the *York House Hotel* opened in Broad Street (where Ask Restaurant now is) and the pub on Lansdown Road was licensed under a new name – the *Marquis of Lansdown's Arms*. An inventory from 1878 reveals that, with the exception of the tap room, it was quite an upmarket establishment. It consisted of:

> Drawing Room with grand piano, flower stands, 3 oil paintings by Hardy, Sr., 3 water-colour drawings by Hardwick, a water-colour drawing by John Syers, Jr., 2 opal lustres with cut glass drops and centre vase, a bronzed tea urn, lots of cut glass ornaments, and a "smoke consumer and cut-glass moon;"
>
> Dining Room with japanned coal vase and large oil painting by Maggs;
>
> Front Bedroom;
>
> Bar Parlour with panelling, engravings, oil paintings and 10 spittoons;
>
> Bar with serving counter with pewter top;
>
> Tap Room, with 6 spittoons, sawdust and sack, and writing on the walls;
>
> Brewery.

Quite what the writing on the walls of the tap room consisted of must, unfortunately for a student of the graffitic muse, remain a mystery. Perhaps they had something to do with the previous landlord's work as a part-time vet and fly proprietor.

In 1976, when Fred Pearce visited the *Lansdown* (as it was then called), it still had public and lounge bars (the public boasting a memorable display of dirty postcards) and "a back room containing darts and a loud juke box, where the young drinkers go." Today the old *Lansdown Arms* is open-plan, but many old features, such as doors and stained-glass, remain.

Mandalyn's is now firmly established as one of Bath's top bars. It bills itself as "a pub for all sexualities," and with sofas, balloons, skeins of flashing lights, a packed social calendar, entertainment, good food, good beer, and a laid-back friendly attitude, it is a splendid example of how an old boozer can be transformed into a popular twenty-first century hangout without losing sight of what pubs are all about.

MARLBOROUGH TAVERN 35 Marlborough Buildings

The *Marlborough Tavern* has one of the most prestigious and unusual locations in Bath. The first part of Marlborough Buildings (the central part) was built by Thomas Baldwin in the 1770s. The *Marlborough Tavern* probably dates from around the same time, although it may be slightly earlier. It stood by itself at the top of what was then known as Milk Street, on the corner of the road to Weston, well away from Baldwin's short terrace.

In the late 1780s, Marlborough Buildings was extended uphill to meet the *Marlborough Tavern*. It was probably intended that the frontage of the house adjoining the *Marlborough Tavern* should be flush with it, but, as can be seen, the builders got their calculations wrong, and it ended up several feet back.

The *Marlborough Tavern* appears on a map of 1788 (when the northward extension of Marlborough Buildings was less than two years old) as "Chivers' House." It was built over the stream which ran behind the other houses – perhaps so that water would be readily available for brewing beer.

The origin of Marlborough Buildings' name is curious. Most people, if asked to make an educated guess, would say that it has something to do with the Duke of Marlborough. It doesn't. It takes its name from the stream at the back, known as the Muddle Brook – or so the story goes. It is claimed that if you say it fast enough, with an eighteenth-century drawl, you'll get the general idea. Perhaps it's the sort of thing that becomes clearer after a few libations.

The *Marlborough Tavern* was first recorded as a pub in 1800, with James Green as the landlord. It was a popular rendezvous for sedan chairmen and servants, so popular, in fact, that the United Servants' Friendly Society used it as their headquarters. In 1839, the Freemen of the City held an anniversary meeting there, at which apprentices were "treated with cakes and ale." Meehan records that the *Marlborough Tavern* is "said to have been visited by Charles Dickens, when he was visiting his friend Walter Savage Landor in St James's Square. Dickens is said to have found his character Quilp in this neighbourhood."

In the mid-nineteenth century, a single-storey extension was built at the back of the *Marlborough Tavern*, fronting Weston Road. By 1903, there were three entrances from Weston Road, leading to a bar in three compartments, a room behind with a bagatelle table and "a seldom-used club room" upstairs.

In 1922, after serving in the Navy and the Royal Marines, Frank Bodger became the landlord. He stayed there until his death in 1940. His widow, Elizabeth Bodger, carried on until 1964, with help from her son and daughter. Despite being badly

Sedan-chair carrying was thirsty work, especially when it involved a climb up to the northern outskirts of the city

damaged in the Bath Blitz, the *Marlborough Tavern* saw few real changes during Mrs Bodger's tenancy, and its old-world atmosphere was much appreciated by the regulars. Among them was Coco the Clown, who, on his last visit to Bath before Mrs Bodger's retirement – at the age of 75 – presented her with a bronze bust of himself.

Sadly, Mrs Bodger's departure heralded the end of the old *Marlborough Tavern*. Courage's brought in the open-it-up-and-knock-it-through brigade (turning two old smoke rooms and Mrs Bodger's living room into the lounge bar, for example) and another Bath pub was brought a-rocking and a-reelin' into the 1960s.

MIDLAND HOTEL 14 James Street West

The *Midland Hotel* dates from around 1870, when the Midland Railway opened their station at Green Park. In its early days it had 14 bedrooms, a sitting room (with a stuffed parrot and a rosewood couch), a conservatory, a smoking room, a bar (resplendent in mahogany and copper), a bar parlour, a coffee room (with a bronzed tea urn and a framed engraving of "The Midland Officials"), a garden against the west wall and a drawing room. The drawing room was full of High Victorian kitsch, including a rosewood chiffonier, seaweed under glass, a figure under a shade, and engravings of "Queen Victoria," "Rustic Felicity," and "Sunday Morning." A photograph of the floods of October 1882 (reproduced in Adrian Ball's *Yesterday in Bath*) shows a solitary figure piloting an improvised raft down James Street past the Midland Hotel. It also shows the long-gone gardens against the west wall, screened from the street, with statues, wall features, shrubs in large terracotta pots, and wires for Chinese Lanterns – it looks as though it would have been a magical place to spend a summer's evening. Today, most of the old public rooms in the *Midland* have been knocked through into one large bar where bands perform.

There were several other pubs clustered around the old Midland station. On the east side of Charles Street, where Government offices now stand, there were two – the *Railway Hotel* (c1868-c1960) on the corner of James Street West and the *Gloucester House* (c1864-1919), which later became the Albion Private Hotel. A little further along James Street West, where Avery Knight & Bowler's car park now is, was the *White Hart*, which opened around 1805, changed its name to the *Midland & Derby Tavern* when the railway arrived, and later changed it again, to the *Edinburgh Arms*, before closing in 1918.

The *Midland* is the only pub at this end of James Street West these days, but, when this book went to press, the site next door was being redeveloped, and the word on the street was that Wetherspoon's had their eye on it for one of their real-ale outlets. Impossible, of course, to comment on a pub that is not even built, but there are enough Wetherspoon's in other towns and cities for the discriminating drinker to form a reasonable idea of what it will be like. But, if a Wetherspoon's does open, with cheap eats and beer at around a pound a pint, it is likely to be the biggest challenge the *Midland* has faced in its 130-year-plus history.

MOORFIELDS INN 73 Third Avenue, Oldfield Park

Only three licences were ever granted in Oldfield Park – and so stringent had licensing regulations become by the time the area was developed in the late nineteenth century, that these were not new licences, but transfers. In order to get a licence for the *Moorfields Inn* – originally known as the *Moorfields Park Tavern* – the Bath Brewery Company had to surrender the licences of no less than three beerhouses – the *Bird in Hand* in Dolemeads, the *Engineer's Arms* on the Lower Bristol Road, and the *Malakoff Tavern* in Claverton Street. The *Moorfields Park Tavern* received a provisional licence on 13 September 1901, and a full licence just over a year later. The 1903 report noted that it stood in a neighbourhood "partly built on." There was a bar with a bagatelle room and a jug & bottle department. "There is also," the report stated, "a large room for billiards, but at present without table, and used occasionally for club meetings." The layout of the *Moorfield Inn* has changed little since. It has been updated and adapted without compromising its essential character. A busy social calendar includes regular live entertainment and sports league fixtures.

NEW BURNT HOUSE 628 Wellsway

The *New Burnt House* appears as Burnt House Farm on Harcourt Masters' Turnpike Map of 1787. At that time, Wellsway had not been built. The only road running past the *Burnt House* was the one at the back, now known as Upper Bloomfield Road. However, at that time, the *Burnt House* faced the other way, and what is now the front entrance was at the back.

The *Burnt House* opened as a beerhouse sometime before 1871. It was a favourite stopping place for coal hauliers en route to Bath from the North Somerset Coalfield. An inventory carried out when the landlord, Thomas Stride, died in 1875 reveals that it consisted of a bar, a tap room and a parlour, none of which had a serving counter, although the bar had a four-motion beer engine. It also had a brewhouse at the back.

In 1898, Thomas Stride Jr, having undertaken extensive improvements, applied for a full licence. He presented a strong case. The accommodation at the inn was excellent. There was a bar with a separate jug & bottle counter, plus a tap room and glass room. Outside was a half-acre garden, a stable for seven horses, a coach house, a brewing house, a cattle stand and a skittle alley. There were also plans to build a tea room for lady cyclists. He also pointed out that the *Burnt House* had brewed its own beer for the past 25 years. The *Cross Keys* was a mile away and both the *Crossways Inn* at Dunkerton and the *Jubilee* at Twerton were around a mile and a half away. The closest pub was the *Red Lion*, but even that was half a mile away, and much of the traffic which passed the *Burnt House* did not pass the *Red Lion*. Despite opposition from the landlord of the *Red Lion*, the licence was granted.

The *Burnt House* stayed in the Stride family until December 1961, when Bill Stride died. The following year it was sold for £10,000. Since then it has been known as the *Lamplighter* and *Strydes** and is now called the *New Burnt House*. Internally, it has changed dramatically, but externally it appears much as it did a century ago. The bay windows added by Thomas Stride are still there, now linked by an elegant veranda, and on the outbuilding to the right there is still a ring to tether your horse to, should you feel so inclined.

There are several stories as to how the pub got its name. In one, the farm, which doubled as a turnpike house, was burnt down by gipsies. In another, the turnpike house stood nearby and was burnt down by local colliers protesting against the tolls they had to pay to carry their coal to Bath.

NEW CROWN 21 Newbridge Hill, Lower Weston

Stripped pine predominates in this street-corner local – in the quiet, orange-painted, orange-lit back bar; in the small, busy, low-ceilinged front bar, with windows on three sides; down by the dartboard, where youngsters congregate. So keen were they on pine when they revamped the *New Crown* that any old dark wood left around was painted to look like pine as well.

It is called the *New Crown*, not to distinguish it from the *Old Crown* in Upper Weston, but because it replaced a pub that stood further down Newbridge Hill, roughly where No 11 is today. Newbridge Hill formed part of the old turnpike road from Bath to Bristol, and the old *Crown* was ideally placed to attract passing trade. However, it was by-passed when Newbridge Road opened and the coming of the railway led to a further decline in traffic. When plans were drawn up to develop the area in the 1870s, it was decided to pull the old pub down and build a new one on the corner of Chelsea Road.

---

* Apparently the Stride family objected to their name being used as the name of the pub, and the spelling was changed accordingly.

This opened in 1878 as the *New Crown*, subsequently changed to the *Crown Brewery*, but later reverted to its original name. The remains of the brewery, which closed around the time of the First World War, can be seen at the back. The single-storey extension on the corner, which houses the front bar, was once the entrance to the pub.

NEW INN 23-24 Monmouth Place, Upper Bristol Road

The *New Inn* is a traditional local with separate snug and public bars, real fires, good beer, cheap food and nicotine-coloured walls. It opened sometime around 1837 as a beerhouse called the *Monmouth Arms*. In its early days a cooper called Sam Gunningham operated from the house next door.

This part of Bath has always been somewhat off the main drag, but if plans for Bath's first railway had gone ahead, it could have been very different. In 1830, three years before the Great Western Railway Company was formed, a group of businessmen tried to get a Bath & Bristol Railway Act through parliament. The line would have followed a similar route to that later chosen by Brunel, except that, at the Bath end, it would have run across the Lower Commons to a terminus just behind the *New Inn*. Vested interests – landowners, stagecoach operators and the canal company – conspired to scupper the scheme, but it is an intriguing thought that, had things been different, jaded travellers might have been nipping into the *New Inn* for a swift pint on their way to catch the train.

NEW WESTHALL
Westhall Buildings, Upper Bristol Road

The *Westhall Inn* was first recorded as a beerhouse run by John Hudson in 1841. Around 1854, for reasons that are obscure, he changed its name to the *Quiet Woman*. It is possible that the name referred to a type of oilcan called a quiet woman and indicated that John Hudson was carrying out some kind of trade there. However, pubs in other parts of the country still called the *Quiet Woman* or the *Silent Woman* carry no reference to an oilcan. The signs of several, in fact, have a sign showing a decapitated woman, suggesting that the name is no more than an anti-feminist jibe.

John Hudson's son, William, changed the pub's name back to the *Westhall Inn* around 1866. It was badly damaged in the Bath Blitz but was rebuilt and is still open today as the *New Westhall*.

According to Meehan, the name of the inn came from "a famous residence once close by – West Hall, the Bath home of Holwell of the 'Black Hole of Calcutta.' The old inn was partly built with stone from Holwell's demolished residence." The Black Hole of Calcutta was a tiny cell into which 146 British captives were crammed by the Nawab of Bengal in 1756, as part of his attempt to kick the East India Company out of India. Conditions were appalling, and the next morning, when the guards came to inspect the prisoners, they found that 123 of them had died. At least that is the story, the only source for which was an account written by one of the survivors, John Zephaniah Holwell. The accuracy of the story has been challenged many times, but the important thing about it is that the British Government not only took it seriously but used it as justification for giving the East India Company carte blanche to do what it wanted. Holwell was eventually rewarded with the Governorship of Bengal. He died in Pinner in 1798.

A curious feature of the *New Westhall* is that it only has windows at the front. Not a black hole exactly, but it is curious to come out of the daylight into a largely windowless space. The main bar, with 1980s-style wooden partitions and deep red décor, is vaguely reminiscent of the Bridge Bar at New Street Station, and seems to be the only one in regular use, although there is a pool room and another bar at the front of the building. It is a pity that it does not get more custom, especially as it is the only Wadworth's pub in this part of town.

OLD CROWN 131 High Street, Twerton

Twerton's *Old Crown* is a venerable old building in which much of the atmosphere of a Somersetshire village inn survives. It dates back to at least 1760 when the following notice appeared in the *Bath Journal*:

> To be sold at the *Crown Inn* at Twerton ... five wagon horses, with their harness, with a good wagon and about five tons of good English hay, now standing near the *Packhorse* on Midford Hill.

When Fred Pearce visited in 1976 he described it as a:

> pleasant little two-bar pub with so little custom that the lounge is often left shut. Sad, because it's a nice place with good beer, a fine old dresser with the original clock set into it, and even a bunch of foliage over the bar (with rail).

Today it has been knocked into one but it still has a distinctly old-world feel, helped by the low ceilings, uneven walls and nineteenth-century framed prints.

The *Old Crown* is the only pub in Twerton High Street today, but there were once five others – the *George*, the *White Hart*, the *Ring of Bells*, the *Queen's Head*, and the *Wheatsheaf*.

The *George*, described in 1787 as "that old accustom'd house ... much the best house in the parish for entertaining travellers," was next door to the *Old Crown* at No 132. It closed around 1878.

A little further along, at Nos 142-144, was the *White Hart*, which dated back to at least 1767. Its demise was tragic. In 1899, the Bath Brewery Company closed it and transferred its licence to the *Victoria Hotel* in Oldfield Park. The Twerton Lodge of Good Templars bought the *White Hart* for £355 and reopened it as a Temperance Institute and Restaurant. At the opening ceremony on 16 May 1899, the Templars burst the old vats and broke "other things connected with alcohol." Although the Temperance Institute has gone, the words *White Hart Templar Institution and Restaurant ... Twerton Lodge* are still faintly visible above the door.

The *Ring of Bells* was across the road at 4 High Street and the *Queen's Head* was between the *White Hart* and the *George*. The *Wheatsheaf*, further up the street, is now a carpet shop.

OLD CROWN 1 Lansdown Place, Upper Weston

Weston's *Old Crown* was first recorded as "the *Chequer*" in 1712. It was later acquired by Moses Collins and renamed the *Crown*. The initials of William Collins, Moses' son, who took over the inn from his father, appear on the end wall of the inn, along with the date 1786. The *Old Crown* is a real hotch-potch of buildings and styles, and, while it is difficult to unravel its development, there is no doubt that it has been around for a very long time

The most celebrated moment in its history came in 1792 when a wake was held there for Samuel Purlewent, an Attorney of Lincoln's Inn in London, to whom William Collins had mortgaged the property 38 years earlier. It was no ordinary wake, and the funeral that preceded it was no ordinary funeral. The terms of Mr Purlewent's will saw to that:

It is my express wish that I may be buried at Weston in the County of Somerset, if I die there, if not to be carried down there (but not in a hearse) nor will I have any parade or coach to attend upon me but let me be carried in any vehicle with all expedition possible so that the same does not exceed the sum of £25, and when I arrive there I direct six poor people of Weston do support my corpse to the grave and that six poor women and six poor men do attend me to the grave, and that I may be buried at 12 noon and that each of them do have half a guinea; and I hereby order and direct that a good boiled ham, a dozen fowls, a sirloin of beef, with plum puddings, may be provided at the *Crown* Inn at Weston, for the said 18 poor people besides the clerk and sexton. And I will allow five guineas for the same: and I request and hope they will be as merry and cheerful as possible, for I conceive it a mere farce to put on the grimace of weeping, snivelling, crying and the like, which can answer no good end, either to the living or dead, and which I reprobate in the highest terms. I desire that after I am buried there be a cold collation provided at the *Crown* –

a sirloin of beef, potatoes, and a fillet of veal, with plenty of good ale, when I hope they will refresh themselves with decency and propriety. No friends or relations whatsoever are to attend my funeral.

The year before Mr Purlewent's wake, the *Crown* had been taken over by William Morgan of Morgan's Brewery in Trafalgar Road, Weston. Brewing continued at the *Crown*, however, and the sign, "Home Brewed Beer," can still be seen chiselled into its

wall today. Around 1800 there was an attempt to attract visitors who had walked over the fields from Bath to stop off at the *Crown* by opening a pleasure garden there. Who knows, perhaps even Jane Austen herself nipped in for a quick cup of tea after one of her rambles over to Weston. Certainly, the *Crown* never seems to have been anything but an eminently respectable establishment.

The same, sadly, cannot be said for all of its customers. The following sorry tale comes from a police report of 1870:

William Fletcher was summoned for assaulting Ann Spratt, the landlady of the *Crown* at Weston ... Complainant said that on Monday night the defendant and another man were drinking at her house, and on leaving the room the defendant followed her and knocked her down, his trousers being unbuttoned at the time, and he attempted to take liberties with her.

Fletcher's defence that he had been led on by Mrs Spratt was dismissed and he was sent down for three months.

Today, the *Crown*, despite being family-friendly, with an emphasis on food, still has much of the atmosphere of an old village inn, while its garden, on a terrace overlooking the Locksbrook Valley, is deservedly popular.

OLD FARMHOUSE 1 Lansdown Road

The *Old Farmhouse* was built in the late nineteenth century, but the farmhouse which once stood on the site was opened as a beerhouse in the 1840s by a pork butcher called Ambrose Cooper. Its original name was the *Old Farmhouse 1632*, suggesting that the building dated – or was believed to date – from the early seventeenth century. No details of the old building have come down to us, but the present building is a splendid example of the arts and crafts style of pub design pioneered by Norman Shaw in the 1870s. The flower on the side of the building recalls the exuberant rococo plant designs on textiles in the Great Exhibition of 1851. An inventory prepared just after it opened gives us a good idea of what it was like inside:

Bar: Carpet. The complete fittings to bar with cathedral and other glass, the whole being in perfect condition.

Jug & bottle: Photo of Old Farmhouse.

Lobby: Coconut mat and label on door: "Gentlemen Only."

Smoking room: Photo of *Old Farmhouse*, gong, marble timepiece, two bronze figures, two oil paintings, framed and glazed map.

The most intriguing items in the list are, of course, the two photos of the Old Farm House. Were they of the building that disappeared – and, if so, what happened to them?

In 1903, the pub was owned by George Biggs, the licensee of the *Crown Brewery* in New Orchard Street, the *Oxford Brewery* in Julian Road (both demolished) and the *White Horse* (now the *Dark Horse*) in Northampton Street. The licensee of the *Old Farmhouse* was Harry Biggs. The bar was in three compartments with a jug & bottle department and glass room, and there was a brewery at the rear.

The *Old Farmhouse* was a beerhouse until 1957, when the *Portland Arms* in Portland Place closed, and its full licence was transferred to the *Old Farmhouse*. A year later, Fred Pearce visited it and found a pub that bears little relation to the one that is there today. This was his description of it:

Cockles (22p a jar), cackle and camaraderie! Small simple working men's (and women's) pub. Red rose plant on the bar has a note: "my sincere thanks to you all" it reads. It's that kind of pub. Simple cream and brown decor in public and smoking room, plus open fire and the supremely knowledgeable Mrs Moore (who calls everyone under 80 "lad") behind the bar, all complete the 1940's feel of the place. No music – just people.

That was before John Bradshaw (whose face appears on the pub sign) moved up here from the *Bell*. Today the *Old Farmhouse* is Bath's answer to Ronnie Scott's. On most nights of the week a jazz combo can be found giving it their all in a room plastered from floor to ceiling with memorabilia from the 'seventies and 'eighties – Private Eye covers, gig posters, Bristol Rovers team photos and so on. The atmosphere is terrific – informal, nostalgic, and above all there is no entry fee. What is more, Abbey Ales, whose Bellringer Beer can be found at many pubs throughout the city and further afield, is brewed at the back of the pub. You cannot really ask for more than that.

OLD GREEN TREE 12 Green Street

Green Street, just round the corner from the North Gate, was one of the first streets to be built outside the city walls. Its first houses date from 1716, when, as John Wood tells us, "a street was begun to be erected upon the new bowling green, the inhabitants of Bath having been animated by the great concourse of strangers to the city, the year before, to increase the private accommodations of the place." Today, Green Street contains one of Bath's best-known and best-loved pubs – the *Old Green Tree* at No 12 – with its three tiny wood-panelled rooms.

The *Old Green Tree* probably dates from 1716 or 1717. In June 1716, John Cornish, a milliner, bought "part of the late bowling green" from Mary and Joseph Walters of Bristol.

The following year, he sold part of the site to Jeremiah Wiltshire, a maltster. The plot he sold was on the southern side of the street, now covered by Nos 15-18. The deed of sale stated that the plot was bound on its eastern side – i.e., where No 14 is now – by a stable and garden. The only part of the street kept by John Cornish was the short stretch now covered by Nos 12-14. If he had erected a stable where No 14 now stands, it seems reasonable to assume that this was attached to a house – possibly a lodging house – next door, at Nos 12 and 13. If this was the case, then it gives the *Old Green Tree* a fairly precise dating of around 1716-1717. Architectural details – such as the step down into the building (indicating that the street was raised after the building was erected), and evidence of a winding cupboard staircase inside the building – also support such a dating.

Like the *Star* on the Vineyards, the *Old Green Tree* appears on CAMRA's national inventory of 242 British pubs whose interiors are particularly well preserved. It has changed very little since it was extensively remodelled in 1928 by the Lamb Brewery of Frome. The frontage, the wood-panelling and most of the bar fittings date from then. The smoke room at the back – where smoking is punishable by hanging upside down and being beaten unconscious with a wet carp – was originally part of the brewery (which closed in the 1920s), and was incorporated into the building at the same time. The beam across the ceiling halfway down the main bar indicates where the back wall of the building was until 1928.

Despite its interior being much more recent than the *Star*'s, it is tempting to think that a regular from a century or more ago would feel equally at home in the *Old Green Tree*. And perhaps he would have a few choice tales to tell of the old days – like this one which appeared in the *Bath Journal* in 1899:

> A well-known purveyor, who lived not far from the *Green Tree*, and sometimes disbursed a deal of his money and his time at that hostelry, on one occasion backed himself for a ten-pound note, although upwards of 60 years of age, to walk to Wells [a distance of 20 miles] in four hours. The feat was accomplished with time to spare, but it took Jacob more than four days to get back, for after arriving at the Cathedral city and partaking of sundry drops with friends, he, to adopt his own phrase, donned his "sitting breeches," and the whole of the ten-pound note he had won and a little besides was expended before he turned his head homeward. (Bath Journal, 22 July 1899)

Ten pounds back then was equivalent to around £500 today. It must have been some bender.

An inventory of the contents of the *Old Green Tree* from 1870 makes an interesting comparison with the scene today. Upstairs, there was a servants' room, a front garret, a WC with a hip bath and water can, and a best bedroom. The smoking room, at the front, had a Kidderminster carpet, three mahogany drinking tables, a sofa, two easy chairs, a cane chair, some folding chairs, window seats with cushions, a small round fancy table, a two-light gasolier, seven oil paintings, four prints, eleven chimney ornaments and two china bowls. The bar had a five-motion beer engine, a metal-top serving counter, and a fixed partition forming a bar parlour. In the bar parlour were a copper kettle and beer warmer, a chimney glass, nine chimney ornaments, five paintings and two prints, fixed seating and two iron spittoons. At the back was a small tap

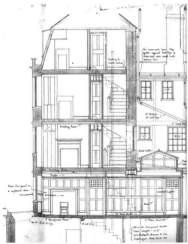

Plans for the refurbishment of the *Old Green Tree*, drawn up bt WA Williams of 20 Old Bond Street for the Lamb Brewery Ltd in 1928.

room with two drinking tables, and the brewery.

Today the *Old Green Tree* is one of Bath's best-loved boozers, with a constantly-changing array of real ales, excellent home-cooked food at lunchtimes (and not a chip or a bowl of microwaved lasagne in sight), and a loyal band of regulars supplemented by those who come to marvel at this wood-panelled oasis in the heart of Bath. The quirky sign, based on Botticelli's *Birth of Venus*, with a bottletop instead of a shell, and Venus clutching a tree, was one of three designs submitted by the artist. The other two can seen inside. On summer evenings the *Old Green Tree* is also the starting point for one of the city's most popular guided tours – the Great Bath Pub Crawl.

O'NEILLS 1 Barton Street

In the nineteenth century, it was not uncommon for pubs to be pulled down to make way for churches. One of Bath's pubs even became a church – the *Shakespeare* in Old Orchard Street, which closed during the First World War, is now the home of Bath's Spiritualist congregation. Recently, however, the tables have turned, and *O'Neill's* is an example of a church which has become a pub. Bath's first Unitarian Chapel, which counted the poet Samuel Taylor Coleridge among its preachers, was in Frog Lane. When Frog Lane was pulled down to make way for New Bond Street, a new Unitarian Chapel was built on the corner of Trim Street. Today, however, it spreads a different kind of gospel – with a distinctive Irish brogue.

PARK TAVERN 3 Park Lane

The *Park Tavern*, originally known as the *Blue Lodge*, dates back at least as far as 1766, when St John's Hospital leased a "messuage or tenement, stable, coach house and summer houses thereto belonging commonly called … the *Blue Lodge*" to Walter Dallamore, who also held the lease of several other pubs in Bath. The *Blue Lodge* is, in fact, one of the city's forgotten pleasure gardens. Although its attractions were modest compared with those

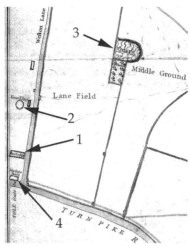

An early nineteeth-century map showing: 1 the *Blue Lodge*; 2 a limekiln; 3 a quarry; 4 the turnpike on the Upper Bristol Road.

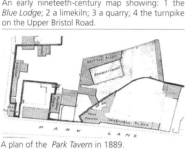

A plan of the *Park Tavern* in 1889.

of Spring or Sydney Gardens, it must have been a pleasant place to wander out to on a summer afternoon when the Upper Bristol Road was no more than a cart track, Royal Victoria Park was pastureland grazed by sheep, and there were no factories to hide the view of the river and the water meadows and green hills in the distance. Industry was confined to some lime kilns up the hill from the *Blue Lodge*, hence the original name of Park Lane – Limekiln Lane.

In 1832, two years after the opening of Royal Victoria Park, Walter Wiltshire took over the lease of the *Blue Lodge* and renamed it the *Victoria Park Tavern*. In August 1832, the *Bath Chronicle* reported that

> the annual carnation feast was held at the *Victoria Park Tavern*, where a highly respectable company sat down to an excellent dinner provided by Mr Wiltshire, the landlord.

Around 1846, a single-storey extension was added to the south wall of the *Park Tavern*, Lark Place was built on the Upper Bristol Road, and five new houses were added to an existing block to form Westhall Place.

On 26 September 1848, a new attraction opened behind the pub:

> On Thursday the excellent racket and fives courts erected by Mr Bussey at the *Park Tavern* were opened for play, when a numerous and respectable company assembled. The game of rackets may be said to be new to Bath, and consequently the trial of skill lay exclusively between strangers.

At the time of the 1903 report the lease of the *Park Tavern* was held by William Mortimer, who also owned the *White Horse* in Larkhall. There was a garden at the back, together with a brewery, and a door opening into "Mr Clarke's stables." The pub's accommodation consisted of a serving bar in the passage, a tap room on the right and a glass room on the left.

The building was badly damaged in the Bath Blitz of April 1942, but was soon rebuilt. Its layout is still much as it was in 1903. However, the thatched roof over the bar and the backlit bowl of flowers in the lounge which Fred Pearce found when he visited in 1976 have disappeared.

PICCADILLY Piccadilly, London Road

Until recently, the *Piccadilly* was known as the *Britannia*. Its original name, however, was the *Hanover Hotel*. It dates back to at least 1796, when John Adams was the landlord. From 1803, it was the meeting place of the Walcot Union Society. In 1828, the *Bath Chronicle* reported that "on Christmas day according to annual custom, JH

Acherley Esq. gave a dinner of roast beef and plumb pudding to fifty old men and women at the *Britannia Inn*, Walcot, whose united age amounted to 3,250 years."

The *Britannia* is an intriguing building. In the absence of documentary evidence, we can only guess how it developed from the evidence of the building itself. It seems likely that it was there before the building next door, and also predated the street on the other side. It seems to have been the misfortune of the original owners of the property to be hemmed in on both sides by aggressive developers. The house next door jutted forward into the London Road, while the street on the other side ran diagonally up the wall of the inn, cutting off most of the light from the ground-floor windows at the back. All the owners of the *Britannia* could do was extend the building forward, and, sometime in the early to mid-nineteenth century, that is what they did, giving us the exceptionally pleasant single-storey frontage which is still there today.

The *Britannia* is a very common pub name, borne by about 150 pubs nationwide. Many, such as the superb old inn on the harbourfront in Ilfracombe, date from the eighteenth century, when the cult of Britannia was at its height. It really took off in 1740, when Thomas Arne set some words by James Thomson to music. *Rule Britannia* has been an unofficial national anthem ever since. The figure of Britannia, which appeared on pre-decimal pennies, though, had been around for a good deal longer, having made its debut on a medal struck in 1665. The model for Britannia was Frances Stewart, the mistress of Charles II and later the Duchess of Richmond. There is thus an obscure (and, it must be said, remarkably tenuous) connection between the *Britannia* on London Road and the *Richmond Arms* in Richmond Place.

At the time of Bath's notorious "drunken election" in 1841, the landlord of the *Britannia* supported the Tory candidates. In the alcohol-fuelled rioting that preceded the election, his pub was naturally a prime target for rampaging liberals. The *Bath Chronicle* reported that:

at the *Britannia Inn*, Walcot, an almost complete demolition of the glass has been effected by the friends of Roebuck and Duncan. . . . The *Hand & Shears*, Walcot Street, the *Crown & Thistle*, Avon Street, Messrs Vezey's coach factory [near the *Long Acre Tavern*] and the *White Horse* Cellar have also shared the "Liberal" furies.

When an inventory of the *Britannia* was drawn up in 1873, it consisted of a bar, a tap room, a parlour, a club room, three bedrooms and a skittle alley. By the time of the 1903 report, the pub was in the hands of the Anglo-Bavarian Brewery of Shepton Mallet. The skittle alley had become a store for baker's trucks. The bar was in three compartments with a glass room adjoining and a small compartment for outdoor trade. At the back was a door leading into Hanover Square, where there were seven small cottages and Bassons' Corn Stores.

In 1976, Fred Pearce found that "the bare walls of the tiny public [contrasted] with the over-fussy decor of the large lounge." The "nice frosted pub glass on the front windows" and the nineteenth-century frontage which he admired are still there, but the partitions between the bars have gone, giving the interior a light, airy feel. The skittle alley, disused a century ago, is very much back in business, and with free pool, curry and a pint for a fiver, seven plays on the jukebox for a £1, and a weekly snowball, it is hardly surprising that it is generally busy.

Today, the *Britannia* has jettisoned its old name and taken the name of the terrace where it stands – *Piccadilly*. Just as Spring Gardens and Sydney Gardens Vauxhall were named after London pleasure gardens, so this part of London Road was called after a fashionable part of the capital to give it a certain social cachet. Oddly enough, however, London's Piccadilly owes its name to someone from this part of the country. Around 1600, Robert Baker, a Somerset tailor, made a fortune by persuading polite society that frilly lace ruffs were a must-have fashion accessory. He dubbed them pickadills (from a Spanish word meaning pricked or pierced) and with the proceeds built himself a grand house in London called Pickadill Hall. The area around the hall later became known as Piccadilly.

PIG & FIDDLE 4 Saracen Street

The *Pig & Fiddle* is one of Bath's newest pubs. Opened in the late 1980s by two Bath brothers – Chris and Paul Clark – in the former fish restaurant on Saracen Street, it has since expanded into Broad Street, taking over what was previously a tapestry shop in 1997. A century ago, as a photograph inside the pub shows, the Broad Street shop was an opticians. Today it specialises in a different type of glasses.

The *Pig & Fiddle* – with one of the biggest on-street patios in the city and fanatical table-footie players – is an up-beat, youth-oriented venue, but also merits a glowing entry in the *Good Beer Guide* for the range and quality of its ales. Always busy, especially when the footie's on the big screen, the heated beer garden at the back is one of Bath's top spots to sit and watch the world go by – if you can get a table. Inside, blazing fires, quirky decor and nice architectural touches add up to a pub that, while attracting a theme-club crowd, is much more than your average theme pub. And if you get bored you can always watch the fish.

Saracen Street, incidentally, is the only street in Bath named after a pub, and was knocked through a load of old buildings in the 1960s to turn the bottom of Walcot Street and the bottom of Broad Street into a maxi-roundabout.

PORTER 15 George Street

It is odd that two of Bath's pubs – the *Porter* and the *Porter Butt* – should be named after a drink which, although wildly popular in the nineteenth century, is rarely

encountered today. It is appropriate that it should be commemorated, though, for in its time it was little short of revolutionary.

Around 1730, Ralph Harwood made one of the most far-reaching breakthroughs in brewing history at his brewery in Shoreditch. At the time, many people drank something called "three threads." Drinkers in many parts of the country still regularly ask for a "half and half" – half a pint of one type of beer mixed with half a pint of another. "Three-threads" took this idea once step further, with three different beers served in one mug. In the days before beer engines, when beer had to be drawn from barrels, this was a tedious process. What Mr Harwood did was to brew a beer which tasted like three threads, but came out of one barrel. He called it "entire butt" or "entire," but it was quickly rechristened "porter," allegedly because of its phenomenal success among the porters in London's markets.

Porter was made from barley roasted at a higher temperature than usual. This charred it and gave the beer its characteristic dark colour. The use of London water gave it a soft taste, in sharp contrast to the gypsum-generated kick of beers from Burton on Trent, which was already gaining a reputation as one of England's top brewing centres. The introduction of porter heralded a revolution in the brewing industry as it was the first beer technically suited to mass production. Not only did it keep longer than other beers, it could be brewed over a longer period. Traditionally, the brewing season lasted from October to May, but porter could be brewed from September to June. One slight drawback was that it needed longer to mature. The problem was not so much one of throughput but of contamination by airborne infection. Brewers solved this by building larger and larger vats, thus decreasing the area exposed to the air relative to the quantity of beer. So not only was mass production of porter possible, it was positively desirable.

The introduction of porter enabled the rich pickings tied up in the licensed trade to be exploited. Like ironmaking before the invention of coke-fired furnaces, or weaving before the invention of mechanised mills, brewing was a localised, small-scale enterprise. Stories like that of Arthur Guinness of Dublin, who in 1799 switched from small-scale beer production to porter in a bid to challenge the English brewers' domination of the Irish market, and never looked back, would simply not have been possible a century earlier. It was in the eighteenth century that the big brewery empires were founded – Whitbread (1742), Charrington (1766), and Courage (1789) in London; Worthington (1744) and Bass (1777) in Burton on Trent; and George's (1788) in Bristol.

In 1837, Martin Hiscox opened a "bottled liquor vaults" at 2 Miles's Buildings, round the corner from what is now the front entrance of the *Porter*. By 1841, John Pasmore, who had held the licence of the *Star & Garter* in Lilliput Alley and the *Pelican* in Bloomfield Terrace, took it over and called it the *Porter Stores*.

By 1903, still confined to 2 Miles's Buildings, the *Porter Stores* consisted of a bar with a glass room behind. Today, the *Porter* has been extended into 15 George Street, formerly Redman's Grocers. In 1995 it was taken over by Phil Andrews, the owner of Moles' Nightclub. Although the *Porter* is very much a young person's pub, it is unlike any other young person's pub in the city. It is, quite simply, a great meeting place, with an interconnected warren of drinking areas, plus a terrific outside area in Miles's Buildings. An imaginative range of vegetarian food is also available until 9pm.

Downstairs, the *Porter Cellar Bar* feels like the sort of place the Beatles played in before they were famous. There is live music there most nights of the week, with a comedy club on Sundays. An imaginatively gloomy colour scheme really cashes in on the atmosphere of the place, while drinking booths in the vaults under Miles's Buildings are vaguely reminiscent of those high-settled cubbyholes that always seem to feature in paintings of old inns. There is more than a whiff of the 1960s about the *Porter* and its cellar bar, but this has nothing to do with retro-chic or hankering for the past. It is just that the energy and enthusiasm that characterised those far-off days, before the marketing men clambered onto the youth bandwagon, still survives there.

All in all, it is not surprising that the *Porter* is rarely quiet. But how many of the *Porter's* patrons know that, high up, on the corner of the building, sits a sphinx?

PORTER BUTT York Place, London Road

The *Porter Butt* was first recorded in 1787 with John Mason as landlord, but it may well be much older. It has always been a sizeable establishment. On Harcourt Masters' Turnpike Map, which also dates from 1787, its grounds are shown stretching down to the river. The Kensington Brewery, next door, also had access to the river.

The *Porter Butt* stayed in the Mason family until at least 1809. By 1816, it had been taken over by John Follett. The alehouse recognizances for that year, however, list Mr Follett as the licensee not only of the *Old Porter Butt* but also of the *New Porter Butt*. What he seems to have done is build a new pub in front of the old one, keeping the old one open until the new one was ready, and subsequently absorbing it into the new premises. 1816 was the transitional year, for by 1817 the *Old Porter Butt* had slipped from the licensing register, leaving Mr Follett with the *New Porter Butt*. A note in the *Bath Chronicle* of 27 August 1917 refers to the "centenary of the opening of the *Porter Butt*," indicating that the new pub opened in August 1817.

By the following year, 1818, the *New Porter Butt* was listed as the *Butt Inn & Tavern*. It continued to be referred as the *New Butt* until at least 1829, however, when it appeared under that name in a list of Bath's principal inns. Its importance was

A nineteenth-century advertisement for the Kensington Brewery, with the *Porter Butt* on the left.

underlined by it being the starting point for a daily coach service to Bristol, introduced around 1819 for the convenience of people living in the Grosvenor area. It was also the first inn travellers from London came to, and, although less prestigious and less convenient than those in the town centre, it was ideally placed to attract visitors seeking a semi-rural location. At this time there were also plans to build a bridge across the river at the back of the *Porter Butt*. This would have given it the inn an even more favourable position, but, in 1827, the scheme was abandoned in favour of a bridge at Cleveland Place.

By 1822, Len Roberts had taken over the *Porter Butt*. He was the victim of something which is still a headache for today's landlords – the passing of forged currency. Whereas today it is Scottish £20 notes, however, forgers in 1822 were more modest in their aspirations, as this report from the *Bath Chronicle* indicates:

> Committed to Shepton Gaol, Charlotte and Catherine Hawkins (mother and daughter), for tendering in payment to Mr L Roberts of the *Porter Butt Inn*, Walcot, a counterfeit shilling, and having in their possession at the same time eleven other counterfeit shillings.

In 1836 the prominent local citizen, Mr JH Acherley, moved his annual Christmas dinner for 50 old Walcotians from the *Britannia* to the *Porter Butt*. In 1841, Daniel Gillen took over the *Porter Butt* and announced that he could supply "landaus, gig and saddle horses on the shortest notice, also a hearse and mourning coaches to any distance."

When the coaching business collapsed because of the opening of the railway, Mr Gillen tried to develop the land at the back of the *Porter Butt* into a Pleasure Garden. On 5 August 1841, the *Bath Chronicle* informed its readers that "a rowing match, for amateurs, is appointed to come off in the water at the back of Mr D Gillen's, the *Porter Butt*, Walcot, on Monday next." Other events were organised, which inevitably attracted a few unwanted visitors. In September 1841, the *Bath Chronicle* carried another story:

> On Monday evening last [a thief called George Williams] went to the Gala at the *Porter Butt* in Walcot, where there was an exhibition of fireworks. Mr Ford, a tailor, residing on the Upper Borough Walls, was present, and while viewing the display he felt someone attempting to extract his handkerchief, who upon enquiry proved to be Williams. He was taken into custody, and the charge of attempting being clear against him he was committed on Tuesday for three months.

Three months for attempting to steal a handkerchief seems a shade draconian. If you reported that sort of thing today, the chances are you would be charged with wasting police time.

The Pleasure Garden idea did not take off and, in 1843, the *Porter Butt* was advertised to let "with skittle ground." George Brinkworth took the lease which he held until his death in 1867, when the inn closed and was put up for sale.

The following year, it was bought by Mark Baggs from the *Bell* on the Lower

Bristol Road. At the time, the *Porter Butt's* public rooms consisted of a bar, a tap room, a long room, a parlour and five bedrooms. The clientele were clearly highly literate, for the bar's contents included a writing desk, Bath, Somerset and London Directories and a dictionary.

A two-gallon jar from Mark Baggs of the *Porter Butt.*

Mark Baggs, who also acquired the Kensington Brewery next door, wasted no time in making changes at the *Porter Butt*. On 4 January 1869 the Council Surveying Committee Minutes recorded that "plans for proposed alteration at the *Porter Butt* Public house were submitted and approved and consent to proceed with buildings given." The description of the layout of the pub in the 1903 report will still, despite certain modifications, be familiar to today's regulars: "Open serving bar in passage with bar parlour on left and room partitioned off inside on right."

In 1880, horse trams were introduced to Bath and a depot for them was established at the back of the *Porter Butt*. The depot was later described by a correspondent in the *Bath Chronicle* as "the equine power station of the old Bath tramway system which extended from the Great Western Station to Lambridge." He went on to recall that, "long after the system of electric trams was opened in 1904, the light narrow-gauge truck used by the horse-drawn trams could be seen in the yard of the *Porter Butt*." There was also a field at the back of the pub for grazing the horses and a landing stage on the river – a distant reminder of the days when Mr Gillen tried to establish a pleasure garden there.

At one time, the part of the London Road where the *Porter Butt* stood was subject to flooding. In November 1894, for example, "the Grosvenor district was cut off from the city by a sheet of water covering the dip by the *Porter Butt Hotel*, and, of course, invading the tram yard and stables to a considerable depth."

The *Porter Butt* is a lively pub, renowned for live music – acoustic sessions shoehorned into the snug on Friday nights, with local rock bands appearing in the Walcot Palais out the back. It has a large walled garden – although this no longer stretches down to the river. It is worth walking round to the back of the pub to look at the range of building styles and try to work out how the inn developed. Although the front part clearly dates from the rebuilding of 1817, parts of it appear to date from well before 1787, when the *Porter Butt* was first recorded as an inn.

PULP 38 Monmouth Street

Pulp, which occupies part of the Seven Dials development – with *Los Iguanas* restaurant upstairs – may seem to have little to do with Bath's early licensed history, but, in fact,

the whole of Seven Dials is on the site of an inn. What is more, the layout of the modern block is remarkably similar to that of the old inn. The Seven Dials courtyard, for example, is virtually the same shape as the old inn yard, while the porticoed entrance to the record shop on the corner stands on the site of the yard's entrance.

The *Londonderry Inn* dated back at least as far as 1717, when Joan Webb leased it from St John's Hospital. It was described as being outside the walls, near the Westgate, between the highway leading to Weston on the south and west, a way leading under the Borough Walls on the east and the "town mixen" or dungheap on the north. (The site of the town mixen, incidentally, is now occupied by the *Garrick's Head*.)

The *Londonderry* was later renamed the *Globe* and became one of the city's top theatrical venues. In 1747, the *Bath Journal* announced that

we hear that the Bath Company of Comedians have taken the Great Room at the *Globe*, without Westgate, which is making very commodious [sic]; and that they intend to perform on Monday next the Tragedy of Theodosius or the Force of Love; with the entertainment of Miss in her Teens, or the Medley of Lovers, as it is now at the Theatre Royal, Covent Garden, London. The prices 2/6 and 1/6.

Other plays given that season included Ambrose Philips' *The Distressed Mother*, *Oroonoko*, *The Lying Valet*, *Jane Shore*, *Tamerlane*, *An Old Man Taught Wisdom*, *Othello* and *The Honest Yorkshireman*. The *Globe* also hosted variety acts, such as "the Grand Turk's Performance on the Slack Rope by Mr Lort" in 1750.

In 1752, an advertisement appeared in the *Bath Journal*:

To be sold, The *Globe Inn* and stables without the west gate of the city of Bath; and also the brick house near adjoining, held by lease from St John's Hospital in the said city.

The old *Seven Dials* pub, successor to the *Londonderry Inn* and the *Globe*, which stood where the Seven Dials development is today

The *Globe* closed around 1770, when its licence was transferred to a new *Globe* on the corner of Avon Street and Kingsmead Square (which is still there, although it has not been a pub for over 200 years). Part of the old *Globe*, however – the south-eastern corner – reopened as a tavern called the *Seven Dials* (a reference to the seven streets which met at this point) around ten years later. In 1780, it was renamed the *Rodney Arms* to commemorate Admiral Rodney's defeat of the Spanish fleet at Cape St Vincent, but reverted to the *Seven Dials* by 1826.

In 1883, it was leased to Edmund Baily of the Bath Arms Brewery in Palmer Street, Frome. In 1889, Edmund Baily joined two other brewers to form Frome United Breweries, based at the

Badcox Brewery in Vallis Way. In 1926, the magistrates decided that the *Seven Dials* should close. Frome United Breweries appealed against the decision to the House of Lords, contesting "the right of the Licensing Justices of a County Borough who had referred a license to the Compensation Authority to act as members of such compensation authority after they had already instructed a solicitor on their behalf to appear before themselves as such members and to oppose such renewal." It was a nice try, but the *Seven Dials* closed anyway and was pulled down in May 1931. Booze, however, has a way of bouncing back. The cocktail quaffers of the ever-popular *Pulp*, whether they are aware of it or not, are following in a venerable tradition.

PULTENEY ARMS 37 Daniel Street, Bathwick

It is not true that the tap room girl at the *Pulteney Arms* is so in love with the handsome chairman that she is obliged to have medical attention.

The *Pulteney Arms* was a well-established and well-known hostelry by the time that piece of scurrilous nonsense appeared in the *Bath Figaro* on 29 June 1838. Now one of Bath's top rugby pubs, the *Pulteney Arms* has a fascinating history. It is also one of the few eighteenth century pubs in Bath which can be dated with any accuracy.

When William Pulteney began to develop the Bathwick Estate in earnest in the late 1780s, it was the start of the biggest building boom in Bath's history. Bathwick New Town, of which Great Pulteney Street was just a small part, was intended to be on a massive scale. The architect, Thomas Baldwin, planned to throw a network of interconnected grand parades around Sydney Gardens. Then, in 1793, the money ran out.

Two of Bath's six banks went bust. The slump which followed was devastating. Terraces barely begun, streets that led nowhere, crumbling foundations, piles of stone and timber, all mocked the developers' dreams. Over one of the most monumental building sites ever seen fell an unaccustomed silence. Weeds sprouted amid the spoil heaps. Dogs and foxes wandered through the shattered landscape. Vagrants sheltered in half-built tenements. Gulleys crumbled. Foundations filled with water.

The human cost was appalling. Architects, builders and the network of craftsmen, tradesmen and labourers who relied on them, lost their livelihoods overnight. An army of workmen were thrown out of work. They faced not only the prospect of long-term unemployment, but, far worse, the paralysing fear that, as the crisis deepened, they and their families would starve or freeze to death.

Although what was left was not technically a ruin (how could it be, having never been completed?), the sight of weed-choked trenches, crumbling heaps of stone, half-built walls, and streets that led into green meadows, was as eloquent a testimony to the transience and folly of human ambition as the ruins of Rome. In 1803, Robert Southey, writing of Bath, drew attention to "the melancholy new ruins, which the projectors were unable to complete, and so were ruined themselves, a sudden check having been given to all such speculations when the last war broke out."

Eventually, financial stability and confidence returned, but the reckless confidence and grandiose visions which had inspired the New Town development did not. It was not until the late nineteenth century that anything approaching the exuberant gesture of the Bathwick development was attempted again – even though Major Davis's Brobdingnagian Empire Hotel was a world away from the classical symmetry of Great Pulteney Street. The vision of a New Town was never resurrected. Many fine buildings were added – the southern part of Sydney Place, designed by John Pinch in 1808, for example – but, compared with the grand sweep of the original plan, these were little more than infills.

Over 200 years later, dead-end streets, intended as grand boulevards – of which Sunderland Street is perhaps the most evocative – still run off Great Pulteney Street. But, for the most telling contrast between the original vision and what succeeded it, you can do no better than go to Daniel Street and stand outside the *Pulteney Arms*.

The alarm bells must already have been ringing when Thomas Baldwin started building Daniel Street, for he got no farther than the first three houses on the southern side. In style and design, they are almost indistinguishable from the houses in Sydney Place. The rest of the street, probably built by John Pinch around 1820, makes no attempt to imitate or blend in with the earlier development. The result is nevertheless very attractive and a graphic illustration of how styles in domestic architecture changed between the 1790s and the 1820s.

The first we hear of the *Pulteney Arms* comes in a newspaper advertisement of 15 November 1792:

> To be lett or sold, that very excellent new built Inn or Public House called the *Pulteney's Arms*, in Grove Street, Bathwick; with a large yard, etc., behind it, where stables and coach-houses, or extensive workshops and ware-rooms, may be advantageously and conspicuously created. Enquire of Mr Clark, Walcot Brewery.

To be LETT or SOLD,
THAT very excellent New-built INN, or PUBLICK-HOUSE, called the PULTENEY's ARMS, in GROVE-STREET, BATHWICK; with a large Yard, &c. behind it, where stables and coach-houses, or extensive workshops and ware-rooms, may be advantageously and conspicuously erected.
Enquire of Mr. Clark, Walcot Brewery.

The *Pulteney Arms* advertised as "new built" in 1792.

It was, therefore, a tied house before it even opened. William Clark had established the Walcot Brewery in 1780 near the Walcot Turnpike on the London Road, and advertised "river water in its greatest purity" as the principal constituent of its products. The first tenant of the *Pulteney's Arms* was John Bagshaw, who held the licence until around 1810. He was succeeded by his wife, Hannah Bagshaw, who was in turn succeeded by James Chilcot in 1816.

One curious point about the 1792 advertisement is that the address of the *Pulteney's Arms* is given as Grove Street. It seems that Daniel Street was not named until it was completed around 1820. The earliest references to the pub give its address as Grove Street, but this soon gives way to "Back of Sydney Place." It seems that Daniel

Street was originally intended to form part of Grove Street, which, instead of stopping at the old gaol, would have been extended in a wide arc over what is now Henrietta Park to meet up with it.

Over two centuries later, the *Pulteney Arms* is still very much in business, lit by gas and with a wooden-floored, multi-roomed interior redolent of a high-class Victorian boozer, with a nice line in chip butties and beer served straight from the barrel. Inside, its eclectic selection of pictures is dominated by rugby memorabilia. Outside, a handsome sign bracket and large gas lamps provide fitting adornment for Baldwin's dignified building. The *Pulteney Arms* was seriously damaged in the Bath Blitz but business carried on as usual during the repairs. The pub described in the 1903 report would be recognisable, in its essentials, to drinkers today:

> Entrance from Sutton Street. Back exit to Sydney Mews. Serving bar with glass room beyond. Also tap room with bagatelle table.

Just off the main tourist drag, with the delights of Henrietta Park and Sydney Gardens on its doorstep, the *Pulteney Arms* is well worth seeking out. The curious cat which features on the pub's logo, incidentally, comes from the arms of the Pulteney family, which can seen in its full glory on a triangular pediment in Great Pulteney Street.

RAINCHECK BAR 34 Monmouth Street

Long, long ago, the *Raincheck Bar* was the *Bell Inn*. The *Bell* opened sometime before 1776 and may have dated from when the street was built in the 1730s. One Saturday afternoon in 1778, it was the scene of a tragic, if rather predictable, accident. It is worth quoting the depositions in the Coroner's Report at length because of their detailed description of beer delivery over two centuries ago:

> James Lewis saith that on Saturday last about the hour of one o'clock in the afternoon as he was coming out of the house of Robert Rymer [the *Bell*] situate in Monmouth Street . . . he heard some person cry out, 'he is dead, he is dead,' upon which [he] ran down into the cellar of the same Robert Rymer in order to give what assistance he could, where he saw one John Taylor lying across an iron rail in a shute which is used for letting down vessels of beer into cellars ...
>
> William Wallis says that on Saturday last about one o'clock

in the afternoon he went with the same John Taylor to put a barrel of ale into the said cellar of the same Robert Rymer. Saith that when the said John Taylor brought the rope which he made use of to let down the barrel into the said cellar he told the deceased John Taylor that he believed the rope being an old one was not sufficiently strong to hold the said barrel and was afraid that it would break and desired him not to trust to it, but the deceased said that he would try it for he wanted to go home very bad. Saith that the said deceased John Taylor fixed the said rope to the barrel and went into the cellar. Saith that they then endeavoured to let the said barrel of ale down with the said rope and that as soon as the weight of the barrel rested on the rope the rope immediately broke, when the said barrel fell down upon the said John Taylor and beat him flat on the ground in the said cellar, by which means the same John Taylor was greatly bruised and by which bruises he this examinant apprehended was the cause of the death of the said John Taylor who died as this examinant hath been informed about five o'clock in the afternoon.

The *Bell* closed in 1815, when Southgate Brewery exchanged its lease for that of the *Bird in Hand* in Corn Street. It later became a butcher's. In the early twentieth century it was Buvington Press. By the 1950s it had become a newsagents, but today, with its licence restored, it is the *Raincheck Bar*. The American-style name is backed up by a New York retro-style ambience that has proved a lasting hit with Bath's drinkers.

Today, Monmouth Street has only one pub and two wine bars – but in the nineteenth century it was a pub crawler's paradise. On the south side of the street were two short-lived beerhouses – the *Old Monmouth Arms* and the *Times Tavern* – but it was on the north side that most of the action took place. There was the *Seven Dials* on the corner of the Sawclose, the *Theatre Tavern* (c1792-1888) where Robins Cinema now stands, the *Victoria Tavern* (c1830-1851) at No 29, the *Midland Arms* (c1868-1910) at No 25, and the *Elephant & Castle Inn* (1794-1841) where Holy Trinity Church stands.

It must have been quite a street.

RAM 20 Claverton Buildings, Widcombe

Claverton Street is a shadow of its former self. It once stretched all the way from the Old Bridge to the bottom of Widcombe Hill, with buildings all the way, on both sides of the road. And, of course, a fair few of them were pubs. Even in the little bit of Claverton Street that is left, there were four. Two have survived – the *Ram* and the *Ring of Bells*. Next to the *Ram*, where the vet's is today, was a pub called, appropriately enough, the *Greyhound*, which closed in 1908. Opposite, at No 4, Widcombe Parade, was a beerhouse called the *Stag's Head*, which closed in the mid-nineteenth century.

The *Ram* opened as a beer house in the 1840s. At the time of the 1903 report, it had a "bar with smoke room and tap room behind." It also had a skittle alley and a brewery. It was one of the last pubs to brew its own beer in Bath. Local residents can still recall seeing brewing operations – some of which took place in the open air. Today, the

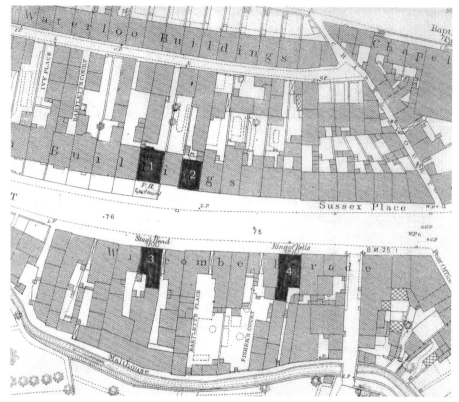

Part of Claverton Street in the late nineteenth-century map showing: 1 the *Greyhound*; 2 the *Ram*; 3 the *Stag's Head*; 4 the *Ring of Bells*.

Ram consists of a large bar with a small lounge separated from it by a glazed partition. Dark wood dominates with exposed ceiling beams, floor boards, high-backed seats and partitions. When Fred Pearce visited in 1975, shortly after it had been revamped, he was appalled by Watney's "attempt to impose an identity on the pub rather than reflecting the existing atmosphere." Funny how something that was jarringly modern a quarter of a century ago now seems one of the most traditional locals in Bath.

RAT & PARROT 38 Westgate Street

Cheap Street and Westgate Street were once lined with coaching inns. They all disappeared years ago – all, that is, except the *Angel*, or as it is known today the *Rat & Parrot*.

Although it is believed to date from 1625, the first record of it we have found comes from 1677, when William Burford leased an inn called the *Three Swans* from the Corporation. In 1689, when Thomas

Eleazer Pickwick announces his move from the *Packhorse* to the *Angel* in 1779.

Carrington took over the lease, he renamed it the *Angel*. He was there until his death in 1704, when his widow, Mary, took over.

Between 1736 and 1749, Thomas Cottle held the lease, but by 1769 it had passed to Thomas Little. Eleazer Pickwick, from the *Packhorse* in Northgate Street, took over in 1779 and placed the following advertisement in the *Bath Chronicle*:

ANGEL HOTEL

WESTGATE STREET, BATH

E Pickwick begs leave to inform his Friends and the Publick that he has taken the above Old-accustom'd Inn, which he has genteelly fitted up with exceeding good beds, and every accommodation for the reception of those who please to favour him with their company.

Neat post-chaises and saddle horses.

The Oxford & Bristol Coaches set out from the above Inn as usual.

Also the Exeter Diligence, which used to set out from the *Saracen's Head* in Broad Street, sets out from the above Inn at five o'clock, and meets the Plymouth Diligence at Exeter every evening.

Mr Pickwick, on his way to building up the greatest coaching business in Bath, was not at the *Angel* for long. He left to take over the *White Hart*, at the top of Stall Street, two years later.

Someone whose sojourn at the *Angel* was even shorter was a nine-foot tall Irishman called O'Brien who spent a few days there in 1792. His arrival was announced in the "What's On" column of the *Bath Chronicle*:

Mr O'Brien, the celebrated Irish giant, lineal descendant from an Irish king named Brian Boreau, whose family has ever been famous for their gigantic growth, may be seen at the *Angel* in Westgate Street.

The *Angel* survived the coming of the railways and retained its old-world character until well into the twentieth century. In 1940 the sale of the *Angel* prompted an article in the *Bath Chronicle* which included several references to its history:

This week has seen the turning of another page in the colourful history of one of Bath's oldest hostelries – the *Angel Hotel*, Westgate Street, which was established in 1625 … It has been taken over by Messrs S Fussell & Son, the well-known brewers, of Rode, Somerset, from Mr Paul Radmilovic, the Olympic swimmer, and today the management was taken over, for Messrs Fussell, by Mr & Mrs HT Hughes from the Cousins Hotel, Plymouth …

An 1846 advertisement for the *Angel*.

The story of the *Angel* is partly the story of Bath itself. From the seventeenth century, when it first came into existence, it watched the progress of the city. It has seen the change from sedan chairs to motor cars, from voluminous skirts to short dresses. When the *Angel* came into being men were hanged for stealing. Wars and threats of wars have passed the *Angel* by, and today it enters into its latest phase with England engaged in a greater struggle for life than in the days of Napoleon.

The oldest hotel in Bath is the *Christopher* in the Market Place, but the *Angel* runs it close … In the coaching days of the eighteenth century, the *Angel* was a well-known posting house, and had extensive stabling premises. Its rivals were the *White Hart* – on the site of which the *Grand Pump Room Hotel* stands – the *Three Tuns* in Stall Street, the *White Lion* in the Market Place, and the *Bear* in Stall Street. This collection of rivals inspired the verse:

> May the *White Hart* outrun the *Bear*,
>
> And make the *Angel* fly,
>
> Turn the *Lion* upside down
>
> And drink the *Three Tuns* dry.

For many years the *Angel* was controlled by proprietors from the West Country. In 1920 Captain GA Maher assumed control, and in 1938, on his retirement, it came into the possession of Mr Radmilovic – "Raddy" to give him the nickname by which he is known by swimmers all over the world. He was licensee of the *York House Hotel*, Bath, many years ago, leaving there to take control of the *Railway Hotel*, Weston Super Mare, from whence he came to Bath. The present owners, Messrs Fussell, are an old-established Somerset firm, so the association of the hotel with West Country owners continues. The *Angel* has been known for generations throughout the United Kingdom as a Mecca for "Knights of the Road," and it has always been a favourite meeting place for local sportsmen and business men.

In 1953 Fussell's gave up the lease of the *Angel*. It was taken by Mr FM Payne from the *King's Head*, Harrow, who appointed Sydney Eade as manager. Shortly before taking over, Mr Payne outlined his plans for the *Angel*:

> We shall entirely redecorate the place inside and out, at the same time doing everything to maintain its essential character. Our first aim will be a really comfortable hotel, although I doubt whether we shall make any structural alterations to extend bedroom accommodation until we can find out how great is the need. We hope to panel the two bars in light oak, and to alter the lighting scheme. The *Angel Hotel* is in such a wonderful position that I don't see how we can go wrong, particularly if we can retain its old character. I must confess I have taken the place as a shot in the dark. Its position and its accommodation struck me as being something really worthwhile.

In December 1965, the *Angel* closed when the owner went bankrupt. It remained closed for the next five years. In November 1967 the lease was acquired by Colmers' Department Store in Union Street. They converted the back of the building to offices and sub-let the front to Gibbs Mew Brewery of Salisbury. Gibbs Mew announced that they were going to reopen the hotel with 23 bedrooms – nine of them *en suite*. There would be two entrances from Westgate Street, one of them leading to a cellar bar. By June 1968, however, nothing had happened, apart from Gibbs Mew putting in a planning application to do away with the "old ornate canopy over the entrance and to replace it with a flat one across the width of the building." Approval for this was eventually given and the canopy was removed in April 1969. The old coaching inn was then gutted to make way for steak bars and a German bierkeller called *Der Engel*. In June 1970, the *Bath Chronicle* gave an update on progress so far:

> The *Angel Hotel* in Bath, opened as a hostelry around 1625 but closed for the past five years, will be selling beer once more in September. The scheme of rebuilding and furnishing is costing Gibbs Mew, the Salisbury brewers, around £100,000. Mr Peter Gibbs, chairman and managing director, said the completion of phase one was expected at the end of August. The bierkeller (which will replace the old

cellar, Captain's Cabin), will be opened in the third week in September. It is hoped to have a ground floor bar ready for Christmas. Bath Estates Committee has agreed to a canopy over the front of the premises, but it will not be like the small ornate one taken down a year ago. The surveyor, Mr J Bevan Jones, said it would go the full length of the building.

The bierkeller opened on Friday 25 September 1970. "Westphalia comes to Westgate Street" declared the adverts, which promised Bathonians "a vivid new experience, full of colour and gaiety in the essential German manner." Innocent of how future generations would misconstrue their words, they enticed customers with the prospect of "gay music and colourful costume." In 1970 that meant lederhosen and accordions – today the image it conjures up is one that would bring a quiver to the most staunchly Teutonic upper lip.

The following April the *Bath Chronicle* announced that:

> … a new restaurant seating 80 people, and a luxury lounge, are now open to mark Phase Two of the restoration of the *Angel Hotel* in Westgate Street, Bath. This week nine bedrooms were also opened and in the final phase another 15 will be completed, plus a residents' lounge. The sauna bath is already in operation. Mr Peter Roome and his wife Annette are looking after the hotel side of the *Angel*, and Mr Colin Read is running the bierkeller, which opened in the basement last September. The spacious ground floor bar was opened at the beginning of April. Rebuilding and furnishing the *Angel* is estimated to have cost £100,000. The sauna bath has been popular ever since it opened. The cost is 65p and half a dozen people can use the baths at any one time … Gibbs Mew, the Salisbury brewery firm which has reopened the *Angel Hotel* will extend the premises above Austin's menswear shop at the corner of Westgate Street and Union Street and this will provide for 15 bedrooms and the residents' lounge.

It was a false dawn. Gibbs Mew soon experienced "management problems" and sublet the *Angel* to a company called Abodian Hotels who put it up for sale. It was taken by Klaus Gottschling, a pastry-cook from Austria, who had come to Britain ten years earlier to work in the hotel trade. His first task was to revamp the bierkeller and make it that bit more authentic by advertising for barmaids in Salzburg.

Sadly, just over twelve months later, Mr Gottschling put the *Angel* up for sale, claiming that the IRA's bombing of the Corridor had kept people away from the city centre and scuttled his attempts to make a go of the business. Despite being put on the market at £42,500 – less than half of the £100,000 which had been spent on refurbishing it less than five years earlier, there were no takers. The *Angel* struggled on till October 1975 when last orders were called once again.

The following March, it was reopened by Gibbs Mew, a director being quoted as saying that "he was sure the company would be able to make the hotel pay." Less than two years later, however, in January 1978, the *Bath Chronicle* reported that:

> The *Angel Hotel* at Bath … is to be renamed the Edwardian. The change, after more than 350 years, is proposed by the new owners, Variety Inns of Bristol. Planning permission has been requested to change the appearance of the frontage of the old coaching inn. The present canopy and lettering will come down – if approval is given. It will be replaced by an ornate metal canopy with gilded lettering. Floodlights will pick out the title, the *Edwardian Hotel*, on the face of the building in Westgate Street. A period door is proposed, glazed and panelled, the glass etched in the Edwardian manner. There will

be brass door pullers and a brass letter box ... Mr Brian Jacobs, financial director of Variety Inns, said they were trying to change the complete image of the establishment. People always thought of the *Angel* as a pub and hotel and for that reason the restaurant has not really succeeded. "We want the Edwardian to be thought of as a place with a marvellous restaurant, with hotel and bar accommodation," he said. The company is spending £40-50,000 on the first stage of redecoration and refurbishing. A further £40,000 may be spent later.

So, less than ten years after spending £100,000 (equivalent to almost £1M in today's terms) ripping out the old fittings, the best part of another £100,000 was earmarked to revamp it with fake Edwardiana. Nothing better typifies the follies and delusions of the decade that taste forgot than this history of misjudgement and miscalculation. Needless to say, the *Angel* did not stay the *Edwardian* for very long (fake Edwardiana tends to have a shorter shelf-life than the real thing). Nowadays, after a spell as the *Westgate Hotel* and another heavy gutting (which at least allowed the Bath Archaeological Trust to see what lay underneath) the *Angel* is the big-barred, many-barred *Rat & Parrot*. It is one of a chain of 15 *Rat & Parrots,* all until recently part of the Scottish & Newcastle portfolio, but acquired in October 2003 by Spirit Amber.

RED LION 468 Wellsway

The *Red Lion* is another pub that moved. The old *Red Lion* stood where Upper Bloomfield Road meets the Frome Road. It opened sometime before 1770, when the following announcement appeared in the *Bath Journal*:

> A fine doe will be turn'd out before the
> Town Hounds, precisely at eleven o'clock
> the morrow morning, at the *Red Lyon* on
> Odd Down near this city.

It was relocated to its present site around 1812 when the new turnpike road to Wells opened. Part of the old inn still survives, however, incorporated into the Odd Down Pharmacy.

The new inn is an elegant late Georgian building, although an entry in the *Journal* of the Rev John Skinner, Rector of Camerton, for 24 April 1820, suggests that it may not always have been the most respectable of houses. A woman had called on him en route from Bath to visit her husband in Shepton Mallet Gaol. He was inside because he had embezzled money from Rev Skinner:

> I gave her half a crown, as she told me her goods in Holloway had been seized for rent, and her
> children were starving. I found out afterwards on enquiry that the woman had been turned out of
> her lodgings on very different grounds, namely, that of having brought home a young man to sleep
> with her, and having gone in his company to the *Red Lion* on Odd Down, leaving her children without
> anything to eat. I certified myself of the truth of this report by going to see the person with whom she
> lodged, of the name of Sims, who told me that was the reason he had locked her room, and that the
> father of the young man who had been at the *Red Lion* with her had separated them at that place.

As late as 1871, the landlord of the *Red Lion*, Arthur Candy, was also a farmer. By 1903, the *Red Lion* had a serving bar, a bar parlour, a tap room, a glass room, and a large walled garden which contained "a WC for women." In 1976, when Fred Pearce visited, it was a "disco and juke box pub with two large bars." An extension in the car park contained the long, low Windjammer Bar. Discos were held most weekends. Live groups also appeared. In 1986, the *Red Lion* was taken over by the Falstaff Group and closed for ten weeks while a 68-seat restaurant and two new bars were put in at a cost of £200,000. It later became a Harvester Restaurant and in 2003 closed for another major refurbishment, eventually reopening as Bath's first Sizzling Pub.

The *Red Lion* has been gutted and revamped so often that, although the building has some interesting external features, such as blocked doorways and windows, internally its history has been expunged. Red, though, is heavily in evidence – red walls, red Roman blinds, red(dish) carpet, red chairs – and the menu features Sizzling Steak, Sizzling Chicken, Sizzling Gammon, and Red Thai Curry, but sadly no Sizzling Red Lion. The Sizzling Pub Co. is, like the Harvester chain, owned by Mitchells & Butlers of Birmingham. Other chains in their portfolio include O'Neill's and All Bar One. The history of Mitchells and Butlers is a complex one. The original company was formed in 1898 when Butler's Crown Brewery merged with Mitchell's Cape Hill Brewery. In 1961, it merged with Bass, Ratcliff & Gretton to form Bass, Mitchells & Butlers. In 1967, the new company merged with Charrington to form Bass Charrington (later shortened to Bass). In 2000, Bass sold its brewing business and became Six Continents. In 2002, the retail divisions of Six Continents was renamed Mitchells & Butlers, while the hotel division was renamed the Intercontinental Hotels Group. Ironically, the readoption of the name Mitchells & Butlers coincided with the closure of the old Mitchells & Butlers Cape Hill Brewery.

RICHMOND ARMS 7 Richmond Place

Richmond Place was built in the early 1800s. Initially, many of its houses were country residences for well-to-do tradesmen in the city. Before long, however, they had started to slide ever so discreetly downhill. By the end of the nineteenth century, the residents of Richmond Place included grocers, carpenters, stonemasons, laundresses, bootmakers, porters, waiters, stokers, basketmakers, warehousemen, coachmen, labourers, and gardeners. Not surprisingly, there was a clutch of beerhouses as well.

No 26 was a grocery-cum-post-office with a beer licence, which survived until the 1960s. No 37 was the *Lansdown Arms*, first recorded in 1837 and closed around 1856. No 39 was a beerhouse called the *Rising Sun*, which opened in the 1840s and closed in 1936. Finally, there was the *Richmond Arms* at No 7.

Until about 1860, a labourer called John Hasey lived at 7

Richmond Place. By 1864 a "provision dealer" called Robert Butler had moved in, followed, around 1870, by another "provision dealer" called David Peploe. He was succeeded by John Oram, who obtained a beer licence around 1872 and called his house the *Richmond Arms*.

Things did not always go smoothly for the early landlords of the *Richmond Arms*. In 1886, for example, when a dairyman called William Bruton held the licence, goods to a value of £35 were seized from him for rent due to the Lacock Brewery. The shop, bagatelle room, kitchen and living rooms were cleared, but enough fittings were left for Mr Bruton to sell some of them to the incoming licensee, Hubert Hingston.

We have been unable to discover when the *Richmond Arms* obtained a full licence, but by 1903 it consisted of a tap room, "with a shop behind where liquors are sold." There was an exit from the back yard to a lane running behind the first ten houses in Richmond Place and a path leading to Summerfield Cottages. Things had not changed much when Fred Pearce dropped by in 1976. His report is worth quoting in full if only to emphasise the changes which have taken place since:

> Up a suburban side street, through the front gate and down the garden path. The *Arms* is a cosy, homely and beautifully kept house. The small lounge looks out onto the garden – where you can sit in summer – and the still smaller smoking room has a TV and darts. The landlady was sitting in the smoking room when we arrived, reading the evening paper for all the world as if it were her private living room. "Would customers please respect our carpet and use the ashtrays," says a sign – do that and you'll be made very welcome. Lunchtime sandwiches and home-made pies are served, so is real Ordinary Bitter, beautifully clear, straight from the metal barrels (Courage gave up wooden barrels long ago). Crib, shove ha'penny.

Today, although the *Richmond Arms* looks much the same from the outside, inside it is unrecognisable. Knocked through, with bare floorboards and bright yellow walls, it is Bath's only pub to make it into the Good Food Guide, on the strength of a nouvelle-cuisinish range of meals that not only cost less than at many similar establishments, but also work out around the same as the chips-with-everything platters served up in some other boozers. If you are wedded to the idea that all pubs should conform to a CAMRA-inspired template of a *faux*-1950s temple to the raising of the wrist, then you will probably hate the *Richmond Arms*. If, on the other hand, if you like places that are full of character, serve excellent food, wine and beer in convivial surroundings, and are as far from brewery-chain inspired insipidities as the equally individualistic but very different *Star*, then you may well find it an inspiring example of how a pub can be transformed and made-over, without compromising its essential quality. On top of all that, the walled, south-facing garden at the front of the building, is a terrific sun-trap. A recent change of ownership has seen the disappearance of the oriental artefacts which once lined the walls and a less Thai-oriented flavour to the menu, but the food is at least as good as it was before, if not better, and the service is impeccable.

Traditionalists may bemoan the blurring of distinctions between pub and wine bar that is exemplified by places such as the *Richmond Arms*, but it is a blurring that has gone on for an awfully long time. The *Richmond Arms* started off as a beerhouse, but many other pubs started off as wine vaults, where beer, if it was sold at all, was very much a poor relation. Two pubs – *St James's Wine Vaults* and the *Belvedere Wine Vaults* still carry the names they had when wine was their primary commodity. Others whose origin is not so apparent include the *Alehouse*, the *Assembly Inn*, the *Boater*, the *Curfew*, the *Grapes*, *Hatchett's*, the *Huntsman*, the *Roundhouse*, and *Smith Bros*. The current reorientation of some pubs towards wine is not the betrayal of a tradition, as some purists would have you believe, but the reversal of a process which occurred a century or more ago.

RING OF BELLS 9-10 Widcombe Parade

The recently-revamped *Ring of Bells* – just opposite the *Ram* – rivals the *Richmond Arms*, not only for the superb quality of its food, but as a model of how a traditional boozer can be taken by the scruff of its neck and transformed into a lively watering hole with not even the merest nod towards the banality of corporate design.

The *Ring of Bells* was first licensed as a beerhouse around 1837. In 1851, the landlord, Thomas Starks, was summoned for staying open after eleven, although, as the house was "generally well conducted," he was only fined a shilling.

In 1870, the *Ring of Bells* consisted of a bar, a bar parlour, a drawing room, a back drawing room, a tap room, a brewery and a skittle alley. The customers were obviously a literate lot, as the drawing room had books and magazines laid out for them to read. The bar parlour had an oil painting and four coloured engravings (including "The Hunting Stud" and "The Thoroughbred") on its walls. The bar had a "cigarette mould," a musical box which played six tunes, a race game, a box of dominoes, two crib boards and five packs of cards. There were also 300 brass cheques or tokens in a box.

By 1903, the accommodation had been reduced to a bar with a smoke room behind it. The skittle alley was still there, but, like the alleys in several other pubs at the time, it was no longer in use. There was also a brewery, which closed around 1914.

Perhaps the most dramatic incident in the *Ring of Bells'* history came in 1915 when the police were called to deal with a man holed up there with a gun, threatening to shoot anyone who tried to enter. When they arrived, they found the house broken up and Albert Rose, the licensee, standing a yard away from his wife, pointing a gun at her. Apparently, he had been given notice to quit, gone on a bender, and ended up losing it completely. A struggle ensued in which he knocked a policeman's helmet off with the gun, but was eventually overpowered and sentenced to six weeks hard labour.

Much later, in 1976, when it was known as *Rosie's*, Fred Pearce described it as:

… possibly Bath's best local. The Saturday jazz and Sunday folk in the upstairs bar are added attractions. The main bar isn't very big, and frankly not in the best state of repair – but if you want Berni decor then don't come here. You'll find a band of TV watchers up the far end, shove ha'penny near the bar and dominoes and chess fitted in somehow. Patrons are a right old mixture of cider freaks, rugby players, Newcastle Brown boozers, skittles fanatics, common or garden locals and people who stumbled on the place by accident and keep coming back. Oh, and don't worry too much about Rosie's sharp tongue – she means it really!

Locals also recall that one of the *Ring of Bells'* landlords was so attached to his racing pigeons that he kept them in his bedroom.

Today, after a spell as the *Hunter's Moon* and the curiously styled *Home@theRingofBells* (with a pair of red slippers acting as a sign), it is once again the *Ring of Bells*, with a magnificent new sign which is not only worth crossing the bridge to see, but makes a cracking excuse for visiting one of the best little bars in Bath.

RISING SUN 5 Claremont Terrace, Camden

The *Rising Sun*, a traditional back-street boozer, is the only pub left in this part of town, but at one time there were many others –the *River's Arms* on Camden Road, the *Crown* and the *Mason's Arms* on Tyning Lane, the *Old Standard* and the *Claremont Arms* in Claremont Buildings, the *Barley Mow* on Margaret's Hill and the *Gay's Hill Tavern* on Gay's Hill. All have closed and all, except the *River's Arms*, demolished. Only the *Rising Sun* still survives to serve Camden's drinkers.

The *Rising Sun* opened in the 1830s, and by 1876 consisted of a bar, a tap room, a sitting room and a brewery. By the time of the 1903 report, the brewery had closed and the accommodation consisted of a bar divided into three compartments, with a glass room on the left. Since then, the *Rising Sun* has expanded, taking in some of the buildings which once stood in Lucklom Terrace, and been knocked through. A skittle alley, garden patio, pool table and wide screen TV have been added, but many links with the past, including some fine frosted glass remain.

RISING SUN 58 Lymore Avenue, Twerton

The *Rising Sun* was opened as a beerhouse by James Tanner in the 1870s. In 1893, its contents were put up for auction. The auction catalogue gives a good idea of what it was like. In the tap room were two deal drinking tables, five deal forms, a fender, a shovel, a poker, a taper beer warmer and spittoons. In the glass room were a deal settle and table. The bar contained a five-motion beer engine and a screen board with shelving at the side. There was no bar counter. In 1976 Fred Pearce described the *Rising Sun* as a "bright little modernised pub perched on a hillside overlooking its constituency of drinkers." It is little changed today.

RISING SUN 3-4 Grove Street, Bathwick

"Bath's Friendliest Pub" reads the sign outside the *Rising Sun* – and it is remarkable that so traditional a local has survived so close to the city centre. Its history – and the history of the street in which it stands – is no less remarkable.

The first building to be erected in Grove Street was the City Gaol, the foundation stone of which was laid in 1772. This may seem a curious choice – after all, Bathwick New Town was intended to rival, if not eclipse, the glories of the New Town build by John Wood & Son to the north of the city. Building a gaol hardly seems calculated to send out the right sort of message.

William Johnston Pulteney, who owned the land, had little choice in the matter. To provide access to Pulteney Bridge he had to build Bridge Street, and to build Bridge Street he had to tear down the old church of St Mary by the Northgate, the tower of which housed the city gaol. He was only allowed to do this on condition that he build a new gaol in Bathwick. As the site he chose for it was – and still is – clearly visible from the other side of the river, he needed to ensure that it did not put people off, so he built it to look like a Palladian mansion. It was Bath's gaol until 1842, when a new one opened in East Twerton, and the old one was advertised for sale "with the terrace in front." Today it is an apartment block, little changed except that the terrace has gone, so that the old ground floor is now the first floor and you enter the building through the old basement.

The *Rising Sun*, at the other end of the street, dates from 1788, when William Tutton opened it as the *Rising Sun & Lark*. A few years later, an advertisement for the newly opened Grosvenor Pleasure Gardens suggested that the best way to reach the gardens was by boat:

> Pleasure Boats for parties may be had by enquiring at the *Rising Sun*, Grove Street, near the new bridge. The fare 2/- for one to six persons, all above 6d per head, and 1/- per hour for waiting.

This indicates that, at that time, there was direct access from the *Rising Sun* to a landing

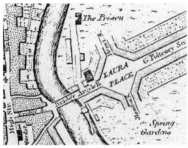

A map from the late 1780s shows the *Rising Sun* was one of the earliest buildings on the east side of Grove Street.

stage on the river. It conjures up an idyllic picture of well-to-do pleasure seekers tripping out of the *Rising Sun* and crossing a grassy sward to where a boat stood waiting by the willow-fringed banks of the Avon. It may not have been quite like that, of course, but whatever pretensions to pastoral bliss the *Rising Sun* may have had disappeared once the Northgate Brewery extended its operations across the river to Grove Street.

In the nineteenth century, Grove Street was a lively area – hardly surprising with a prison at one end of it. A newspaper report from 1846 gives some idea of the kind of thing that went on down there:

Hannah Pearce was summoned for assaulting Louisa Wickham, by throwing water over her in Grove St. The assault was admitted by the defendant, but in her defence she pointed out that the water was clean. The magistrates told her this did not excuse the act and fined her 10/- and costs or in default 14 days in prison.

BATH.
Grofvenor-Gardens Vauxhall.

WHEWLETT refpectfully acquaints the Nobility, Gentry and Public, that thefe delightful and extenfive Pleafure-Gardens, beautifully and romantically fituated near the River Avon, are now opened for the Seafon, where Families may be accommodated with Breakfaft-ing, Afternoon Tea, Dinners, &c.— Every attention will be paid to render it a place of Fafhionable refort.

A BAND of HORNS and CLARIONETS will attend every TUESDAY evening during the Seafon.—Subfcription for Walking and Bowling 10s. to Chriftmas, or 5s. for walking only to that time.—Families by Agreement.——Admittance to Non-Subfcribers Sixpence, the value in Wine &c. of the beft quality.

There are Two Bowling-Greens and Two Swings. A pleafant way thro' the Fields by Bathwick to the Gardens.—Large parties are requefted to give timely notice for Breakfafts, &c.

☞ Pleafure Boats for Parties may be had by enquiring at the Rifing-Sun, Grove-ftreet, near the New Bridge.—The Fare as. from one to fix perfons, all above 6d. per head and 1 s. per hour for waiting.—A Boat attends to convey perfons acrofs the Ferry to the Garden gratis.

A 1795 advertisement for Grosvenor Gardens, with details of boats for hire at the *Rising Sun*.

Next to the prison was one of Bath's most notorious pubs, the *Ostrich*. Despite being built, presumably as a respectable tavern, by John Eveleigh in 1791, it went rapidly downhill. The gardens at the back were turned into a warren of tiny hovels known as Ostrich Court. The *Ostrich*, along with Ostrich Court and much of the east side of Grove Street, was pulled down in 1890 in an early example of slum clearance.

The *Rising Sun*, which managed to avoid the rapid descent into disrule which affected the rest of the street, survived. The Loyal Bathonian United Society, Bath's oldest friendly society, used it as their headquarters throughout much of the nineteenth century. When an inventory of the pub was drawn up in 1874, it consisted of a bar, a glass room, a tap room, another small drinking room, a dining room, a drawing room, a skittle alley, a malt room, a water closet, and stables.

In 1916, the landlord of the pub was William Heizman, of German descent, but born in England. Because of anti-German feeling, he changed his name by deed poll to Hayman, and, once this was done, appeared before the licensing authorities to have the name on the licence changed as well. The application was granted.

Today, the *Rising Sun* retains a two-room layout, with a newly-refurbished skittle alley at the rear. It remains very much a locals' pub, with a friendly informality which so many city centre pubs have long abandoned.

ROSE & CROWN 6-7 Brougham Place, Larkhall

Larkhall was a growing suburb when Worthy Baker opened the *Rose & Crown* as a beerhouse in the 1840s. In 1898, the Bath Brewery Company tried to get a full licence for it and offered to shut the *Malakoff* on Holloway as a sop to the licensing magistrates. The application was rejected, as the *Royal Oak* in Dafford Street (now the *Brains Surgery*) was being rebuilt, and was in line to be upgraded to a fully licensed house. The *Rose & Crown* had to wait over 60 years to get a full licence. It was only when the *White Lion* opposite the *Larkhall Inn* closed in 1959 that the magistrates finally agreed to an upgrade.

At the time of the 1903 report, the *Rose & Crown* had two entrances from Brougham Place and one from Dafford Street. The bar was in two compartments, with a tap room and glass room behind, and a club room upstairs. A revamp a few years ago enhanced rather than detracted from the pub's Victorian ambience. Until recently, the *Rose & Crown* was very much a regulars' pub. A change of licensee and a "fairly hefty clean up operation" has since transformed it into a lively bar, where, as *Venue* magazine puts it, "a woman can wander in unaccompanied for a pint without worrying."

ROSE & LAUREL 118 Rush Hill

The *Rose & Laurel*, with its rough, whitewashed walls, looking out over the Avon valley, on one of the steepest bits of Rush Hill, looks for all the world like a country alehouse. Which, to all intents and purposes, it is.

It started off, so the story goes, as two poor houses belonging to the Parish of Englishcombe. It first appeared as a pub called the *Laurels* in the 1884 *Postal Directory*, with Thomas Riddick as the landlord. However, there was an earlier pub on Rush Hill called the *Cross Hands*. This was first recorded in 1872 with William Toogood as the landlord. By 1876, Benjamin Toogood had taken over, but by 1880 the *Cross Hands* had disappeared from the records. It is possible that the *Cross Hands* later reopened as the *Laurels*.

Today the *Rose & Laurel* survives as a busy, friendly, old-fashioned local in an area which never had many pubs – and, thankfully, with an emphasis on the raising of the wrist rather than the wielding of the fork.

ROUNDHOUSE 2 Stall Street

The *Roundhouse* may not immediately spring to mind when drawing up a list of Bath's oldest pubs, but it has been licensed since 1809, when Benjamin Atkinson set up in business at 2 Stall Street as a wine merchant. By the time an advertisement for the *Abbey Wine Vaults* appeared in the *Bath Chronicle* in 1842, extolling the virtues of its Guinness Extra Stout and Burton Ale (from the wood and in bottles), it was a pub as well. In the late nineteenth century it was extended and took over the property on the corner of Stall Street and Cheap Street, which was rebuilt at the same time. The 1903 report described the *Abbey Wine Vaults* as having a smoking room and a drinking bar, with entrances from Stall Street and Cheap Street. It was subsequently renamed the *Roundhouse*, and in 1976 Fred Pearce (who wasn't impressed)

summed up its decor as "Watney's Red Carpet, wall to wall background music, eye-straining wallpaper design and vast array of keys over the bar." Early in 1985 it was closed for six weeks for renovation, which included putting in the spiral staircase to the restaurant on the first floor. This obtrusive addition, which caused considerable friction with the Planning Department at the time, is still there, despite the pub having received a minimalist makeover in August 2003.

ROYAL HOTEL Railway Place

In 1842, a year after the railway opened from London to Bath, an advertisement appeared in the *Bath Chronicle*:

> To be lett … a newly-built house, situated in Railway Place, immediately facing the Bath station of the Great Western Railway; which has been erected especially with a view of being opened as an inn and for which a victualling licence has been granted. Apply to Mr Hoare, Plumber, Dorchester Street.

This became the *Royal Hotel*, on the east corner of Manvers Street. It is primarily a hotel rather than a pub, although you can still nip into one of its two bars for a drink. Some Bathonians remember the 1960s jazz club in the old skittle alley in the cellar with affection, and Fred Pearce's 1976 description of the *Royal* will no doubt ring a few bells (remember bierkellers? remember the Gay Nineties Bar?!):

> Berni Royal: Restaurants and bars complex but the bars seem to be very much an afterthought … Scotch bar has tartan fabrics on the wall, silly pictures of Scottish soldiers and lots of people rushing in and out from the station with suitcases … Gay Nineties bar is similar and the Bierkeller has jazz on Tuesday evenings.

On the other side of Manvers Street was the *Argyle Temperance Hotel*, whose architecture matched that of the *Royal Hotel*. Although the architect is unknown, it is possible both buildings were designed by Henry Goodridge (who was closely involved with the GWR) in association with Isambard Kingdom Brunel. Although markedly different to Brunel's station across the road, their Greek Revival style echoes the Brunel-designed Railway Hotel in Bristol (now Brunel House), as well as other Greek Revival buildings by Goodridge, such as those in Cleveland Place.

ROYAL OAK 8-10 Summerlay's Place, Pulteney Road

This area was once stiff with pubs. Dolemeads – which lay between Pulteney Road and the river – once had eight pubs, most of them strung out along the river bank. Today there is just one, the *Royal Oak* on Summerlay's Place.

Summerlay's Place was built in 1836, and there seems to have been a beerhouse called the *Royal Oak* there from the start. It started off in No 8, before moving into No 9 as well. In 1892, Henry Rossiter, who came from Surrey, married Rosina Stride (of the

Stride brewing dynasty), and took over the *Royal Oak*. At the time of the 1903 report, the *Royal Oak* consisted of a tap room, a bar, a glass room and a brewery. Shortly afterwards, Henry Rossiter took over No 10 Summerlay's Place as well. In 1915, his son, Bill Rossiter – later Alderman Rossiter – took over, and, in 1923, added a "bowling saloon." Although the pub was always officially known as the *Royal Oak*, it was universally referred to as *Rossiter's*.

Among the non-alcoholic entertainments put on by Bill Rossiter were children's picture shows, which attracted large crowds. He was also the first landlord in Bath to have both radio and television in his pub. Among the societies which met at the *Royal Oak* were the Bath Birdcage Society, the Bath & District Rabbit Club, the Bath Central Flying Club and the Bath & Western Counties Bulldog Association. Before the Second World, the *Royal Oak* was also a venue for mouse racing. Brewing at the *Royal Oak* continued until around 1946. When Bill Rossiter left, in 1962, there were four bars, a smoke room, a skittle alley and a show room.

The *Royal Oak* was bought for £10,000 by Grosvenor Steak House (Bath) Ltd., who acquired the *George & Dragon* at Batheaston and the *Claremont Arms* in Fairfield Road at around the same time. They got rid of the partitions and today the *Royal Oak* consists of one large bar with log-cabin inspired walls, prominently displayed Holsten Pils posters and a nice vine down by the toilets.

POSTSCRIPT: Since writing the above, new and enthusiastic licensees have taken over the *Royal Oak*. The Holsten Pils and the bunting that once bedecked the inside of the pub have gone and home-cooked food is on the agenda. The vine by the toilets, however, is still there.

RUMMER 6 Newmarket Row

The *Rummer* started off, sometime before 1776, as the *Chequers*, becoming the *Rummer* in 1809. From 1803, it was the meeting place of a benefit society called the Bath Independent Britons.

In 1840, an advertisement appeared in the *Bath Chronicle*:

HOME BREWED PUBLIC HOUSE:

To be let … that well-accustom'd Public House,

the *Rummer Tavern*, situated next to the Market Place,

now in full trade, with an excellent stock of strong beer

In 1883, Joseph Jefferies, the landlord, went bankrupt and the *Rummer* was acquired by Usher's Brewery. The inventory drawn up at the time paints a

The *Rummer* advertised to let in 1840.

picture of a comfortable if not opulent establishment. The bar had a panelled counter, two screen boards in the window, a partition and a door between the bar and the smoking room. There was a glazed lobby with a serving hatch, and another glazed partition at the foot of the stairs. The smoking room had stuffed seating around the room, a cloth on the floor, two spittoons, a mahogany drinking table, and a Windsor chair.

In the late 1890s, Usher's were unceremoniously bounced out of the *Rummer* in an quite breathtaking display of partisanship. But to understand what happened we need to go back and look at a pub which once stood round the corner.

At one time the area behind the *Rummer* was awash with pubs – hardly surprising, seeing that the market was there as well. They included the *Beefsteak Tavern*, the *Grove Tavern*, the *Noah's Ark*, the *Jolly Butcher's*, the *Old Tumbledown Dick*, and, in the lane leading down to the river, the *Red Cow*. They ranged from the decidedly dubious to the reasonably posh – and the poshest of the lot was the *Grove Tavern*.

The *Grove Tavern* had a variety of addresses, not because it moved around, but because it stood on one of those faultlines between lanes, rows and courts which were a legacy of the piecemeal way the old city had developed. In 1792 it was in Eastgate Lane, in 1800 it was in Orange Court, and in 1805 it was in Newmarket Row. In other words, nobody – even though they might have known how to get there – was quite sure where it was.

So comprehensively was this area redeveloped when the *Empire Hotel* was built that it is almost impossible to visualise what was there before. The *Grove Tavern* stood above the old East Gate, where the *Empire* stands today, looking out onto Eastgate Lane. The entrance to it, however, was from a court which also lies under the *Empire*.

It was first recorded in 1782 when a Mr Charley moved from the *Plume of Feathers* in Horse Street to "a large and commodious house called the *Grove Tavern* [with] exceedingly good lodgings . . . neat wines, London Porter, etc." In 1789 Signor Invetto, the celebrated firework impresario, was lodging at the *Grove* when a dreadful tragedy occurred:

> Saturday afternoon about four o'clock a melancholy accident happened at the apartments of Signor Invetto, at the *Grove Tavern* ... occasioned by some powder taking fire, which communicated to several pieces of fireworks in the room, by the explosion of which his wife and son were instantaneously suffocated, and afterwards scorched so as to render them dreadful spectacles. This very ingenious foreigner was from home when the catastrophe happened – on his return, finding the situation of his wife and child, his agonised feelings cannot well be described; whatever can be conceived of despair, frenzy and horror were depicted in his countenance. He has lost everything he possessed in the world; but above all what he prized superior to every other consideration; for he was exemplary in his attachments and duties as a husband and father.

Despite this tragedy, Signor Invetto stayed in Bath and continued to make his living from firework displays. He moved to Frog Lane – which later became New Bond

Street – and you cannot help feeling that it must have been a very understanding landlord who took him in after what had happened at the *Grove*. Nevertheless, he was still giving firework displays in Sydney Gardens ten years later.

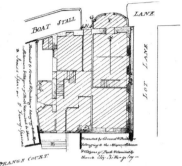

An early nineteenth-century plan of the *Grove Tavern* with Boatstall Lane and the old East Gate on the north.

The Northgate Brewery took over the lease of the *Grove Tavern* and, in 1810, added bow fronts to its windows. Apart from that, nothing much seems to have happened until plans for the *Empire Hotel*, which involved the demolition of the *Grove Tavern*, were drawn up in the late 1890s. The Bath Brewery Company, who had acquired the lease, submitted plans for a new pub, in a similar style to the *Empire*, next to the market. These were rejected, because it had been decided that the licence of the *Grove* would be transferred to the *Empire*.

What happened next all but beggars belief. The Corporation bounced Usher's out of the lease of the *Rummer Tavern*, which they had held since 1883, and offered it to the Bath Brewery Company. The Bath Brewery Company accepted the offer, moved in, and renamed the *Rummer* the *Grove*.

The 1903 report on the new *Grove Tavern* reads as follows:

> Entrances from Newmarket Row, Grand Parade and Market. Exit from cellar to Slaughterhouse Lane leading from Orange Grove to side of river under Grand Parade. Open urinal on stairs leading to market just outside smoke room door. Bar in three compartments and smoke room beyond and little room beyond latter, sometimes used.

The door through to the market (with the urinal on the stairs) was to the right of where the bar counter now stands. A door to the left of the bar led through to a small triangular-shaped bar. Both had gone by the time Fred Pearce visited in 1976 and described the *Grove* as follows:

> Two small bars – the Castle and Eastgate, the former overlooking Pulteney Weir. Old cast iron tables, a fine wooden settle and clock have been kept as this pub moved from serving regulars to plying for the tourist trade. A few regulars remain, however – a merry band with a penchant for singing.

In 1980 the future of the *Grove* was threatened when Bath City Council put the pub on the market instead of renewing Courage's lease. David Stubbs, a council spokesman said that the property had "potential for other uses [which] could yield a greater income. It might be used for a variety of things – a shop, restaurant or wine bar. It could even be a public house again." Happily, wiser counsels prevailed, and after being closed for two months' refurbishment, it reopened – as the *Grove Wine Bar*. Later it went back to its old name – the *Rummer* – and it is still open today (although without the urinal on the stairs). In the two public rooms on the first floor (one a TV sports lounge) some fine eighteenth-century features can be seen. The front room, overlooking Pulteney Bridge, has some impressive plasterwork and a buffet niche in the corner. The pub's name, incidentally, has nothing to do with rum. A rummer was a large glass, so called after Dutch "Roemer" or "Roman" glasses.

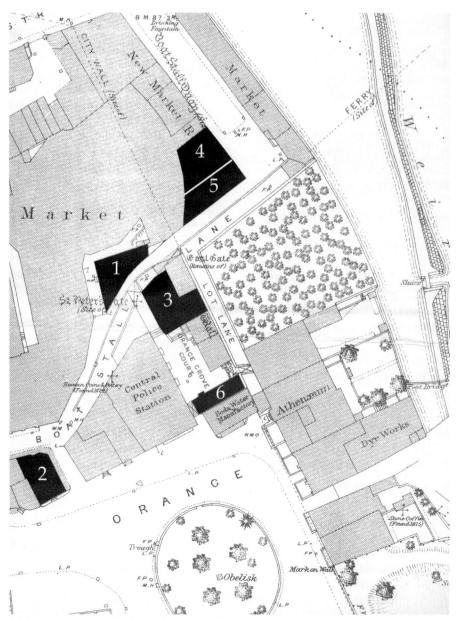

Pubs in the Orange Grove and Market area in the 1870s: 1 the *Beefsteak Tavern*; 2 the *Cross Keys*; 3 the *Grove Tavern*; 4 the *Newmarket Tavern*; 5 the *Rummer*; 6 the *Sun*. Only the *Rummer* remains. The *Sun* and the *Grove Tavern* were demolished to build the Empire. The *Cross Keys* and the *Beefsteak Tavern* have also disappeared. The *Newmarket Tavern* is now the Marmaris Restaurant, while the Police Station (to the left of the *Sun*) is now Brown's Restaurant.

ST CHRISTOPHER'S INN   1 Broad Street

St Christopher's is Bath's newest pub, the successor to the *Oliver*, named not after Oliver Reed but after Dr William Oliver, whose face appears still appears on a plaque above the entrance. Dr Oliver made a fortune from the sick people who came to Bath to seek a cure, prescribing them a dry biscuit whose exact recipe was a closely-guarded

secret and of which he was the sole supplier. Bath Olivers can still be found, but they cost rather less than they did in the eighteenth century.

The opening of the *Oliver* was recorded in the *Bath Chronicle* on 2 June 1962:

> Almost exactly 200 years ago Dr Oliver passed on the recipe for the Oliver Biscuit to his coachman, Atkins, who set up shop in Green Street. Since then an unlicensed restaurant has always existed on the site. On Thursday the *Oliver Inn* opened on the site to provide a fully licensed restaurant for the middle-brows. On the ground floor of this spacious and carefully restored historic house, there will be a chicken and ham bar seating well over 100 diners and on the first floor a steak bar catering for more than 50. Of four drinking bars, one is called the Doctor's Bar as a direct compliment to Dr Oliver, and here Oliver Biscuits will be supplied with the drinks. Another bar has been erected in the 600 square foot cellar of the building, where existing stone walls from the seventeenth century have been retained.

The story about Atkins' biscuit factory is probably apocryphal. Certainly, the shop was not always a restaurant. It was a grocer's for many years, with spells as a chemist's and a bookseller's, until it was taken over by James Fortt in 1908. One story that is not apocryphal concerns a mid-nineteenth century wager:

> At the rear of 1 Broad Street were the private stables, yard and coach house, belonging to Mr Wiltshire, and where his horses and carriage were stabled whenever he came into Bath. Access was gained to these through a pair of high folding gates in Green Street. There is a very interesting incident connected with this place which occurred some short time after the introduction of railway travelling, when the old Jehus had to give place to the engine driver, and like Othello discover their occupation gone. It became hard lines with many of these old chaps and some of them were reduced to the position of driving pony carriages about the streets of Bath. As in all classes, some, on the other hand, were more provident, and made hay while the sun shone, so that when they were superseded they had a little wherewith to sustain themselves. Such a one lived for years at No 2 Richmond Place, by the name of Lock, and amused many with his coaching anecdotes and adventures. The preliminary part of the incident I have alluded to took place in the smoke room of the Castle [where the main post office stands today]. A conversation having arisen as to the dexterity of the old stage coach drivers and the wonderful accuracy of their measurement in passing each other or any object with only the most minute margin of space being left, one of the disputants was outlandish enough to assert he could produce one of these old jarveys who would perform the apparently utterly impossible feat of turning a stage coach and four in that narrowest of all thoroughfares in Bath, Green Street. The party who questioned the possibility of this exploit being accomplished, having been assured there was no catch in the transaction and that everything was fair and above board covered the stake posted, maintaining such an achievement could not be accomplished. A few days after this, in the early morning a well-known aged four-in-hand man, seated on the box of the old stage-coach which for years adorned the showrooms of the late Mr Benjamin Newnham, coach builder, whilst in Grove Street, as well as in Broad Street – where the

YMCA rooms now are – accompanied by a number of friends, some on the coach, others walking, were to be seen descending the thoroughfare. When the rumble of the coach arrived parallel with the opening into Green Street, the old hand with the ribbons took his dimensions; the coach was cautiously backed along the street until it reached the *Green Tree*; then the large folding gates were opened; the coach, together with the wheelers, was backed into the yard, and the faces of the leaders, standing in the roadway, brought straight with the shop of Mr Fortt [now *St Christopher's*]; they were then gently pulled for Milsom Street, the wheelers and the coach following out of the yard without the least hitch taking place; the quidnunc, who had not given the yard a consideration, admitting the bet was honourably made, and fairly won.

In 1968, the *Oliver* was regarded as the place to go for chic meals. Not only could you have a steak cooked to your liking, but there was a special treat – the house ice cream. When Fred Pearce visited in 1976, however, he was not impressed:

> Comfy seats, quiet muzak, adjoining restaurants and lots of middle aged people sitting cross-legged and hands clasped slightly uneasy amidst the failed opulence of Bernis. Lots of wine and sherries. Doctors Bar serves Tartan; the Cellar Bar has a juke box.

The 2001 *Itchy Guide to Bath* described it as "one to bring your gran to." Not any longer. 2003 was but a few days old when it shut up shop for good and the gutters and revampers went in to transform it into Bath's latest backpackers' hostel – *St Christopher's*, complete with a minimalist, classically-inspired bar downstairs.

ST JAMES'S WINE VAULTS 10 St James's Street

St James's Street was built, like the Square it leads to, by John Palmer in the early 1790s. On 30 June 1791, the following advertisement appeared in the *Bath Chronicle*:

> John Halpen (late servant to the Rt Hon Lady M Stanley)
> Begs leave to inform his friends and the public
> That he has opened a Commodious
> INN & TAVERN
> Known by the name of *St James's Hotel*
> Back of the Old Crescent.

He was not there very long. By the following year, John Davis had taken over. In 1796 another advertisement appeared:

> For sale by auction, part of the property of Richard Hewlett ... Nos 8 & 9, St James's Street, adjoining St James's Square, being those extensive premises planned and built for a tavern, and now called *St James's Coffee House*, together with four coach houses and eleven stall stabling. The whole let to Mr Clark, Brewer at £130 a year, 15 years unexpired of his lease.

The sale was due to Mr Hewlett's bankruptcy. He was among the victims of the biggest slump in Bath's history, when two of its six banks went bust. The sale of his estate, however, does not seem to have disrupted the running of the hotel. In the early

1800s, it was kept by Matthew Hudson. By the late 1820s, Henry Roberts had taken over and renamed it *St James's Tavern*. Among the societies that met there was St James's Patriotic Benefit Society.

By the 1840s, when a wine and spirit merchant called William Brett took over, the hotel side of the business was in terminal decline. When John Brett (who already had a wine & spirit merchant's at 20 Kingsmead Square) took over in 1849, he closed the hotel and renamed the premises St James's Wine Vaults. Gradually, it became less of a wine merchant's and more of a pub. By 1903, it was owned by John Rawlings of the *Devonshire Arms* on Wells Road. When Fred Pearce visited in 1976, he noted that "an unusual feature of the lounge decor is a fine wood bar with frosted glass panel and arched wooden hatchway," while the public bar was "more chatty." Today St James's Wine Vaults is open plan, but still retains an individual atmosphere. It is open all day, and despite being well out of the town centre, always seems busy in a laid-back sort of way.

SALAMANDER 3 John Street

For most of its history, John Street – built by John Wood in 1730 – has remained aloof from beer. Today, however, it not only has an extract from the Magna Carta written on the side of Bonham's auction house – "let there be one measure for wine throughout our kingdom, and one measure for ale, and one measure for corn" – but also Bath's newest real ale pub, the *Salamander*.

The *Salamander* was one of the hippest places to hang out in 1960s Bath. By the 1970s, however, it had – according to Fred Pearce at any rate – gone down in the world. His comments on the place are worth quoting in full:

> A small bar under the restaurant. It's tatty but appears to trade on the fact. Bohemian or something. Ripped wallpaper on the ceiling, stuffing falling out of the seats and bar padding, dirty floor. On top of that lot the prices for nasty cold Trumans beers start at 28p. Low lighting and loud juke box. Some nice pictures and basketwork, but it hardly compensates.

Many who remember the old *Salamander* with affection will strongly disagree with Fred's assessment. After all, he hated the *Hat & Feather*, and seems to have disliked the *Salamander* for much the same reasons. The old *Salamander* has gone, however, and its place has been taken by Bath Ales's second outlet in the city. Although some of the old decorative features have sadly disappeared, the Bath Ales team has managed to create, from scratch, an ambience which feels as though it has developed over generations. Although tucked away in a back street, the *Salamander* is rapidly developing a reputation as one of Bath's top real ale pubs. Good food, good beer, great service, and a terrific atmosphere – in a John Wood building. The Bath Ales' colour scheme – midnight blue and dark orange – creates the perfect setting for downing their range of ales – while the upstairs restaurant is, like the *Hop Pole* – getting rave reviews in all the right places.

The name of the pub, incidentally, is only indirectly linked to the creature which appears on the sign. "Salamander" comes from a Persian word meaning "lives in fire," reflecting the erroneous belief that salamanders could walk through fire and remain unharmed. As a result, the word was applied to various objects which could withstand great heat, such as pokers, brands or griddles. The *Salamander* in John Street acquired its name because it was noted for its seared chops and steaks. A sign on the wall at the back of the pub declares that the *Salamander* is Bath's famous old chop house. A former landlord found the sign in the cellar in the 1970s behind a pile of rubbish, but, although it appears old, it only dates from the late 1950s. Certainly, we have found no record of No 3 John Street being an eating house earlier than 1957.

In 1856, when records of John Street first appear in the *Bath Directory*, the building was occupied by William Smith, a pattern drawer. By 1870, he had been replaced by Miss F Harford, a music seller. She was only there a couple of years, before John Barry and his wife moved in. He was an accountant, she was a milliner, and they did not stay very long either, for by 1874, the wonderfully named Mrs F Trash, a "servant's registrar," was sharing it with Mrs Frances Savage, a dressmaker.

In 1878, a Mr Bull took over the lease. The firm of law stationers and accountants he established there lasted till 1909, when Messrs Walker & Ling, a drapery business which also had premises at 2-3 Milsom Street and 4-5 Quiet Street, moved in. They later moved into the shop next door (now the *Firehouse Rotisserie*) as well. Around 1952, Leoni's Ladies' Hairdressers took over Nos 2 & 3 John Street. Although Leoni's continued in what is now the *Firehouse Rotisserie* until around 1965, a coffee bar and restaurant called the *Salamander* opened in No 3 around 1957.

On 12 April 1957, the *Salamander* got a licence to serve wine to diners. Just under a year later, on 7 February 1958, it got a licence to serve beer to them as well. Finally, on 11 May 1962, it got a full pub licence, so that its patrons no longer needed to scoff as well as sup. The *Salamander* may be one of Bath's newer pubs, dating back just over 40 years, but it is one no lover of real ale should miss on even the briefest visit to Bath.

SAM WELLER'S 14 Upper Borough Walls

Although some Bath pubs – the *Star*, the *Saracen's Head*, and the *Bell*, for example – have kept their original names – the majority have had at least one change of name, often in the dim, distant past. Although some modern renamings – particularly those inspired by a quest for corporate identity – are pretty unforgivable, it is no use saying

such things did not happen in the good old days. Nevertheless, there is one Bath pub whose renaming is a matter of particular regret, simply because its old name lasted so long. This is *Sam Weller's*, known, for over 250 years, as the *Full Moon*.

The original *Full Moon* was built in the late seventeenth or early eighteenth century. It backed onto the old city wall and was probably a fairly basic two-storey alehouse. The distance between "the path by the Borough Wall" (later widened into Upper Borough Walls) and the wall itself was not very great, and the building would almost certainly have been no more than one room deep. To compensate for this lack of depth, it was twice the length of the present building, extending to what is now the corner of Burton Street.

The first reference to the *Full Moon* comes in a council minute of 1739, in which Daniel Milsom was granted the lease of a piece of ground "abutting against the *Full Moon* on the east, a way from the Westgate to the Northgate on the south, and the said Milsom's Garden north, on condition that he do not build upon the town wall nor have any way out of the ground … nor to build above one storey above the way that goes by the wall." The terms of the lease are interesting, as they almost certainly indicate the terms on which the *Full Moon* itself was built – that is, it could not go on top of the city wall, could not breach it, and could not be more than one storey higher.

Just over a decade later, the council abandoned their protective attitude towards the city walls and embraced a policy of demolition and redevelopment. The only bit of the old walls to survive above ground was a short stretch in Upper Borough Walls, which can still be seen today. It only escaped because George Trim's development north of the walls at that point, dating from the early eighteenth century, ruled out further development there. The rest of Upper Borough Walls was redeveloped in the 1770s, with many of the old buildings, including the *Full Moon*, being forced to set their frontages back several feet so that the road could be widened.

In 1773, Jeremy Willsher (or Wiltshire) was obliged to give up the lease of the *Full Moon* and apply for a new lease, which laid down terms for developing the site. The text of the new lease ran to several pages, full of legal prolixity and obfuscation, copperplated on crumbling vellum by some long-departed scribe. It is, nevertheless, full of fascinating detail for anyone who takes the trouble to decipher it. Here, for example, is the description of the plot of land granted to Jeremy Willsher:

> All that plot of ground (late parcel of a messuage or tenement, malthouse, millhouse, stable and yard with a wash house and also of a plot of ground with another messuage or tenement with its appurtenances called the *Full Moon* severally demised as aforesaid) … and also being some part of an ancient messuage or tenement heretofore called the school house … containing in front south-west to a street called the Borough Wall 23 feet 6 inches and in breadth backwards 24 feet and in length on the west side 39 feet 10 inches and on the east side 43 feet 2 inches. And also

all that messuage or tenement hereinafter agreed and intended to be erected and built by and at the costs of the said Jeremy Willsher on the said plot of ground being the first house from the south-east corner house in Burton Street ... which said plot of ground and the said messuage and buildings to be built thereon are bounded on the north by another plot of ground and a messuage building on some part thereof demised ... to the said Jeremy Willsher for the like term, ... on the south by the said street called the Borough Wall, on the west by other plots of ground and messuages building thereon demised ... to the said Jeremy Willsher, being another part of the said premises.

The quill pushers who drew up leases like this were paid by the word, which goes a long way to explaining why they are so full of repetition and interminable detail. One thing missing from the lease, however, is any reference to the old wall, or even to the line of the old wall. Nor is there any mention of the ditch which lay on the other side of the wall. John Leland, writing in 1542, had pointed out that, "from inside the town the wall appears to be of no great height, but from outside the height from ground level is considerable." Confirmation of this can be obtained by a quick peek over the eastern end of the surviving stretch of wall in Upper Borough Walls into the yard below. We can presume – although we cannot be sure – that the wall came down before Jeremy Willshire signed the lease (to provide stone for building, no doubt), but what of the ditch behind it? Had it already been filled in, or did it provide the foundation for the *Full Moon's* cellars?

Although the wall is not mentioned in the lease, one relic of old Bath does put in an appearance – the "ancient tenement ... heretofore called the school house." This was the first King Edward's School in Barton Lane, outside the wall. It was only used as a school for just over 30 years, between 1552 and 1583. By 1631, it was leased as "a messuage or tenement with a garden thereunto adjoining" to John Simons. The *Full Moon*, therefore, lies on top of the original King Edward's School as well as part of the city wall.

The lease granted to Jeremy Willsher also goes into great detail about the type of building he was to erect. It had to be four storeys high (including garrets), two feet further back from the street than the old building, and built "with all speed." The frontage had "all to be of ashlar stone, well jointed and executed." A pavement, four feet two inches wide, "with the best pennant stone well faced," was to be "laid down according to the rules of good workmanship" in front of the building. Jeremy Willsher also had to "make, pitch and finish" the roadway, from the edge of the pavement to the middle of the street, "with good blue lias stone." Finally, he had to build a conduit from his property into the main sewer "for the conveying of foul and nasty water and other such offensive matters."*

Perhaps the most startling detail of all, however, comes right at the end of the lease. Jeremy Willsher was clearly a man of means – maltster, brewer, and property developer. Yet there, at the bottom of the final page, appear the words, "Jeremy

---

* "Offensive matters," incidentally, only meant the liquid variety at this time. Until well into the nineteenth century, solid ones still had to be collected by those most odoriferous of our forefathers, night-soil men.

Willsher his Mark," and a shaky X scrawled beside it.

It is not known whether the *Full Moon* is haunted. Spectral scratchings at the window, however, may come from the ghost of an unknown woman, about 80 years old, who called into the tap room one raw night in 1819 and asked for a pint of beer and a chance to warm herself by the fire. The request was refused, on the grounds that she looked penniless. She went outside and sat on the pavement until a passer-by took pity on her and helped her along to the Guildhall. She was taken into the Beadle's Room and sat in front of the fire, where she died. It was later found that she had enough money for a beer in her pocket.

Alternatively, they may come from the spirit of James Harding who worked at the *Full Moon's* brewery. One day in 1821, James Wine, the brewer, asked Harding to pump up some wort into the copper, which was about ten feet deep. He left him alone for about a quarter of an hour, and, when he returned, found Harding in the copper, which was about 30 inches deep in boiling wort. He managed to haul him out, but he died about ten minutes later. At the inquest, he said that he had frequently seen Harding sit on the side of the copper, whilst engaged in brewing, to eat his lunch, despite being warned of the danger.

By the mid-nineteenth century the *Full Moon* had a smoking room, a tap room and parlour (both with framed prints on their walls), a bar and a brewhouse. It was an eminently respectable pub, where "tradesmen and artisans rubbed shoulders together [and] any evening you could make sure of hearing instructive and intellectual conversation on the topics of the day."

In 1880 a new frontage was added to the building, which, according to a report by Major Davis, not only "ignored the structure of the old building" but caused "serious settlement" and threatened to bring the whole building down. The owners were ordered to take immediate remedial action. The ground-floor frontage, a particularly well-preserved piece of pub design, probably dates from this time. The rather haphazard appearance of the upper floors bears witness to the convoluted history of the building and, no doubt, to the ill-advised revamp of 1880, although it is likely that any cracks and settlement from that period have long since stabilised.

The 1903 report on the *Full Moon* tells us that the bar was "in four compartments" and that there was an "undersized billiard table in the small room at the back." It was still called the *Full Moon* and still had two bars when Fred Pearce called in 1976. Today, it has been knocked through into one – although the layout of the old pub can still be traced by looking at the beams on the ceiling – and renamed *Sam Weller's*. Whilst it is fitting that Dickens should be honoured in a city which provided so much inspiration for his *Pickwick Papers*, it is a pity that it had to be the *Full Moon*, with such a rich history of its own. The pub sign, showing Sam Weller standing over a snoozing Mr Pickwick with a foaming tankard in his hand, has, however, been singled out for especial praise by members of the Pub Sign Society.

SARACEN'S HEAD   42 Broad Street

Talking of Dickens brings us neatly on to the *Saracen's Head*, one of Bath's most famous pubs. The building goes back at least as far as the early eighteenth century, although the date of 1713 cut into the facade looks like a later addition. The idea that pubs called the *Saracen's Head* or the *Turk's Head* date back to the time of the Crusades, when knights called into them on their way to the Holy Land, is, in almost all cases, unfounded. Families whose members had taken part in the Crusades included a Saracen's Head in their coats of arms. When pubs opened in buildings owned by them, Saracen's Heads appeared on their signs in the same way as other heraldic devices. There was, incidentally, a *Turk's Head* further up Broad Street, at No 14, which closed in 1935.

The first record we have of the *Saracen's Head* as a pub comes from 1728, when it formed part of a marriage settlement. Although never in the first rank of Bath's coaching inns, it was the starting point for regular coach services to London, Bristol, and other cities.

City of BATH. **B**e it remembered, that on the *Third* Day of *December* 1776 *William Davis* of in the Parish of *St Michael* in the said City, *Innholder* and *Joseph Thwaits* of the fame City, *Victualler* came perfonally before us *Henry Wright Esqr. Mayor* No. *104.* and *Edward Bushell Collibee and John Horton Esqrs* Juftices of the Peace in and for the fame City, and each of them feverally acknowledged to owe to our Sovereign Lord *George the Third* King of Great-Britain, &c. the Sum of Ten Pounds, *each*

Upon Condition that if the above-bounden *William Davis* who is this Day licenced by us to keep a common Inn and Alehoufe for one whole Year from the Date hereof, or until the next General Licenfing of Victuallers for the faid City, in the Houfe wherein he now dwelleth, fituate in *Broad Street* in the Parifh of *St Michael* within the faid City, and commonly called or known by the Name or Sign of *the Saracens Head* do from henceforth keep the true Affize in felling Bread, Beer, Ale, Victuals, and Liquors, according to Law and the Tenor or Purport of his faid Licence, and fhall not have, or keep, or permit, or fuffer any Perfon or Perfons to have or play at or with Cards, Dice Tables, Bowls, or any other unlawful Game or Games, in his Houfe, Out-houfe, Yard, Garden, or Backfide, nor fuffer any Perfon to be drunk, or remain tipling or drinking there, nor any Diforder to be committed therein contrary to Law, but on the contrary, if he fhall maintain and keep good Order and Rule in the fame according to the Laws of this Realm, then this Recognizance to be void, or elfe to remain in full Force.

Taken and acknowledged at the faid City of *Bath*, the Day and Year above, } before us,

Hon: Wright Mayor
Ed. Collibee
John Horton

The licence granted to William Davis of the *Saracen's Head* in 1776.

Legend has it that Charles Dickens stayed at the *Saracen's Head* in May 1835, while working as a reporter, covering Lord John Russell's visit to Bath. The chair which he reputedly slumped in after a hard day's scribbling was shown to curious visitors in Victorian times and – so it is said – sold to them on several occasions.

In 1850, David Aust, a developer, was given the go ahead to build a house on "ground adjoining the back of the *Saracen's Head* in Walcot Street" by the Corporation. However, Mr Acres, who held the lease of the *Saracen's Head* objected to the plan. It is unclear whether the objection was upheld, or whether David Aust went ahead with the building. It is possible, however, that what is now the back part of the *Saracen's Head*, forming the entrance to the pub from Walcot Street, dates from this time, and was originally a separate building.

At the end of the nineteenth century, the right-hand side of the *Saracen's Head* (looking from Broad Street) housed a shop. At one time this was an antique shop known as the Pickwick Curio Stores. It later became a bookshop. There was a back entrance to the *Saracen's Head* from Walcot Street. The entrance to the stable yard (now bricked up) was next to it. Inside the pub were two bars, a tap room, a smoke room and a private glass room. In 1888, there were eight bedrooms to let. By 1903 the number had fallen to three. A "long dining room" on the first floor was also described as "seldom if ever used." The possible reason for this is that the licensee, Alderman Rubie, who also held the license of the *Castle Hotel* in Northgate Street (on the site now occupied by the Post Office), only used the rather outmoded facilities at the *Saracen's Head* if the *Castle* was full. On the whole, the *Saracen's Head* seems to have seen better days by the end of the nineteenth century. Perhaps the most telling remark made by the Corporation official who inspected it in 1903 was that it had "no urinal, customers making use of the stable."

Today, of course, it is a very different story, but what appears to be one of the pub's most interesting historic features – its highly ornate ceiling – is the result of a skilful makeover in the 1960s. The pub has been knocked through, and the old stable (no longer used as a urinal) now forms part of the drinking area. The *Saracen's Head* is a Steak & Ale Pub, part of a chain formerly owned by Scottish & Newcastle, but acquired in October 2003 by Spirit Amber. Like the *Bear* on Wellsway, it is festooned with banners bearing the motto, "serious about steaks." It's a snappy catchphrase – perhaps the start of an ongoing campaign. Still to come – "cheerless about chicken," "pessimistic about pork," "troubled about toad in the hole." Who knows?

Before the advent of all-day drinking, the *Saracen's Head* had a licence to stay open till 4pm on Wednesday afternoons because it was market day. It was naturally very crowded. Just one of those quaint English customs (like hanging around waiting for the pubs to open at 5.30) which those who mastered the art of raising the wrist in those halcyon pre-all-day-drinking-days of auld lang cider remember with dewy-eyed affliction.

SLUG & LETTUCE York Buildings, George Street

The *York House Hotel*, part of which now houses the *Slug & Lettuce,* opened on Bonfire Night 1769. We know this because the previous Saturday a notice appeared in the *Bath Chronicle*:

> The proprietors of *York House* beg leave to acquaint the nobility and gentry that their house will be open on Tuesday next for their business.

Designed by John Wood the Younger, the *York House* was not only one of the

biggest coaching inns in Bath, with its yard occupying what is now Broad Street car park, but the most up-to-date. In 1778, a local writer called Philip Thicknesse, who was not known for dishing out compliments, described it as "an excellent hotel, the only house of reception which is situated in an open, airy part of the city; and, to the advantage of its excellent situation, the stranger will find what can be found scarce anywhere else in England, a sensible, honest host, who is not only a man of good family, but one who has a liberal education. From such a man, every person who comes to his house is sure of meeting with politeness, diffidence and a proper reception ... When the *York House* is full, the *Bear* is the next best inn, and, for people of inferior rank, the *Greyhound* or the *White Lion* in the Market Place."

Over forty years later, Pierce Egan was still able to describe the *York House* as "one of the largest and best inns in the kingdom out of London." The "sensible, honest host" mentioned in 1778, Robert St John Lucas, was still there. Around 1805 he went into partnership with Bradshaw Reilly, and by 1830 Mr Reilly was listed as sole licensee. At the height of the coaching era, the horses from the coaches serving the inn were stabled not only in the yard in Broad Street, but also in Princes Mews, Edgar Mews, and Circus Mews.

It was not only coaches which ran to and from the *York House*. Carriers were based there as well. One day in 1819, a cart from the *York House* was found at Midford with its splinter bar broken and the carter lying in the road in a state of advanced inebriation. A group of locals put him on top of the cart and took him along to the nearby *Fox Inn*. There they fixed the splinter bar, dumped the carrier, swearing mightily, inside the cart on top of some old sacks, and set off for Bath. When they arrived at the *York House* they went to get him out, only to find that he had rolled over on to his front and suffocated.

In the same year that Philip Thicknesse published his eulogy in praise of the *York House*, early morning excitement was provided when an Irish nobleman, Count Rice, was carried wounded to the *York House* after killing Count Du Barré in a duel on Claverton Down.

Further excitement came on Christmas Day in 1827, when

a destructive fire ... broke out on the York House premises, between two and three o'clock of the morning. It was first discovered issuing from the windows of a shop in Broad Street, immediately under the large assembly room of the hotel ... The bells of St Michael's Church, and the bugles of the Cavalry, quickly alarmed the whole city, and drew an immense concourse to the spot. The engines of the different fire offices arrived with great expedition; but, notwithstanding every effort, the flames raged with unabated fury, till the whole wing was consumed. Fortunately, the fire was prevented, by a party wall, from reaching the front buildings of the hotel, the principal part of which remained untouched.

The following week's *Bath Chronicle* picked up the tragic consequences of one woman's rush to see the fire:

> Tuesday last a child named Langford, one month old, was left in the bed of a neighbour at 18 Ballance St, while the mother went to see the fire at *York House* – the husband coming home in the absence of his wife, and not knowing that the child was in the bed, folded it up; and on the return of the mother the child was found suffocated.

The proprietors of the *York House* soon got over the fire and within a month had placed an advertisement in the paper saying that rumours of a lack of rooms at York House were being falsely put about by their competitors.

In the 1830s, bottled sauces started to be extensively advertised in the local newspapers. Sauces had been available in Bath throughout the eighteenth century, as accompaniments to the plain boiled meats which were prepared for residents of lodging houses, but it was not until the early nineteenth century that sauce-bottling really took off. Crosse & Blackwell's was one well-known brand. York House Sauce was another (at least in Bath), but unfortunately has not proved to have the same staying power.

In 1840 the *York House* was taken by John Emeny from the *Bath Hotel* at Clifton. The following year he placed an advertisement in the *Bath Chronicle*:

> J Emeny begs to inform the nobility, gentry and public … that he has always in hand a large supply of fine lively turtle which he sends, alive or dressed, to any part of town or country

Such were the culinary delights of the early Victorian period.

Today, after standing empty for several years, the *York House* is once again one of Bath's most popular hotels. The thirtieth *Slug & Lettuce* bar in the chain opened in part of it in November 1999. The lavish opening ceremony included free beer and dancing on the tables. The *Bath Chronicle* reporter was certainly impressed – "the decor of the place is very posh; it smells of London bars and high-class society … The layout is one big 'L' – there are no nooks or crannies in which to hide, which states pretty much from the off that this is not your average local … The surreal notion that somebody could walk in with their dressing gown and a cup of tea was ever present, but that just adds to the charm."

The *Slug & Lettuce* chain is owned, like the *Litten Tree*, by SFI (Surrey Free Inns), which has taken a radical approach to pub design. To quote the company's profile, "SFI high street concepts are designed as 'chameleon' bars." This means that, by subtle changes to the presentation, different types of customers will be attracted at different times – shoppers and business people at lunchtime, party animals at night. They recognises that "a potential pitfall with large retail premises is that, whilst they may work well when full, there is a danger that the customer will feel lonely during quieter periods. SFI units are designed to avoid this problem through the provision of more intimate areas within the bar with varying 'look and feel.' Lounge type seating, dining areas, intimate corners, zones for partying groups and poser tables (to name a few) integrate to create an electric feel." So it is not just a question of pub versus superpub. Even in the aspirational-customer-profile world of the superpub, there is a battle between those who favour the wide-open approach, such as *All Bar One*, and those, like SFI, who go for multi-zoning. Fifty years hence, will traditionalists perhaps be campaigning to have interiors like that of the *Slug & Lettuce* preserved and listed as rare examples of late twentieth-century pub design? After all, who could have predicted, when the *Star* got its shiny new Gaskell & Chambers fittings in the mid-nineteenth century, that they would be so cherished at the beginning of the twenty-first?

One pub that we cannot feature in this book is the third of the bars which SFI planned to open in Bath. In January 2001, plans to open a 550-capacity Bar Med pub in Westgate Buildings (just up from Smith Bros) received the thumbs down from councillors after a vigorous residents' campaign, even though B&NES planning officers had recommended acceptance.

SMITH BROS 11-12 Westgate Buildings

The vibrantly modern *Smith Bros* was once a wine and spirit merchant's dating back at least as far back as the 1840s. Before that, its cellars allegedly formed part of Bath's debtors' prison. In 1863, when Thomas Toleman sold what was then the *Borough Wine Vaults* to William Wilson of 4 Norfolk Crescent, it consisted of a shop with a serving counter, a counting house and a stable in the yard.

By the beginning of the twentieth century, the *Borough Wine Vaults* was owned by Emma Tutton of the Bathwick brewing dynasty. The licensee was Edwin Ponter, a director of Smith Bros, Wine & Spirit Merchants. Part of Westgate Buildings was destroyed in the Bath Blitz and the frontage of the *Borough Wine Vaults* was blown off. However, it was repaired and by the early 1970s the *Borough Wine Vaults* had become the *Spirit Vaults* public house. When Fred Pearce visited in 1976 he found a "surprisingly traditional" public bar – "all high ceiling and smoky yellow paint" – and

LEFT An 1848 advertisement for the *Borough Vaults* (now *Smith Bros*)
RIGHT An adverisement from 1916 featuring Beckford Whisky, whose trademark was the tower on top of Lansdown.

a large lounge bar. He also noted that trade was slack – even though it sold the cheapest pint in town – Courage Best at 19p. It sounds cheap – and indeed it was. If the price of that 19p pint had risen in line with inflation it would cost you a mere 83p today. So much for EU harmonisation and all those claims of reduced taxation.

STAR   23 Vineyards

It is no exaggeration to say that the *Star* is a national treasure. The part of Bath it lies in has an atmosphere like no other, with high stone walls and buildings crowding in on all sides. The pub, too is just the sort of wood-panelled bolthole where you would not be surprised to see Dylan Thomas scribbling away in the corner with a Woodbine in the corner of his mouth. If you're not into poetry, then think of the pubs in those black and white films which always seemed to have Stanley Holloway in them.

Where are they now? Gutted or gone – but if you want to see what they were like and have Draught Bass poured out from a jug or help yourself to a complimentary pinch of snuff on "Death Row" – then come to the *Star*. It looks like pubs used to look before they were Red Barrelised, made over, departitioned, Laura Ashleyfied, fruit-machined, nitro-kegged, alco-popped, Al Caponed, distressed, bamboozled or just plain ******ed up. Put another way, its survival is about as surprising as that of a Meissen figurine in a bull-battered china shop. It very nearly disappeared. The Luftwaffe narrowly missed it – the plans for the extensive restoration work which had to be carried out after a bomb fell across the road are still on display in the bar – but a more insidious threat came in 1991, as reported in the *Bath Chronicle*:

> The *Star*, in the Paragon, unchanged for more than 100 years, may now lose most of its drinking space in favour of offices in a deal between owners Bass Brewery and a London-based property company, which hopes to buy the site for offices, then lease back the ground floor to Bass. Under the scheme all the wood-panelled rooms would go – reducing the pub to one room instead of five. Rooms above would also become office space.

But, thanks to all those who fought to preserve the *Star*, including the landlord, Alan Perrett, Bass was foiled in its bid to destroy a piece of Bath's heritage as important, in its own way, as the Abbey and the Roman Baths. Finally, in 2000, the *Star* was taken over by Alan Morgan of Abbey Ales, Bath's only brewery.

It is easy, now that the future of the *Star* is assured, to dismiss the fears of the 1990s as exaggerated. They were not. There are plenty of examples of pubs falling to corporate vandalism as late as the mid-1990s. There was a pub in Birmingham, the *Prince of Wales*, which stood in the way of plans for the area around the National Convention Centre. Although less well-preserved than the *Star*, with some of its partitions already gone, it was still recognisably a nineteenth-century street corner local, one of very few left from the 1960s Sack of Birmingham. A vociferous campaign (supported by, among others, the brass section of the City of Birmingham Symphony Orchestra, who found it a handy place to whet their whistle after a hard evening's blow) eventually succeeded in saving it. But it survived, only to be gutted and turned into an Irish theme pub-cum-eatery – ironic for those who remember the Irish licensees and the Sunday night ceilidh sessions shoehorned into its tiny back bar. Just try and imagine the *Star* as one big bar called *Doonican's* or *Paddy McGinty's* and be thankful that wiser counsels prevailed in Bath.*

OLD STAR ALEHOUSE?

A map of 1742 showing an earlier building on the site of the *Star*.

A fragment from a half-gallon jar from Richard Osborne, who was at the *Star* from around 1847 to 1861.

The date of the *Star's* building is uncertain but it is thought to have been put up around 1760 by Daniel Aust, a builder who worked on many of the houses in the Paragon. It is likely that, like many other eighteenth-century developers, he used the pub as an office and paid his men there. It would have been a neat way of recirculating money back into his own coffers. Regarding the shape of the building, the story goes that Mr Aust also made coffins and made the *Star* coffin-shaped to advertise his business. It is a good story, but it is possible he made it that shape to fit it onto a rather awkward site.

There was a building on the site of the *Star* before 1760, however. Thorpe's map of Bath, dating from the 1740s, shows a solitary building at the junction of what later became the Vineyards and Guinea Lane. It is a totally different shape to the building there today, lying across the site. A trip down to the cellars clearly reveals that Daniel Aust built the *Star* on the foundations of an earlier building – possibly an old alehouse – which he pulled down when he started developing the area. Given the antiquity of the roads around here and the proximity of Walcot Church, it could have been centuries old. The *Star* is also a very old pub name, associated with the Virgin Mary, and often borne by alehouses used by medieval pilgrims en route to shrines such as Glastonbury. The *Star* would have been an odd name for Daniel Aust to choose if he had been building the pub from scratch – the *Mason's Arms* or the *Paragon Tavern*, for example, would have been more

---

* According to recent reports, wiser counsels have now prevailed in Birmingham, and the *Prince of Wales* has been revamped as a traditional English pub. It is just a pity they did not prevail before the old interior was destroyed.

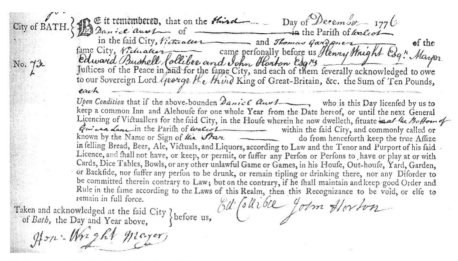

The licence granted to Daniel Aust for the Star in 1776.

obvious choices – but, in the absence of any further evidence, the theory that an older pub once stood on the site must remain just speculation – at least for the present.

By 1792 the licence passed to Daniel Aust's son, Peter who was there until at least 1811. From 1774, the Bath City Patriotic Benefit Society met at the *Star.* Not that it was all plain sailing in the old days. This report comes from 1834:

> On Wednesday week, John Hicks, a notorious character of Walcot, was fined four shillings and costs,
>
> for entering the *Star* public house and maliciously breaking two tables with a poker.

For many years there was a brewery at the back of the *Star,* the smoke from which on at least one occasion caused local residents to complain to the council. The fittings which make the *Star* so unique were installed in the mid-nineteenth century by the firm of Gaskell & Chambers.

TRINITY 49-50 James Street West

The area round here was once full of pubs – three on the south of Kingsmead Square, six in Corn Street, eight (at least) in Avon Street … the list goes on. The only one left is the *Trinity*, named after the nearby Holy Trinity Church, designed by John Lowder around 1817, and destroyed in the Bath Blitz.

The original building on the site of the *Trinity* dated from 1774, when Messrs Jelly, Fisher and Ford leased the land off St John's Hospital to build a house. Around 1839, Thomas Lye opened a beerhouse and brewery there. In 1844 the following advertisement appeared in the *Bath Chronicle*:

TRINITY BREWERY

To be sold ... the above small concern, including two store pieces of 1,600 and 800 gallons; smaller ditto and barrels, 150 gallon copper boilers, forcing pump, 20 bushel mash tub, two large coolers, capital four-motion beer engine, about 1,000 gallons of strong beer, and implements of business.

The *Trinity Brewery* advertised for sale in 1844.

It was bought by Matthew Stevens, who appears in subsequent *Postal Directories* as a beer retailer. Brewing ceased around 1898. The 1903 report on the property described it as being in a fair condition. Its trade was chiefly "off." Despite serious bomb damage in World War Two and extensive rebuilding, the *Trinity* has survived as a popular local, its sense of history reflected in a poster on the wall: "Beer – Helping Ugly People Have Sex Since 1862." Its sign features an ingenious interpretation of the pub's name – a pint of beer, two stocks of barley and a sprig of hops.

TROWBRIDGE HOUSE 128 Coronation Avenue, Twerton

Just down the road from the *Trowbridge House* is one of Bath's most striking architectural features, but because it is tucked away down a side street in South Twerton few people know about it. South Twerton Junior School, built in 1893, could have been just another late Victorian school, solid and functional, in that pseudo-public-school, East Midland Jacobean style they were so fond of back then. Perfectly respectable, but hardly anything to set the pulse racing. But the architect decided to go that bit further, stepping a circular turret out from the corner of the building and capping it with a bulbous copper spire. The school's hilltop site, with two roads leading up to it, gives it a prominence which the architect capitalised on in a magical way.

From the outside, the *Trowbridge House* has no such architectural distinction. It was built by Usher's of Trowbridge in 1923 as an off licence. Nine years later, with new housing springing up at the top of Coronation Avenue, they considered that "the development of the neighbourhood had reached a stage where it was reasonable and proper that the inhabitants should have a full licence." Rev Bert Bailey, the Moravian Minister, and the Oakhill Brewery both opposed the application, but, after a poll of local residents showed a clear majority in favour, it was approved. The first landlord was Mr RG Smith.

As the magistrates would not grant a new licence, Usher's had to transfer one from somewhere else. They chose the *Cleveland Arms* on Sydney Wharf. This had opened around 1830 and had its own brewery until 1926. But the virgin territory of

Coronation Avenue promised richer pickings than the old canal wharf, so the *Cleveland Arms* had to go.[*]

Although, from the outside, the *Trowbridge House's* functional design betrays its origin as an off-licence, inside it is fascinating. The leaded lights dividing the public and lounge bars are a remarkably well-preserved piece of inter-war pub design, and while the public bar – with bar footie, Karaoke and Quiz nights, blue lights and a state-of-the-art trophy cabinet – is sleekly modern, the lounge bar is anything but. A deer's head, guns, buffalo horns, bottles, warming pans, antlers, beer crates, prints, Tubular Bells and Queen on the CD Player are among its delghts. The pièce de résistance, however, is a fading, framed, handwritten list of Bath's pubs in 1833.

Here you can sit and wonder what they were like, those long lost inns and alehouses – the *Elephant & Castle* on the Lower Bristol Road, the *Sedan Chair* in Bridewell Lane, the *Heart & Compass* in Cumberland Row, and the *Darby & Joan* in Guinea Lane. All long, long gone, and long forgotten. But, rest assured, all will feature in a companion volume to this – *Bath's Lost Pubs*. And, if you think the stories of the ones that are still open are good, wait till you hear the stories about the ones that have gone.

VICTORIA HOTEL Millmead Road, Oldfield Park

The *Victoria Hotel* at Millmead Road was first recorded in the 1898 *Postal Directory*, the licence having been transferred from the *White Hart* in Twerton High Street. From the outside, it looks a typical product of the closing years of Victoria's reign, confident, grandiose and dignified, the architectural equivalent of Elgar's *Pomp & Circumstance* marches. Inside it is a different story. The public bar is a temple to sixties rock. Sketches and paintings of Dylan, the Stones, Hendrix, Clapton, and the Floyd (with Syd hovering in the background) cover the purple-painted walls. The lounge is more sedate, with a painting of waves breaking over the fireplace and books on the mantelpiece, although Bob Marley still puts in an appearance. The back bar, with wide doors leading to the sheltered garden, has a motor racing theme.

The *Victoria* still has its original layout, complete with a separate entrance to its jug and bottle department, where a stained-glass hatchway opens into the bar. It is very much a locals' pub, with a real old-time feeling, not because it has been let go, but because the regulars like it that way.

VOLUNTEER RIFLEMAN'S ARMS 3 New Bond Street Place

In 1824, John Plura and Henry Mant put forward a proposal to the council for "a footway from Upper Borough Walls into New Bond Street in continuation of Union

---

[*] The old *Cleveland Arms* still survives, with part of its painted sign – on which the word "Usher's" can clearly be seen – on the wall.

Passage." The following year, the council approved the scheme, and New Bond Street Place was built.

The *Volunteer Rifleman's Arms* dates back to around 1858, when William Ponter, who had been a "shopman" at 8 St James's Parade, moved to 3 New Bond Street Place and opened a beerhouse called the *Porter Stores*. By 1868 it was known as the *Oakhill Porter Stores* (because its beer was supplied by the Oakhill Brewery).

By 1874 it had become the *Rifleman's Arms*, later changed to the *Volunteer Rifleman's Arms*, indicating that it was the meeting place of a volunteer regiment. The 1903 report described it as having a "glass room behind bar, partitioned off, and smoke room at the back." In 1976, when it still had two bars – a public and a snug – Fred Pearce described it as a "superbly friendly little city centre local." Today it has been knocked through into one, but it would still be difficult to argue with Fred's summing up.

There were once dozens of little beerhouses like this in the city centre. There were four in Union Passage alone – the *Albert Tavern*, the *Union Tavern*, the *Rising Sun* and the *Military Arms*. Today only the *Volly* (as it is known to regulars) and the *Coeur* survive to remind us of a bygone age. The *Coeur* holds the record as Bath's smallest pub (although there were plenty smaller a century ago), while the *Volunteer Rifleman's Arms* holds the record for the longest pub name in Somerset.*

WANSDYKE INN 49-51 Upper Bloomfield Road

Wansdyke is something of a mystery – a massive defensive earthwork to the south of Bath. Some say it was built by the Romano-British to keep the Saxons out; some say the Saxons built it to keep the Romano-British at bay. Nobody is really sure. It was the Saxons who called it Woden's Dyke after their chief god, however, and Woden's Dyke – or Wansdyke – it has remained ever since. In more recent times it has given its name to, among other things, a parliamentary constituency and a pub.

There is no such mystery about the *Wansdyke Inn*, which lies just below the *New Burnt House* at 49-51 Upper Bloomfield Road. Originally, it housed a grocer's

---

* The national record for the longest pub name is held by the *Old Cheshire Astley Volunteer Riflemen Corps Inn* in Stalybridge, Cheshire.

and a dairy, but when the *Circus Brewery* in Circus Mews, which dated back to the 1830s, was destroyed by enemy action in April 1942, its licence was transferred to the *Wansdyke Inn*. Today it is the only Wadworth's pub in Bath south of the river.

WESTON HOTEL Newbridge Road, Lower Weston

The *Weston Hotel*, which opened around 1897, was fitted out on a lavish scale. The entrance hall led to a private and a public bar. The private bar had polished light oak fittings, hot and cold running water, "three sliding sashes with coloured glass panels, three fixed sashes, casings and framings over the beer engine counter," and a speaking tube connected to the kitchen. There was a smoking room with stuffed settees, an oak centre table and four spittoons. There was a coffee room, a billiard room, a private parlour, and a lavatory which must have been one of the wonders of Weston, boasting a sponge bowl, two china urinals with plated taps and "Doulton's Patent Flushing Apparatus." The floors of all the downstairs rooms were covered with lino. Upstairs were nine bedrooms, all carpeted. At the back was a massive hall with a portable platform in six sections and 200 chairs, a coach house and stables.

After being known as the *Sportsman* for some years, it is known as the *Weston*. Although it has been knocked through and decked out in generic big-pub style, traces of its former grandeur survive amid the five pool tables and wide-screen TVs. Other attractions include Karaoke on Wednesdays, Student Nights on Thursdays, and monthly Lap-dancing Nights (for which patrons are advised to book early to avoid disappointment).

Architecturally, the *Weston Hotel* is a muddle of different styles. The entrance is a skilful recreation of seventeenth-century vernacular design, and would not look out of place on a Cotswold manor house. The building it is joined to, however, bears little relation to it architecturally, being firmly in the arts and crafts style developed by Norman Shaw. The hall at the back is quite remarkable. Although it is easy to miss, dwarfed as it is by the hotel, if it were to stand alone it would dwarf not only most church halls but also many late Victorian churches.

WHITE HART Widcombe Hill

This is the pub that came back from the dead. When it closed and was turned into a backpackers' hostel, most people thought that, to all intents and purposes, it had gone for good. The bar area downstairs was kept for the use of the hostel's residents, however, and now it has reopened to the public. Real ale, courtesy of Bath Ales, is available, and there is live music on Wednesday evenings. Décor-wise there is not much left of the old pub. Instead, it is a clean, light, and very enjoyable place to while away a couple of hours over a drink or two. The inn yard at the back,

where the old skittle alley has acquired a second floor to accommodate backpackers, is a continental-style oasis of calm in the heart of Widcombe. It is not really stretching a point to say that, despite its modern décor, the *White Hart* has gone back to its roots as an inn, providing food, accommodation and alcohol for travellers.

Those roots go back at least as far as 1778 when Joseph Windsor moved from the *White Hart* to take over a long-forgotten inn at the bottom of Holloway called the *Angel*. The *White Hart* almost certainly dates from the early eighteenth century, however, when Ralph Allen built a tramway down what is now Prior Park Road to carry stone from his quarries at Combe Down to a wharf on the River Avon. As the tramway went past the *White Hart's* door, it is likely that the men in charge of the trams were regular visitors.

The *White Hart's* position at the bottom of Widcombe Hill had its drawbacks, as was discovered in 1828 when a dam burst near Widcombe House:

> The affrighted inhabitants of the adjoining dwellings hurried to their upper stories, the lower part being instantly filled to the depth of several feet … The torrent continued its devastating course along Prior Park Buildings; and, washing down a wall, rushed through the *White Hart* Public House, across the road into the houses opposite, called Sussex Place. In the lower apartments of one of these dwellings, lay a poor old man and his wife, each of them between 60 and 70 years of age; and so totally unconscious were they of the approach or existence of danger, that before the least assistance could be offered, they both perished in their beds.

A half-gallon jar from Edward Archer who was at the *White Hart* in the early 1880s.

In 1884, when the licence of the *White Hart* was transferred from Emily Orchard to John Herd, the property consisted of a bar, spirit vaults, a smoking room, a parlour, a club room, seven bedrooms, a dressing room, a skittle alley, a brewery and cooperage. The bar, lustrous with mahogany, was astonishing. Along its back wall, a five-columned fixture with carved capitals topped by a cornice stretched to the ceiling. Another panelled fixture filled the window. Gilt lettering, glass panels and silvered backs added to the effect. The circular-fronted counter was hardly less elaborate. If it all got a bit too overwhelming, you could slip outside to the garden, where there was a summer-house. Alternatively, you could just nip into the stone urinal, with its matchboard screen and roof.

Just before midday on 20 January 1960, a rep from Stroud Brewery, which owned the *White Hart* at the time, pulled up outside on a routine visit. No sooner had he got out of his car than he saw flames coming out of the windows and heard the distant sound of several fire engines rushing to the scene. The fire, which was described in the *Bath Chronicle* as "the sharpest fire Bath has experienced for some time," soon attracted a large crowd of onlookers, but was eventually brought under control. Although the building was saved, the main bar had to be completely pulled down and rebuilt.

The most memorable feature of the old *White Hart* was the figure of a deer, made of lime, mahogany and oak, over the entrance. It originally stood over the entrance to the *White Hart* in Stall Street, one of Bath's major coaching inns. When the inn was demolished in 1867, the carved figure was removed to the *White Hart* In Widcombe. In 1988, having deteriorated badly, it was taken away to be restored. After being fitted with a new set of legs and liberally coated with lead-based paint for protection, it returned the following year, only to disappear one night in 1999. Eventually, it turned up, minus its head, in the stream in Prior Park. After a lengthy restoration and the fitting of a new head, it was restored to its rightful place and unveiled in a moving ceremony by Lady Margaret Oswick (aka Ralph Oswick of the National Theatre Company) in March 2003.

WHITE HORSE 42 Shophouse Road, Twerton

The *White Horse* was opened as a beerhouse by James Simmonds, a foreman at the cloth mill in Twerton, around 1870.

In 1851, James Simmonds' father had given him "land bounded on the south by the road from Twerton to Englishcombe and a dwelling house with the wash house and privy some years built." In 1856, James Simmonds bought "premises" and "a parcel of ground" next to the dwelling house to build an extension. The original building, possibly dating from the seventeenth century, with ammonites in its wall, forms the top part of the present *White Horse*. The original front entrance, now largely hidden behind a modern extension, faces up the hill. Most of the present building, however, dates from James Simmonds' extensions in the 1850s. The *White Horse* was granted a full licence in 1949.

BATH'S OLDEST PUB

If you have read this far, you may still be pondering the question we have been asked more than any other while researching the history of Bath's pubs – which is the oldest? The chances are, though, that you saw the title of this chapter on the contents page and turned to the back to find out the answer straight away.

If only it were that simple.

The further back you go, the less records have survived. If Pompeii is anything to go by, Roman Bath was packed with pubs, but they have disappeared without trace. The same goes for the medieval city. It is only when we get to the late eighteenth century that full records begin to be kept. Up till then it is very hit and miss.

One of the contenders for Bath's oldest pub is the *Saracen's Head* in Broad Street, with the date 1713 carved on one of its gables. Although the carving may be a nineteenth-century addition, the building is certainly early eighteenth century, if not older.

Several other pubs date from this period. The *Old Green Tree* in Green Street was built around 1716 on the site of a tree which shaded a bowling green. *Sam Weller's* – originally the *Full Moon* – was built against the city walls sometime before 1739. The *Griffin* in Monmouth Street was built in the 1730s, possibly taking its name from the griffin on the newly-erected monument on Lansdown.

The *Star* was probably built around 1760, and, while this does not qualify it for Bath's oldest pub, it may have been built on the site of an old alehouse, traces of which can still be seen in its cellars. The *Bell* in Walcot Street, which dates from before 1728, may also be on the site of an earlier pub.

Other pubs built on the site of old inns include the *Crown* at Bathwick and the *Bear* on Wellsway. The *Hat & Feather* may date from the time when disaffected Royalists – whose emblem was the hat and feather – met there during England's brief flirtation with republicanism in the mid-seventeenth century. The present building, however, is only about a century old.

The *White Hart* in Widcombe dates from the early eighteenth century, and was probably a welcome stop for the men working on Ralph Allen's tramway, which ran past the door. The *Cross Keys* at Combe Down opened around 1718, while the *Old Crown* at Weston dates back to at least 1712.

The *Grapes* in Westgate Street has a potted history painted on one of its beams, claiming that it dates back to 1302. There is certainly a building lease for the site dating from then, but the present building is basically seventeenth century, with an eighteenth-century frontage. Although it was a wine merchant's in the early eighteenth century, it only opened as a pub around 1794.

Another pub housed in an ancient building is the *Delfter Krug* – originally the *Sawclose Tavern*. It was built around 1636 but only became a pub in the 1840s.

Then there are – or rather were – Bath's coaching inns. These were imposing buildings, patronised by the wealthy. Not surprisingly, records of them have survived rather better than those of lowly alehouses. The centre of Bath was once full of them, but in 1841 the railway opened from London, and within a few years most of them had gone. Only two have survived.

All Bar One in the High Street was the *Christopher Inn*, while the *Rat & Parrot* in Westgate Street was the *Angel*. Both date from the seventeenth century, possibly earlier. Although both have always been licensed premises, they have changed so much that to claim either as Bath's oldest pub would perhaps be stretching a point.

There is, however, a surprise contender for the title of oldest pub. The *Hare & Hounds* on Lansdown, although much altered and extended, has at its heart a seventeenth-century alehouse. We even know the name of its landlady – Jane Wait – who took over in 1695. Although, as with all licenses at this time, the pub was not named, there has only ever been one pub in the Parish of Charlcombe – the *Hare & Hounds*.

Other possible contenders for the title, such as the *King's Arms* in Monmouth Street, which may well date from the seventeenth century, have no such records to support their claims.

So the answer to the question of Bath's oldest pub must remain veiled in mystery. Perhaps it's better that way. After all, if the mystery was solved, it would put paid to all those endless, inconclusive debates over a beer or two – or three …

IN CONCLUSION:
A PERSONAL SELECTION

If the question of Bath's oldest pub is contentious, that of the city's best pubs is, not surprisingly, even more so. It is also highly subjective and subject to change. A new licensee can transform a dingy, unpopular back-street boozer into a vibrant, award-winning bar where you have to fight for a table. Sadly, the reverse can also happen. We have, therefore, ducked the issue of question of which are Bath's best pubs, offering instead a few pointers to visitors whose time in the city is limited.

It is important to bear in mind, however, that any information on what Bath's pubs are like will soon be out of date. You should treat all of what follows with the greatest caution, supplemented, if possible, by an up-to-date guide. The *Good Beer Guide*, published annually, is a reliable guide to those pubs whose beer meets the stringent criteria of those good people from the Campaign for Real Ale (CAMRA), while for those whose taste is a bit more eclectic, the *Itchy Guide to Bath* is worth a look. This only deals with city centre pubs and is aimed at a young(ish) audience, but its no-holds-barred approach (with comments like "this bar is really, really crap") is entertaining if nothing else.

HERITAGE PUBS

Two pubs which no visitor to the city should miss are the *Old Green Tree* and the *Star*. These are both on CAMRA's National Inventory of "pubs whose interiors are of outstanding heritage interest." Less than 250 pubs in the UK (out of a total of around 60,000) feature on this list, a measure of how pub interiors have suffered at the hands of the modernisers since the 1960s. Bath is lucky to have to have two. The *Star's* interior dates from the mid-nineteenth century, while the *Old Green Tree's* dates from 1928. Both pubs also have terrific real ale (the *Star* is the tap for Abbey Ales Brewery) and a terrific atmosphere. The *Old Green Tree* also has great lunchtime food.

REAL ALE

For those in search of the best real ale, an up-to-date copy of the *Good Beer Guide* is essential. It should be stressed, however, that this is a guide, not a definitive list of the pubs that serve good beer. Many pubs not in the guide serve a decent pint of real ale, although sadly some do not. For the record, the pubs that featured in the main section of the 2003 Guide included the following:

Bell, Walcot Street
Coeur de Lion, Northumberland Place

Cross Keys, Midford Road, Combe Down
Hatchett's, Queen Street
Hop Pole, Upper Bristol Road
Lambretta's, North Parade
Old Farmhouse, Lansdown Road
Old Green Tree, Green Street
Pig & Fiddle, Saracen Street
Pulteney Arms, Daniel Street
Salamander, John Street
Star, Vineyards

POSTSCRIPT: As we went to press it was announced that the Rummer was to be added to the line-up of Bath pubs in the 2004 Good Beer Guide.)

PUB FOOD

Most pubs in Bath serve food, at least at lunchtime. Many provide standard pub fare, with chips featuring prominently. It is difficult to single any out, although, if you are really into chips, the chip butties in the *Pulteney Arms* are justifiably famous. The chilli in the *Rising Sun* in Grove Street takes some beating as well, while the *Pig & Fiddle* is getting something of a reputation for its burgers.

The *Porter* has a wide-ranging vegetarian menu, featuring favourites such as cashew nut curry, served all day till 9pm. Excellent vegetarian rolls, with fillings including humus, roasted aubergine and mozzarella, are also available in the *Bell*.

The only pub in Bath to get a mention in the *Good Food Guide* (so far) is the *Richmond Arms*. Other pubs that may well be nudging towards an entry include the *Salamander* and the *Hop Pole*, both owned by Bath Ales and both recipients of awards and glowing reviews in the local and national press. The *Old Green Tree* also has a very imaginative lunchtime menu – high quality food at extremely reasonable prices. Across the river in Widcombe, the *Ring of Bells* is fast gaining a reputation as one of Bath's top food pubs, while the open-plan kitchen behind the bar in the *Delfter Krug* is also attracting rave reviews. Out of town, the *Cross Keys* at Combe Down is well-known for the range and quality of its menu. Finally, if you are into tapas bars, the *Belvedere Wine Bar* is one not to miss.

MUSIC

It would be easier to draw up a list of Bath pubs that do not have live music than one of those that do. Music in pubs goes back a long way, although it has not always found an appreciative audience. Take this newspaper report from 1841, for example:

> Francis Comley was fined 10/- and costs for an assault upon Leonard Lye. It appeared that on Friday evening the defendant, who is a wandering violin player, went into the house of the complainant, who keeps a house for the sale of intoxicating liquors on Holloway, and expressed an anxiety to "discourse most eloquent music" on his four-stringed instrument. The landlord had a decided objection to the instrumental display, and upon refusing permission, many words ensued, and the defendant suddenly struck the complainant a blow on his face, which materially damaged it. For this conduct a warrant

was obtained, and for the assault in question the fine was inflicted.

When the Vicar of St James's Church (which stood where Clinton cards in Stall Street is today) campaigned to have a notorious dive called the *Bell* on Lower Borough Walls closed down in 1881, he complained of the "dissolute women, half dressed … soliciting passers-by. At night, riots, fighting and piano playing disturbed the whole neighbourhood." The Vicar got his way. The *Bell's* piano fell silent and the pub was closed. Today, the building has found a rather different use as the Faerie Shop.

The other *Bell*, on Walcot Street, has always been, of course, much more respectable. Sunday lunchtimes, Monday and Wednesday evenings see the stage at the *Bell* transformed into one of the town's top live music spots. Expect just about anything – from ska to bluegrass, from blues to funk, and from folk to jazz. Local bands alternate with world-class musicians, and the standard is awesome.

Wednesday nights also see class acts at the recently reopened *White Hart* in Widcombe.

The *King's Arms* in Monmouth Place is another terrific venue, with loud music on Friday, Saturday and Sunday nights – blues, punk, and some of the best rock bands you are likely to hear.

The *Old Farmhouse* – Bath's answer to Ronnie Scott's – is the number one spot for jazz in all its manifestations, from trad to avant-garde and everything in between, almost every night of the week, while the *Green Park Tavern* is fast gaining a reputation as a top venue for country and bluegrass.

The cellar bar at the *Porter* generally attracts a younger crowd, but here the standard is awesome as well, with just about anything likely to turn up. *Moles* night club, which attracts top bands on a regular basis, is next door.

The *Hat & Feather* is another terrific venue. Great live music – although the highlight of the week for many is DJ Derek with his collection of ska and reggae records every Wednesday.

The *Porter Butt* on the London Road has an Irish and roots acoustic session every Friday night, while an eclectic and impressive assortment of bands line up in the Walcot Palais out the back on a regular basis.

Other bars with live music include the *Belvedere Wine Vaults*, the *Salamander*, the *Weston*, the *Larkhall Inn*, the *Midland*, the *Trinity*, the *Centurion*, the *Huntsman*, and the *Hobgoblin*.

The best place to find an up-to-date run-down of who's playing where is in the *Bath Chronicle's* "What's On" Guide. This appears every day, and there is a special "Bath Time" supplement every Friday, with features on forthcoming gigs.

GLOSSARY

BAR
In medieval times, innkeepers erected a rail to divide the body of the inn from a space near the entrance to which travellers of low degree were admitted for refreshment. This effectively barred them from the rest of the inn. In time, the railed-off area came to be known as the bar, a term which is still with us, although now it applies both to the counter at which drinks are served and the room in which they are served.

BEER ENGINE
A device consisting of apparatus holding the handpumps in the bar and connecting them to the cellar.

FREE HOUSE
A pub not tied to a brewery, and therefore free to sell whatever beers it likes.

JUG & BOTTLE
A small off-sales department in a pub, sometimes entered through a separate door and generally screened off from the rest of the pub.

LAGER
The main difference between beer and lager is that beer is top-fermented while lager is bottom-fermented. This sounds more technical than it is. All it means is that some strains of yeast float on top during fermentation while others sink to the bottom. Originally, all beer was top fermented. Bavarian monks pioneered the use of bottom-fermenting yeasts in the fifteenth century. The resulting product was called "lager bier," as it kept longer than traditional brews – "lager" is the German word for "store." Virtually all the beer brewed outside the UK today is "lager bier," made with bottom-fermenting yeasts. Although lager in this country is almost invariably a light golden colour, indicating the use of lightly malted barley, this is not essential, and there are many excellent dark European lagers. Almost all the lager served in this country is non-real ale, although there is also no reason why this should be the case. One real-ale lager which can sometimes be found on tap at the *Old Green Tree* and the *Bell* is Great Dane, brewed by a Danish master-brewer at Stonehenge Brewery. It is well worth looking out for, whether you are a confirmed lager drinker or not.

LOUNGE
Originally a verb meaning to move indolently, by 1775 it had come to mean a place – not necessarily a room – one could lounge in. In Sheridan's *The Rivals*, for example, Mr Fag describes the City of Bath as "a good lounge." Later, it came to mean a place in a hotel or inn where one could indulge in lounging.

MESSUAGE
A legal term signifying a building together with any outhouses, land, etc., attached to it.

PUBLIC HOUSE
Originally, a house which provided food and lodging for the general public. Later it came to mean a house in which the principal business was the sale of alcoholic liquors to be consumed on the premises.

PUB

Public house was abbreviated to public by the early eighteenth century. A century later, public had been shortened to pub. Further abbreviation being impossible, the term is still with us today.

REAL ALE

A book could be written about real ale. Many have been. Put in the simplest possible terms, it is beer which is still "live" – i.e. still fermenting – when it leaves the brewery. All beer is brewed with malted barley, hops and water, plus yeast to promote fermentation. With real ale, fermentation is in two stages. The primary fermentation takes place at the brewery. Once this is complete, the beer (complete with yeast) is put in barrels and sent to pubs, where a secondary fermentation takes place. The barrel has to be left undisturbed so that sediment can sink to the bottom. Soft and hard wood pegs are tapped into plugs in the barrel to control the release of carbon dioxide (generated by the fermentation process) until the beer is considered ready to serve.

SNUG

An obsolete term for a small parlour screened off from the rest of the pub. Originally known as snuggeries, snugs were particularly favoured by female drinkers anxious to avoid swearing and ribald talk.

TAP

An word of Anglo-Saxon origin, signifying a cylindrical peg through which liquid could be drawn off from a vessel. The big leap forward in tap technology was the fitting of a device for shutting off or regulating the flow. For centuries, tapping barrels of beer or casks of wine was the only way to get the contents out. This was only done after they had had chance to settle and mature. Knowing the optimum time to tap a barrel or cask was crucial. In the days when people had precious little to amuse them, the date on which a barrel of new beer or a cask of new wine was tapped often assumed quasi-mystical significance. The closest we get to it today is the hullabaloo which accompanies the arrival of Beaujolais Nouveau. Nevertheless, the sound of the tap being hammered gently home has bequeathed us a meaning of the word tap which has nothing to do with barrels or cylindrical pegs. Just think of that the next time you tap on a window or watch a Fred Astaire movie.

In the seventeenth century, however, and right up until the early 1900s, tap had other meanings as well. The 1933 edition of the *Oxford English Dictionary* gives, as one of the definitions of tap, "the liquor drawn from a particular tap; a particular species or quality of drink." A tap room was the room in an inn where barrels or casks were tapped. It was also the place where servants and coachmen of those staying at the inn would gather to pass the time. In time, it became called simply the tap. By the mid-nineteenth century, virtually every pub had a tap room, where the less salubrious customers were expected to drink.

As inns expanded, taps expanded as well, and often took over adjoining buildings. These not only served drinks, but also accommodated coachmen and servants of the gentry staying in the inn. Thus, a tap, originally just a way of describing the room where the barrels were kept, came to mean a particular type of pub.

Add to that range of meanings the humble tap-root (so called because its shape recalls that of the taps once tapped into barrels), and you have an object lesson in how language develops.

UNREAL ALE

This is brewed in exactly the same way as real ale, but, before it leaves the brewery, it is chilled and the yeast is drained off so that fermentation ceases. The beer is then pasteurised and the barrels are sealed. Unlike real ale, keg beer (as non-real ale is generally called) lacks the fizz caused by continuing fermentation and has to have gas (either carbon dioxide or a mixture of carbon dioxide and nitrogen) added when it is pumped up from cellar to bar. Not surprisingly, all this tinkering about has a marked impact on the way it tastes. To mask this, it is generally served much colder than real ale. The big advantage with non-real ale is that serving it is virtually foolproof. When it arrives at the pub all that has to be done is to link it up to a gas cylinder and start pouring. Another advantage is that it lasts much longer than real ale.

BIBLIOGRAPHY

Primary sources include a vast range of material held in the Bath, Somerset and Wiltshire Record Offices, as well as the Mompesson Records in Buckinghamshire Record Office.

An invaluable source of primary material has been local newspapers held in Bath Central Library, Bristol Reference Library and the British Newspaper Library.

Bath Postal Directories, a near-complete run of which is held in Bath Central Library and Bath Record Office, have been consulted extensively. We have also consulted Kelly's Directories for Somerset, especially for outlying parishes not covered comprehensively in early Postal Directories.

Other works consulted include:

Kegs & Ale: Bath and the Public House, Bath, 1991.

Old English Coffee Houses, London, 1954.

Report to the Licensing Justices of the City of Bath on All Houses in the Said City Licensed for the Sale of Intoxicating Liquors (Except Grocers and Chemists), Bath 1903.

Weston Parish (Building of Bath Museum Publication), Bath, 2000.

Barber, Norman, *A Century of British Brewers, 1890-1990*, New Ash Green, 1994.

Beaton, Mark, Mike Chapman, Andrew Crutchley & Jane Root, *Bath Historical Streetscape Survey*, 2 vols, Bath, 2000.

Bickerdyke, John, *The Curiosities of Ale & Beer*, London, 1889.

Bold, Alan, *Drink to Me Only: The Prose and Cons of Drinking*, London, 1982.

Bone, Mike, "The Rise and Fall of Bath's Breweries, 1736-1960," in *Bath History, VIII*, Bath, 2000.

Boston, Richard, *Beer and Skittles*, London, 1976.

Butler, Richard, *Bath City Police: A Brief History*, Bath, 1985.

Chapman, Mike, *An Historical Guide to the Ham and Southgate Area of Bath*, Bath, 1997.

Chapman, Mike & Elizabeth Holland, *Bimbery and the South-Western Baths of Bath*, Bath, 2001.

Chisholm, Kate, *Fanny Burney*, London, 1998.

Clark, Peter, *The English Alehouse: A Social History, 1200-1830*, London, 1983.

Dallimore, Keith, *Exploring Combe Down*, Bath, 1988.

Davis, Dorothy, *A History of Shopping*, London, 1966.

Davis, Graham, *Bath Beyond the Guide Book: Scenes from Victorian Life*, Bristol, 1988.

Davis, Graham & Penny Bonsell, *Bath: A New History*, Keele, 1996.

Delderfield, Eric, *British Inn Signs and Their Stories*, Exmouth, 1965.

Dillon, Patrick, *The Much Lamented Death of Madam Geneva: The Eighteenth-century Gin Craze*, London, 2002.

Dunkling, Leslie & Gordon Wright, *Pub Names of Britain*, London, 1987.

Egan, Pierce, *Walks Through Bath*, Bath, 1819.

Fawcett, Trevor & Francis Kelly, "Northampton Street: An Outline of Its Historical Development," Bath, 1999.

French RV, *Nineteen Centuries of Drink in England*, London, 1884.

Girouard, Mark, *Victorian Pubs*, London, 1975.

Grafton, Frank, *Tipple & Temperance*, Unpublished article, Bath Record Office.

Hackwood, Frederick, *Inns, Ales and Drinking Customs of Old England*, London, 1985.

Hargood-Ash, Joan, *Two Thousand Years in the Life of a Somerset Village; Weston, Bath*, Weston, 2001.

Haydon, Peter, *Beer & Britannia: An Inebriated History of Britain*, Thrupp, 2001.

Hecht, J Jean, *The Domestic Servant in Eighteenth-Century England*, London, 1980.

Holland, Elizabeth, *The Kingston Estate*, Bath 1992.

Holland, Elizabeth & Mike Chapman, *Bath Guildhall and its Neighbourhood*, Bath 2000.

Hudson, Thomas, *Temperance Pioneers of the West*, London, 1887.

Hunt, Henry, *Memoirs*, 3 vols., London, 1820.

Manco, Jean, *The Spirit of Care: The 800 Year Story of St John's Hospital, Bath*, Bath, 1998.

Meehan, JF, *Famous Houses of Bath & District*, Bath 1901.

Minnit, SC, J Durnell & AJH Gunstone, *Somerset Public House Tokens*, Bridgwater, 1985.

Morris, Dr Claver, *The Diary of a West Country Physician*, ed Edmund Hobhouse, London, 1934.

Neale, RS, *Bath: A Social History, 1650-1850, or A Valley of Pleasure, yet a Sink of Iniquity*, London, 1981.

Parfitt, Robert, ed., *The Book of South Stoke with Midford*, Tiverton, 2001.

Pearce, Fred, *The Critical Guide to Bath Pubs*, Bristol, 1976.

Penrose, Rev John, *Letters from Bath, 1766-1767*, ed. Brigitte Mitchell & Hubert Penrose, Gloucester, 1983.

Pound, Christopher, *Genius of Bath: The City & its Landscape*, Bath 1986.

Robertson, Charles, *Bath: An Architectural Guide*, London, 1975.

Scott, Maurice, *Discovering Widcombe & Lyncombe*, Bath, 1993.

Shickle, Rev CW, ed., *Ancient Deeds Belonging to the Corporation of Bath*, Bath, 1921.

Skinner, John, *The Journal of a Somerset Rector*, ed. Howard & Peter Coombs, Oxford, 1971.

Snadden, Brenda, *The Last Promenade: Sydney Gardens, Bath*, Bath, 2000.

Southey, Robert, *Letters from England*, London, 1807.

Stone, Barbara, *Bath Millennium*, Bath, 1973.

Sydenham, S, *Bath Pleasure Gardens of the Eighteenth Century Issuing Metal Admission Tickets*, Bath, 1907.

Sydenham, S, *Bath Tokens of the Seventeenth Century*, Bath, 1905.

Symons, Katherine E, *The Grammar School of King Edward VI, Bath, and its Ancient Foundation*, Bath, 1934.

Wilcox, Ronald, "Bath Breweries in the Latter Half of the Eighteenth Century," in *A Second North Somerset Miscellany*, (pp. 23-31), Bath, 1971.

Wroughton, John, *A Community at War: The Civil War in Bath and North Somerset, 1642-1650*, Bath, 1992

Wroughton, John, ed., *Bath in the Age of Reform*, Bath, 1972

GUIDED TOURS

If you have enjoyed reading this book, why not come along on the Great Bath Pub Crawl to find out more about Bath's boozy past. Regular walks take place throughout the summer, and party bookings can be arranged throughout the year. Group bookings can be tailored to individual requirements. For more details see our website, www.greatbathpubcrawl.com.

If, on the other hand, you feel that you would like to give pubs a rest and find out a bit more about Bath's non-alcoholic history, then log on to www.bathwalks.com for details of other walks and talks we can arrange.

HOUSE HISTORY RESEARCH

Kirsten Elliott has worked for various clients, including architects and breweries, researching the history and development of historic buildings for planning applications. This research involves tracing the history of an individual building back to the time it was built, discovering the name of the developers, original occupiers and the uses to which the building was put. For pubs, this also entails looking at licensing records and other sources to come up with a list of licensees. If your house is being renovated, converted or adapted, or if you just want to know more about its past, we will be happy to quote a price for the work you require. Contact us on info@akemanpress.com or call on 01225 310364